–A–
Nation
SEIZED

For Tom + Mona –
Thanks for dinner with
E.J. Dionne – and thanks for
your leadership &
St. Mary's University.

Bill Israel
3-19-13

OTHER BOOKS OF INTEREST FROM MARQUETTE BOOKS

James Gillett, *A Grassroots History of the HIV/AIDS Epidemic in North America* (2011). ISBN: 978-0-9826597-7-9 (paperback)

John C. Merrill, *Farewell to Freedom: Impact of Communitarianism on Individual Rights in the 21st Century* (2011). ISBN: 978-0-9826597-5-5 (paper)

John Markert, *The Social Impact of Sexual Harassment: A Resource Manual for Organizations and Scholars* (2010). ISBN: 978-0-9826597-4-8 (paper)

Jennifer Henderson, *Defending the Good News: The Jehovah's Witnesses' Plan to Expand the First Amendment* (2010). ISBN: 978-0-922993-84-0 (paperback)

John C. Merrill, *Call to Order: Plato's Legacy of Social Control* (2009). ISBN: 978-0-922993-81-9

John W. Cones, *Introduction to the Motion Picture Industry: A Guide for Students, Filmmakers and Scholars* (2008). ISBN: 978-0-922993-90-1 (paperback)

John Schulz, *Please Don't Do That! The Pocket Guide to Good Writing* (2008). ISBN: 978-0-922993-87-1 (booklet)

John W. Cones, *Dictionary of Film Finance and Distribution: A Guide for Independent Filmmakers* (2008). ISBN: 978-0-922993-93-2 (cloth); 978-0-922993-94-9 (paper)

Hazel Dicken-Garcia and Giovanna Dell'Orto, *Hated Ideas and the American Civil War Press* (2008). ISBN: 978-0-922993-88-8 (paper);

Mitchell Land and Bill W. Hornaday, *Contemporary Media Ethics: A Practical Guide for Students, Scholars and Professionals* (2006). ISBN: 0-922993-41-6 (cloth); 0-922993-42-4 (paperback)

Joey Reagan, *Applied Research Methods for Mass Communicators* (2006). ISBN: 0-922993-45-9 (paperback)

David Demers, *Dictionary of Mass Communication: A Guide for Students, Scholars and Professionals* (2005). ISBN: 0-922993-25-4 (paperback)

–A–
Nation
SEIZED

How
KARL ROVE
and the
political right
stole reality,
beginning
with the
news

BILL
ISRAEL

MARQUETTE BOOKS LLC
Spokane, Washington

Printed in the United States of America

Library of Congress Cataloging Number
2011920445

ISBN for this edition:
978-0-9826597-6-2

MARQUETTE BOOKS LLC
3107 East 62nd Avenue
Spokane, Washington 99223
509-443-7057 (voice) / 509-448-2191 (fax)
books@marquettebooks.com / www.MarquetteBooks.com

For Eileen

and to the memory of
Park Rinard and Harold E. Hughes,
mentors, templates, friends

Contents

TABLES

Introduction

The news media "are like sheep!" Karl Rove exclaimed to a rapt audience of students at the University of Texas at Austin. Journalists focus more on the horse race — who is leading — than on the substance of a campaign. The irony, he added, is that even though "we're more dependent on the press ... they're uniquely unable to see" what really happens during an election campaign.[1]

The date was February 10, 1998. Rove was speaking to juniors, seniors and graduate students who were enrolled in "Politics and the Press," a course that Rove, political journalist Dave McNeely and I were team-teaching. Rove was taking time off from managing George W. Bush's 2000 election campaign, flying regularly to and from Austin and Washington, D.C. At the time, I was in the last year of my Ph.D. program at UT. I previously had worked as a reporter, press secretary, consultant and educator.

Rove's presentation to the students reinforced a comment he made three weeks earlier. Most journalists who cover politics, he said, have little understanding of what happens in political campaigns. The same is true of business reporters, "who don't know business,"[2] he added.

The students didn't respond to the attacks on journalists. Rove's intensity and stimulating presence held them spellbound. Indeed, Rove was witty, full of energy and insightful. But the moment reminded me of a question Italian political philosopher Antonio Gramsci once posed: Why do people yield to power, rather than act in their own best interests? Gramsci, a leader of the Italian Communist Party, raised this question in the 1920s as Fascism seduced his countrymen. He concluded that because powerful people tend to control politics, common people need to build their own institutions, to alter their political destiny. For criticizing the regime of Benito Mussolini, Gramsci was sent to prison and died shortly after his release.

As the semester progressed, Rove revealed many of the secrets of how he helps elect candidates and maneuver through political logjams and the media (see Chapters 1-9). "Democrats were the first to use polls, but Republicans perfected them for campaigns and policymaking," Rove said, rolling a piece of chalk between his right thumb and forefinger while speaking to another class that day. He then tracked the A to Z of how he uses polls — when and why. On other days he talked about television, radio ("great on a negative attack"), advance work, candidate debates and direct mail.[3]

Rove, McNeely and I began preparing for the course in late 1997. On the surface, it seemed that Rove and I were a good match. Both of us came from strong Republican roots; he from Utah, the son of a geologist who was frequently gone; and I from Iowa, the son of two music teachers. Utah is home of hardscrabble mountains and a seat of western conservatism, but conservatism runs just as deep in the topsoil of northwest Iowa.

Rove dropped out of the University of Utah in 1970 to travel the country and to campaign and organize for the Republicans. In our first extended phone call before we taught at UT, he talked about how, at age twenty-two, he had become executive director of College Republicans, an organization formerly associated with the Republican National Committee. Two years after that, he traveled the Gulf States in a Ford Pinto with John Carbaugh and Lee Atwater, campaigning for the chairmanship of College Republicans and broadening his political network. As executive director of College Republicans, he worked under Republican National Committee chairman George H. W. Bush and campaigned for Richard Nixon, master of the political dirty trick and "plausible deniability" — the term for exacting political damage without leaving fingerprints.

At the time, I was in my early 20s and, like Rove, I studied politics. My goal was to become a better reporter. I moved from Iowa to Washington, two months after Nixon's 1972 reelection, to become press secretary to Senator Harold E. Hughes, an Iowa Democrat. Hughes served three terms as governor and became the template Democratic political leader for my generation in Iowa. While I worked for him, Hughes chaired a Senate Armed Services subcommittee investigation of Nixon's secret Cambodia bombings. Two members of Hughes' staff led the investigation, while I wrote and edited press releases and commentaries for the news media,[4] handled press inquiries, set up interviews and backed up my mentor, Park Rinard, Hughes' administrative assistant. The investigation ultimately contributed to the House Judiciary Committee debate to impeach Nixon, which ended after he resigned in disgrace.

By the time we taught together, Rove had helped run seventy-three campaigns, many for U.S. Senate and House seats in two dozen states, and even worked for a parliamentary campaign in Sweden, close to his Norwegian roots. He, like Nixon, had used questionable tactics to win election campaigns, but Rove covered his tracks better, at least for a time.[5] Now he was heading up George W. Bush's election campaign.

In 2000, many people in the United States and abroad thought Bush had no chance of winning. He was a governor but inexperienced in national politics. Four years later they wondered how Bush could have been elected again when his administration cut taxes mostly for the rich, cut social expenditures for the poor, dismantled environmental and antitrust regulation, upended the balance of trade and the dollar's strength, engorged the national debt by trumping up a war in Iraq, and destroyed America's reputation for justice around the world. How could Bush be reelected with that unenviable record?

Many political pundits believe the credit goes to Karl Rove. In fact, after Bush "won" the 2000 election — even though he lost the popular vote — Republican senators created a logjam at the White House in the cabinet room doorway, each stopping to shake hands with the principal architect of the Bush presidency.

"The line backed up because every one of them stopped and said, 'Hello,'" Senator Bill Frist of Tennessee said at the time. "They know how important he is. Everybody knows that in terms of putting it all together, in terms of the politics, in terms of strategy positions and also policy, that Karl is the hub, the central node of activity that surrounds the presidency."[6]

Indeed, my observations of Rove in and out of the classroom three years earlier, in 1998, reinforced that scene in the cabinet room doorway. Rove was the most able political operative I'd seen in twenty-five years as a political reporter and political staffer. His centrality to the Bush campaign was never in question. When Bush called Rove on his red cell phone, Rove responded, "Yes, sir," and dashed upstairs to the privacy of a rear hallway to take the boss's call even when class was in session. Back in Texas, before he became "the architect," Rove held no official Bush appointment — yet news people called him "the prime minister," for when it came to Bush politics and policy, Rove was the man. Whether it was a small political tiff or a full-scale fracas, Rove fought with intelligence, intensity, tenacity, urgency, secrecy and will, as if he were at war, and he usually won.

Why was Rove so successful?

Intelligence is obviously one factor. He could consume massive amounts of political news and history. This knowledge commanded respect among and gave him access to Republican/conservative leaders and many audiences beyond. Stories and historical references rolled off his tongue, in class and out. He demonstrated a knowledge of American political history unlike anyone I had encountered in practical politics. He combined all this with a boisterous, kinetically extraverted personality and a deep conviction in the morality and opportunity of libertarian capitalism. I'd grown up with strongly conservative friends, some deeply involved in the cause. But no conservative I'd known came close to Rove's ability to exploit the resources in his environment.

Another one of Rove's greatest strengths was his ability to act as deal-maker and political entrepreneur, running interference through the gamut of the GOP and conservatism, charming liberals as needed to drum up majorities and disable opponents. In Texas, he worked as a consultant to big oil, big land interests, big tobacco and corporate polluters. He brought to class a beautiful leather briefcase emblazoned with "King Ranch," a token from one of Texas' wealthiest elites.

Knowledge, personality and deal-making definitely factored in his success, but equally important, in my opinion, was his command of negative campaign tactics. He perfected them. He was the king of Texas political direct mail, and the Bush campaign used negative political advertising as effectively as any campaign in history. Just ask Senator John McCain, who was brutally attacked in the South Carolina Republican primary, which cost McCain the Republican presidenial nomination in 2000.

Although Rove and I shared a deep interest in the tools of electoral politics and the importance of public policy in American life, I believed that negative campaign tactics undercut the democratic process, making voters cynical. After working as press secretary for politicians in Iowa, California, and Washington, and reporting for newspapers, radio, television and magazines, I'd become disgusted with dirty politics and the near ideological convergence of Democrats and Republicans in the 1990s. That's one of the reasons why I decided to pursue the Ph.D.

Despite our philosophical differences, I respected Rove for his depth of knowledge and experience and considered him a friend.

The political sociologist Philip Schlesinger once observed that news had become "the exercise of power over the interpretation of reality."[7] To control that exercise, politicians and others compete every day to shape the meaning of news. That's a reason why, a few years after Rove and I taught together, I decided to write a book tentatively titled, "The Lessons of Karl Rove." My goal, in part, was to distill the lessons Rove presented, to show his impact on news. These lessons are outlined in the first part of this book (Chapters 1 to 9). But I discovered, as I wrote, deeper themes to all of this, which didn't end with the Bush era. After studying the methods of Rove and the political Right, I realized they had gone well beyond outstripping Democrats by controlling the news and winning elections. Instead, by mastering political communication and propaganda — through public relations campaigns, advertising, polling, marketing, branding, information technology, linguistics, and journalism itself — Rove and the Right had succeeded in stealing reality. As Chapters 27-31 show, it's a phenomenon that many journalists themselves may neither see nor be able to expose — but one that has shifted the United States to the political Right.

The book is organized into six parts. As noted above, the first part addresses the question: Why is Karl Rove so effective? It tells the story of Rove's preparations and lessons for our class, much of it in his own words, as well as the lessons offered by the political advertising people, advance "men," image-shapers, and journalists who guest-lectured in the class. Many of them are well known.

However, Rove's success also roots deeply in the long development of the political Right and propaganda. Part two, therefore, traces that development, reviewing the importance of propaganda, especially to waging war. Part III, in turn, connects the rise of the American political Right to its mastery of improvements in propaganda and the connections to Rove. It also hints at the Right's success at changing the nature of news, by observing an about face at The Washington Post.

Part IV returns to Rove, to track his political emergence during the era of Watergate. It highlights dirty tricks with which Rove became associated during Watergate and later, as he rose to prominence in the Right. Part IV then outlines the potency of the propaganda Rove and the Right deployed to drive the nation to war in Iraq, eliminate dissent, and render two of the nation's leading news institutions inert.

Part V seeks to evaluate how this new force shapes our news, politics and everyday reality. It does so through a study of 32 American journalists, who give greater definition to these phenomena, including attributing responsibility for these effects to the Right, Rove, and President George W. Bush. The journalists, many of whom are well known to the public, also talk about why mainstream journalism is unable to shake this potent force.

Part VI summarizes the evidence supporting the main theme of this book — that American political reality has been stolen. It then outlines evidence from Rove's recent book to illustrate why Right and Rove continue to succeed in stealing reality.

Bill Israel
San Antonio, Texas
December 2010

The Lessons of Karl Rove and Friends

Chapter 1

DEMAGNETIZING ISSUES

Karl Rove's consulting office in Austin was humming with activity when I arrived and his receptionist asked me to wait until "Karl" finished business down the hall. A minute later he emerged, grinned "hello" to me, and whirled her down the hallway.

I spotted a pile of faxed news releases from the campaign not of George W. Bush, but of his brother Jeb, who was running the first time for governor of Florida. From the looks of it, Rove was almost as involved in running Jeb for governor as he was in running George for reelection as Texas governor and for president — all at the same time.

Moments later, Rove's receptionist landed in her chair, smoothed her hair and composed herself. But within two minutes, he buzzed her on the phone with more instructions and projects while he shoveled still more her way by e-mail.

Rove reappeared and ushered me through Karl Rove + Co., the political consulting firm he'd formed eighteen years earlier after leaving the employ of then Texas Governor William Clements. As we walked down the hallway, Rove introduced me to a half-dozen staff members and then paused with pride in his backroom computer shop, where seven-foot-tall racks of magnetic storage tape testified to the political direct mail work for which he'd become known. He introduced me to his information technology assistant, Kevin Shuvalov, and then to others producing press releases, editing mail lists, writing speeches, booking engagements, and handling arrangements for an array of campaigns. Rove's political shop, in a leafy Shoal Creek office neighborhood not far from the Capitol in Austin, was moderate in size but had earned the attention of most of political Texas and some of the rest of the country.

A year earlier, Journalism Department Chairman Rusty Todd asked me to help Dave McNeely, then state political editor for the Austin *American-Statesman*, to assist with a class titled "Politics and the Press." McNeely set out to teach the course with Paul Begala, who, with James Carville, had run the first Clinton-Gore campaign and consulted on the second. Begala had just returned from Washington to work at Public Strategies Inc. (PSI), the Austin lobbying firm. I had been teaching young reporters on an assistantship at the university and was doing dissertation research. Todd pulled me from teaching to run a program to introduce minority high school students to journalism as a potential career, then asked that I also assist McNeely and Begala with their class. Todd, who had worked for a member of Congress himself, thought I'd be a good match for the course. I had been a political reporter for newspapers, magazines, and broadcast news and had worked as a press secretary for a gubernatorial candidate in Iowa, for the majority leader of the California Senate, and for a U.S. Senator in Washington, D.C.

I enjoyed McNeely, a long-time Texas journalist. Begala was good at his work, especially at debate. He brought interesting speakers with him, including Carville, George Stephanopoulos, and political television specialist Mark McKinnon. At one class, he brought John F. Kennedy Jr. I wasn't informed in advance, so just before class I hustled to the journalism department's photo lab upstairs to find a photographer, certain I'd hear complaints from our dean if we didn't record the moment. As it turned out, word of his appearance had already sped around our building. When Kennedy — who'd recently been chosen the "Sexiest Man Alive" by *People* magazine — used a public phone down the hall from the dean's office, women pushed out into the hall, and he grinned back as he made his call.

But in class, when the student photographer I recruited began methodically shooting close-ups with flash, Kennedy objected and Begala came to his defense. Begala wanted to keep the appearance of his friend low-key. But this was a public institution, and I wasn't pleased that Begala shouted at the student photographer, who became upset. McNeely interceded and defused the situation. The photographer, by the way, got some good pictures.

That fall, Begala left for Washington to defend Clinton in the Monica Lewinsky scandal. I was writing my dissertation when McNeely called to ask if I'd help with the class again. With Begala gone, McNeely recruited Rove. By this point, McNeely's wife, television journalist Carole Kneeland, was fighting a recurrence of breast cancer. By the beginning of January, I was growing nervous about our class. McNeely wasn't always available. Other than the previous year's syllabus, we had no class plan, and I had not even met Rove. With thirteen days before the first class, I told McNeely I'd contact Rove to get things moving. I faxed him.[8]

We talked by phone the next day and agreed to keep the same class format he and McNeely had begun to work up. We agreed, too, to keep roughly the same topics covered in the previous syllabus, including: how the political press works, campaigns, polling, political advertising, debate, statehouse reporting, political public relations, and public journalism. Rove asked me to recommend theoretical and practical readings on each topic to get students started. I made some suggestions but he emailed two days before class began.

"I've revised the syllabus," he wrote, "and will either bring copies for the class or turn it over to you to copy. In addition, I have articles to hand out for the next class meeting. Might you arrange to copy them?"

Rove added, "I'm also redoing Dave's book list but will bring it with me tomorrow since I'm adding more books tonight. How many copies should I bring?"[9]

People say Rove is a take-charge kind of guy. They're right. But I was able to squeeze in several readings, including some from a couple of mass communication and political scientists and a couple of chapters from Timothy Crouse's popular book, *Boys on the Bus*.[10] The book popularized the term "pack journalism," a phenomenon in which journalists from less prominent newspapers often borrow the ideas of journalists at more prominent media when writing their leads while covering presidential political candidates. Crouse pointed out that one reason for the copycat behavior is that editors back home would often chide reporters who wrote stories that differed from the major news services. Homogeneity, in other words, was more important than creativity or uniqueness.

A short time later I went to Rove's office to meet him in person. At first, we were reserved with each other, perhaps for good reason. Rove knew I was a former staffer for Sen. Harold E. Hughes of Iowa, who was No. 6 on Nixon's White House Enemies List. Hughes had headed the Armed Services Committee investigation of the Nixon-Kissinger secret Cambodia bombings, which contributed to the debate to impeach Nixon. In turn, I'd heard unkind things about Rove, including the fact he torpedoed Governor Ann Richards' protégée and nominee for Texas Railroad Commissioner, Democratic state representative Lena Guerrero. Rove called a reporter with the well-timed leak that Guerrero had claimed she had graduated Phi Beta Kappa from the College of Communication at University of Texas. She had not. Through a series of missteps, her candidacy imploded. There were more stories about Rove, including several that he had attacked Richards for appointing too many gays to her administration.

At least since the days of Lyndon Johnson, Texas has been as notorious for vote-stealing and political dirty tricks as Chicago once was for voting by the dead.[11] Rove, however, began developing his skills in that area not as a Texan but as an outlander. Once, early in his career, as he light-heartedly acknowledged to our class, Rove disrupted the opening of the campaign headquarters of Illinois state treasurer candidate Alan Dixon in 1970 by handing out a thousand fliers to hippies and the less fortunate in poorer sections of Chicago promising "Free beer, free food, girls, and a good time for nothing." Two years later, in an incident I do not recall him mentioning in class, he drew attention for teaching dirty tricks during weekend seminars to College Republicans,[12] even after the discovery of the Watergate burglary. This, according to former Nixon counsel John Dean, earned Rove a brief review from a Watergate special prosecutor (no action came of it).[13] He also drew mention in testimony before the Senate Watergate Committee for instructing a Republican National Committee employee to collect political intelligence by attending, under an assumed name, a youth leadership conference for the campaign of 1972 Democratic presidential candidate Sen. Edmund Muskie.[14]

But it turned out that we got along very well together. The morning of our introductory class, I dropped by Rove's office to pick up the revised syllabus and his contributions to the readings we'd been assembling. He checked in by e-mail at midday, believing there was a long list of people who wanted to take the class, who might show up that afternoon. He asked: "What's the maximum number of students we can accommodate?"

Rove's enthusiasm was admirable, but my concern was whether we could get enough students to take the course. Many students have difficulty seeing opportunities like this — to have one of the greatest political campaigners in history teach a class. Fortunately, though, by four that afternoon we had a bustling group of eager student journalists and student politicos, about two dozen — some seated, some half-seated or talking to others up and down the steep bank of chairs that rose theater-style from the front well of our large lecture room in Burdine Hall. I staked out a chair and table at the front and stage left, close to the crowd, to best distribute an array of materials. I set up a table and two chairs front and center for McNeely and Rove. McNeely introduced all three of us and we discussed what we'd be covering in the weeks ahead.

Shortly after 4 p.m., one week later, a hush fell over class a row at a time as McNeely, looking ashen, descended the theater steps from the back of the classroom to the well in front. In an orderly way, he told the students of his wife's death and said he would be in class in the weeks ahead as best he could. A short time later, he left. Rove and I filled in.

Two experienced campaign managers joined us as guest presenters that day. One was Dale Laine, who'd been deputy executive assistant to Governor Bush and helped manage his 1998 gubernatorial campaign. The other was Greg Hartman, a Democratic campaign manager and executive assistant and director of communications for Texas State Comptroller John Sharp. Rove was third.

In our first extended conversation a week before, Rove had made it clear, without condescension, that he believed most journalists know little about the business of electing candidates.[15] In class, he elaborated.[16] Elections are won, he pointed out, by simplifying issues, by making choices clear and stark, black and white, either/or; by preparing the campaign battlefield long before the conflict begins; and by attacking when tactical and strategic advantage are clear. Essential to that process is "demagnetizing issues to ... get to core principles," to penetrate the screen of the news media to reach voters directly.[17] He did not specify those principles at that moment, though over the semester he would laud the ideas of eighteenth-century political economist Adam Smith, twentieth-century economist Friedrich von Hayek, the political philosophy of Ronald Reagan, and Thomas Jefferson, who observed that government is best which governs least. To illustrate the point, he used the 1994 gubernatorial race in which Bush defeated incumbent Governor Ann Richards.

Preparation for that campaign, he said, revealed opportunity on four fronts: public schools, juvenile justice, welfare, and tort reform.[18] Rove listed each issue on the board, defining each with a chalk spike below and to the left and right, effectively outlining either/or positions—right and wrong—with a figure that looked, in each instance, like a bottomless equilateral triangle.[19] He defined a "good" public school as one in which students do well on standardized tests and the local school district exercises local control. If the students performed poorly, schools should be warned to improve or face a voucher system.

He defined juvenile justice as good if it disposed of "super-predators ... who should be sent to prison"; bad, if society failed to confront such young people "who are more violent and more random" than the typical criminal. Rove defined welfare as "jobs versus dependency." Good versus bad. He presented tort reform as a single good: the passing of legislation to end "too many lawsuits brought by too many greedy lawyers, tying up the courts" — and, therefore, implying that the civil torts system is bad.

The power of Rove's approach lay, first, in snapping the issues from their context and redefining them in ways that would advantage Bush. Second, the either/or spikes on his charts not only presented choices, but effectively outlined a wedge. The issues picked, and the wedges he created, however, were aimed not at the issues themselves, but at voters who cared about them — usually Democratic- and independent-leaning constituents, or "swing voters," who might go to either party, depending upon the issue definition. The point of the issues chosen, and the wedges by which he defined them, was to split those voters off as a group, away from traditional patterns of voting for Democrats and traditionally Democratic issues.

For Rove, context and history were not the point; rather, the point was to redefine the issue, in order *to move the constituency itself to the right*, and advantage his candidate. The role of government is to support a philosophy of economic libertarianism, even if that means protecting the wealthy to pursue their interests and pushing lower classes out of the way. "Demagnetizing," Rove called it — the uncoupling of social issues from history, the re-insertion of nineteenth-century economic libertarianism as government's philosophical foundation, and redefining the issues to benefit the Right.

The issues addressed during that first lecture appeared to center on the old divisions of wealth, class, race, and power. When a student in class tried to question Rove's approach to politics, and I joined in to challenge more deeply, he roared at us, cutting us off before we could finish speaking.

"What are you trying to do," he thundered, "engage in class warfare?"

A hush fell over the room. Rove, who until then appeared congenial and witty, showed that he could intimidate. On the other hand, Rove could not have better demonstrated an important principle of his work: that the best defense to some challenges is not debate, but counterattack. If challengers suggest you've fuzzed the issues, attack the challengers by accusing *them* of practicing "class warfare." Scholars call it *ad hominem* attacks: If you can't win the argument, discredit your opponent.

At a subsequent class, Rove talked about Timothy Crouse's *Boys on the Bus,* which tracked reporters in the 1972 presidential campaign and found that the Associated Press often sets the news agenda for other media. Crouse called it "pack journalism." Reporters would consult with one another and, in particular, with Walter Mears of AP as to the lead and focus of the story. The campaign reporters had learned that if the editors at home saw Mears's story coming over the wire, they demanded to know why their own reporters didn't have a similar angle. The end result is that stories emerging from the campaign bus were highly homogeneous.

Rove's response was to accuse the press of ideological bias, asserting that reporters are elite liberals, unrepresentative of Americans. He suggested a disconnect, for example, between the press's performance and the fact that President Clinton's job approval ratings remained high, despite the Monica Lewinsky scandal. The following week, Rove argued that it is not the press that should tell voters the positives and negatives of the opposing candidates, but the opposing candidates themselves.[20] Indeed, he maintained that often it's best to ignore the press altogether. He recalled that President Reagan's image maker, Michael Deaver, learned to surround the president with flags and national monuments, or to utterly confound the written message by overwhelming it with visuals.[21] Sometimes, he said, it doesn't matter what the story is, if you can promote the right picture.[22]

Chapter 2

POLLING

On another day,[23] Karl Rove traced the signal debacle of 1936, when *Literary Digest* polled a sample of automobile owners and predicted Alf Landon would defeat Franklin Delano Roosevelt. Roosevelt went on to win all but two states. Rove also noted seminal polling work by Sinclair and Merriman, Whitaker and Baxter, and Gallup, from the 1930s through the 1960s. He said that FDR began limited use of polls in the White House and that by 1960 John F. Kennedy relied on Louis Harris's survey research. By the 1970s, polls were central to campaigns.

"Democrats were the first to use polls," Rove smiled. "But Republicans perfected them, for campaigns and policymaking." He cited the book *The Superpollsters* by David Moore, and recognized especially the work of Reagan pollsters Richard Wirthlin and Robert Teeter.[24]

Moving to the blackboard, Rove wrote:

Baseline poll. Twenty- to thirty-minute interviews of a large sample of individuals, conducted to gauge the strengths and weaknesses of issues and candidates, the relative partisanship and ideological make-up of the constituency, and major issues' volatility and intensity — intended to determine what a candidate should address, and when.

Panel back survey. Empanel up to 800 respondents in early February, and by June/July re-question 400 to 600 of them to learn whether voters have "moved" on issues for the purpose of assessing the impact of campaigns and events.

Brushfire poll. Survey a smaller sample of respondents to gauge the immediate impact of campaign messages, particularly from television and radio.

Tracking poll. Sample 150 to 200 new voters sequentially every night, average the findings into the preceding nights, while dropping off the first. Intended to gauge movement in a constituency and to fine-tune the impact of messages on voters.

Focus groups. Gather a handful of people, sometimes small or target samples of specialized audiences, to analyze their perceptions. Sometimes employ an electronic "perception analyzer" whose dial participants use to give immediate feedback, especially on advertising.

Campaigns now can easily poll for message, Rove said, because the capital cost of computer analysis has plummeted. As a result, "Now, we have dozens of polls going on in more than five or six major races," while "the press is stuck post-1936" in its ability to track public opinion. As a consequence, journalists don't have access to much of the knowledge about what happens in a campaign.

Earlier in the semester, Rove applauded an author who criticized the tendency of some journalists to treat campaign coverage no more carefully than an announcer track-side might call a horse race.[25] Nonetheless, he said, for political strategists, "The purpose of polls is to play the horse race — to get a snapshot at that point" in time to evaluate the candidates' strengths, weaknesses and standing, in order to best decide the next steps to take in the campaign. "It's intensely subjective," Rove explained, but "campaigns rely on their subjectivity — how your slant will play — especially in the back and forth with your opponent." That level of analysis is invaluable, he suggested, because good data help guide strategists and candidates toward the steps needed to win. But the press tends to use polls only for horse race coverage. Such coverage may neither motivate nor evaluate how people ultimately feel about an issue, nor even accurately predict the outcome of an election, he said.

By the time Rove finished and we took a brief break, Republican pollster Mike Baselice and Democratic pollster Jeff Montgomery joined the discussion, elaborating on the points made. Baselice was helping poll for Rick Perry, the Republican running for lieutenant governor at the time, and who later became governor. Montgomery consulted on an array of Texas Democratic races.

Asked by a student to describe "push polling," Baselice said its point is to put "information out to get people to not want to vote for your opponent." Indeed, according to the American Association of Public Opinion Research[26] and the National Council on Public Polls,[27] a push poll is not a poll but a telemarketing technique used to pass large numbers of potential voters false or damaging "information" about a candidate under the guise of taking a poll to see how this "information" affects voter preferences. The point of a push poll is not to measure opinion, but to "push" the voters away from one candidate and toward the opponent, often with the use of innuendo.

Another important use of polling, Montgomery added, is to simulate the flow of a campaign three to four months down the road in time, by assembling and mixing up the questions in a way that may accurately reflect the play of issues in the campaign. In effect, it is a way to experiment with what the issues' respective influences may turn out to be.

"A survey is like a blood test," Montgomery said. "It uses a sample to give you a reading on what's going on in the body. Political analysts like Karl are the doctors who shape the message, based on that reading."

Rove gave the impression that polling is an intelligence function, in which interpretation is key. As class broke, Baselice handed him a thin folder with what appeared to be the latest polling data on one or another campaign. The two discussed them in a brief aside by the table at the front of class, before Rove took the file in hand and departed. He may have commissioned lots of polls, but it became clear from Rove's presentation, from the discussion that followed, and from the care with which he took the folder of data from Baselice, that in the end he alone interpreted and decided what the data might mean.

Chapter 3

TELEVISION

The subject for the next class was television. Just as Rove delegated to others the mechanics of polling, he delegated the production of television messages to others, too — once he determined what the picture should be.

Rove's control over television was so effective that he helped turn Texas from a conservative Democratic state once in the spell of Lyndon Johnson to an enclave of Republican officeholders. Rove had rolled so many Democrats that by 1998 he was able to recruit Mark McKinnon, former media man for President Clinton and a campaign manager for Governor Richards, to produce campaign television for Bush. The trim and athletic-looking McKinnon had been to campus before. Now he was invited to comment on a half-century of campaign television ads, while Rove filled in some gaps.[28] McKinnon told us that Rove had so trounced him in an earlier race that it made more sense to join him than to try to beat him.

Political television commercials have consumed the largest share of a presidential campaign's resources since 1952.[29] TV is the primary tool of politics simply "because lots of people watch it," McKinnon said. Even though "an elite 2 to 3 percent of watchers are highly informed and not persuadable....you're really trying to get to [less-informed] 'others' in an election," he explained. The point of campaign television in reaching such voters "is to wash over 'em, and stick, while they're leading their lives."

Negative ads, in particular, can have a powerful effect, especially on undecided voters, McKinnon said. Although almost everyone claims to hate negative ads, they change votes and using them is fair game. Among the examples of negative ads McKinnon screened for class was the "revolving door" commercial produced by the George H. W. Bush campaign in 1988 to attack Governor Michael Dukakis as soft on crime. The commercial showed supposed prisoners filing in to a state penitentiary for incarceration only to turn around and come out again at once, through a revolving door. The ad implied that Dukakis had furloughed 268 first-degree murderers, who had then raped and brutalized or otherwise done violent harm to still more victims. McKinnon and Rove focused on the commercial's visual effectiveness. I did not know it at the time, nor do I recall any discussion from either of them that, in fact, the implication was false. Only one of the Massachusetts' inmates furloughed during the Dukakis administration went on to commit a violent crime.[30]

To have an impact on voters, McKinnon said, political television must:

- *Tell a story — a narrative.* "It's best if there's a villain, a threat, a victim, a hero, and a solution, or resolution." McKinnon emphasized the importance and power of telling a story, and McKinnon recalled Ronald Reagan's metaphorical 1984 ad, "Morning Again in America."[31] In that ad, McKinnon said, "There was no wasted breath — you know where it's going." The ad featured images of Americans going to work and a calm narrator suggesting that improvements to the economy since 1980 were due to the policies of President Reagan. The ad is considered among the most effective campaign ads ever because of its simple, optimistic message, and the phrase, "It's morning again in America," used literally to refer to people going to work, and figuratively, as if to ask: "Why would anyone change a successful administration? "

- *Be brief.* "The average news clip has gone from a minute and thirty seconds to seven seconds." Citing the observation of former Clinton campaign associate Paul Begala, McKinnon noted that the Bible through the single verse, John 3:16, digests all of Christianity into less than eight seconds. "For God so loved the world, that he gave his only begotten Son, that whosoever believeth in him should not perish, but have everlasting life."

- *Be emotional.* Hook the viewer's heart before head, McKinnon said. Touch hopes and dreams, as Ronald Reagan sought to inspire hope and optimism.

- *Be relevant.* The most effective television ad in American political history remains Tony Schwartz's 1964 "daisy commercial," an ad for then-President Lyndon Johnson. The ad sought to capitalize on fear that Barry Goldwater was an out-of-control bomb-dropper who would lead America into nuclear war.[32]

- *Be unique.* Show why you're a better candidate. Although Teddy Kennedy survived the political disaster of Chappaquidick, McKinnon said, he failed the uniqueness test in 1979 when he opened himself to an exclusive interview at the family compound in Hyannis. When television journalist Roger Mudd asked, "Why are you running for President?" Kennedy seemed unprepared with a convincing answer. When the senator responded with no clear message, rationale, or uniqueness, McKinnon said, Kennedy's candidacy sank.

- *Repeat.* Governor Ann Richards faced a problem in 1994 similar to Kennedy's in 1979: overconfidence. The campaign, McKinnon said, seemed so secure that when a reporter one noon time asked her to specify her message, Richards responded, "I didn't think I was going to have to work for my lunch." Richards, though a popular governor, had no deliberate rationale for keeping her office. Although the re-nomination was hers for the taking, "she never articulated a message for reelection," McKinnon said. "She didn't know what she wanted to do." Because she wasn't clear on her message, she lost the opportunity to reinforce its power through repetition, and by that failure undercut her potential for re-election.

  In contrast, President Clinton, in his acceptance speech after his nomination in 1996, sought to "Build a Bridge to the 21st Century" and he repeated the theme incessantly throughout the campaign and in his second inaugural address, McKinnon said. In turn, when Clinton was besieged on Whitewater and Monica

Lewinsky, as McKinnon demonstrated with a tape from "Meet the Press,"[33] Clinton aide Begala zeroed in on special prosecutor Kenneth Starr, calling him "corrupt" and suggesting that he met the test set by Lord Acton, "that absolute power corrupts absolutely." Begala gave a bravura performance, making Starr the issue instead of Clinton, and repeating that message during the show. (Indeed, it stuck so well with me that I later asked McKinnon to produce another copy of the tape for my own use in other classrooms.)

Political messages are less about party identification than about providing clues as to what one cares about, McKinnon said. Messages should clearly focus a candidate's concerns.

Asked by a student why politicians seem to avoid talking about abortion, McKinnon hinted at the dangers of a candidate being ripped apart by tackling such a volatile issue. Instead, he said, he took another lesson from Rove, who introduced McKinnon to the term "heuristics." The word expresses the idea of an interpretive impression, based on some set of observations. In sum, McKinnon explained, instead of overtly confronting an issue like abortion, a candidate may instead through a variety of messages seek to give an impression of who he is and what he wishes to do. Rather than confront such volatile issues head-on, the approach seeks to educate viewers on the candidate's view of life and to get them to like him, so that they'll transfer their trust and vote for him, whatever his view on abortion or any other hot issue.

Building on McKinnon's comments, Rove added: "Whoever raises abortion in election media first, loses." Governor Richards raised the issue in her election media in the 1994 race and suffered from a Bush campaign counterattack. When it comes to abortion, he said, "the counterpunch has a greater opportunity to hit home — especially on Christian radio," which can be targeted to energize a fundamentalist-leaning audience without enraging others who tend more to watch mainstream media.

On hot-button issues such as abortion and gun control, "it's better to narrowcast," Rove explained. Both issues tend to attract conservative audiences that may never watch mainstream media. In that situation, he said, "Radio is really good, great on a negative attack ... . It's also tough to figure out what the opposition's doing."

At the receiving end of such an attack, he said, there's an even greater danger, a more potent weapon that can be used to bypass the press in a campaign's last moments.

"The only thing worse to face than radio," Rove said, "is mail."

Chapter 4

DIRECT MAIL

Direct mail's great advantage, Karl Rove explained, is the element of surprise.[34] As a result, it is effectively "immune from press coverage" — reporters can't tell where, to whom, or in what specific variation a specific piece may be addressed; they can only guess. Direct mail permits a targeted delivery of messages to designated recipients; and the messages, and images, can be changed, depending on which audience is targeted.

Direct mail has been a substantial factor in politics for more than thirty years. "It's not a recent phenomenon," he said. He traced its use to a Mississippi fund-raising letter associated with Colonel William Crane, dated Oct. 19, 1864, which encouraged the giving of money for a campaign in exchange for political patronage; to 1856, when preprinted envelopes helped the candidacy of Californian John C. Fremont; even to 1688, the first known example of direct mail.

With individual pieces costing from 25 to 75 cents and up, direct mail can be expensive, especially if one sends out a hundred thousand pieces or more, he said. On the other hand, it can be quite inexpensive relative to producing TV ads and buying air time — yet just as effective in delivering strong visuals. Such mail generally is sent to as narrowly focused a group as possible, Rove said, to target those it may most affect and to avoid the media, the opponent, or the opponent's known supporters. Mail, he implied, can be especially effective for negative campaigns, enabling the smearing of an opponent while providing a comfortable distance between the candidate and the political hit itself.

Direct mail helped damage presidential aspirant Pat Buchanan's bid in the Michigan primary in 1992, Rove explained, when a mailed piece noted that while running in a state dependent on the failing Big Three automakers, Buchanan had at home, parked in his garage, a German-made BMW. In Senator Kay Bailey Hutchison's campaign, Rove used mail to show voters that she was the logical candidate in sync with H. Ross Perot. Rove compiled a list of Perot voters, a valuable list, he said. Direct mail houses make a nice living by compiling such lists and renting them out to candidates on a pay-per-use basis — and patrolling their use by putting fake names and addresses specific to that list and watching for them to come in, to indicate misuse, he said.

The range of lists, he explained, varies from users of supermarket-savings cards, to specific audiences, such as those who buy ruby red grapefruit; or, from a different list, those who've bought used cars in the past ten years. Some political operatives — Karl named no names, but his smile and the racks of tapes I'd seen in his office suggested he was speaking for himself — have lists of two million people or more, ready to slice and dice into myriad categories. An important resource for a state campaign, he said, would be a list of everyone who contributed to Texas campaigns in the last ten years.

Direct mail was important in George W. Bush's first gubernatorial race. It helped marginalize Governor Ann Richards' effort to equalize funding between wealthy and poor schools. Richards sought to level resources between wealthier districts and poorer districts. Because Bush needed swing Democrats and independents to win, Rove used direct mailings aimed at those upper-income swing school districts to defeat Richards. Television "treats everybody alike," Rove said. "Mail," he said, "is for Maoists!" It permits hitting potential voters in nearly revolutionary ways; it enables the targeting of voters in a thousand different school districts, with the potential to reach each with a slightly different message, thereby turning those voters toward one's candidate without alerting either reporters or the opposition.

The surprise element of direct mail campaigning can have great impact even when opponents are of the same party. For example, when Rove helped Lamar Smith run against his fellow Texan and boyhood friend Jeff Wentworth, Smith appeared ready to allocate "$500,000 for the GOP primary, $400,000 of it to Jeff's neighborhood," beginning by papering Wentworth's home precinct with direct mail. The idea that he'd face that kind of money and direct mail attack "made Wentworth crazy,"

Rove said. "By October and November, we floated the rumor" through the Republican grapevine that Smith might dump even more into the race. The fear of losing drove Wentworth to run even more expensive campaign advertising three months before the election, Rove said — "and Wentworth ran out of money."

"So it was a psychological game!" Rove said. "Get him to spend money! There was a $70,000 debt for Wentworth by the end" of the campaign. All it took to win, Rove said, was a little direct mail and a phone bank.

Having contributor lists is especially important because of campaign contribution limits. Rove leaned back and smiled as he explained to the class the irony that 1974 campaign contribution limits set by Congress, the legislative fruit of the Nixon-Watergate scandals, created the market for a new kind of political operative. That legislation and the one-thousand-dollar individual campaign contribution limit it prescribed put a premium on the ability to aggregate hundreds and thousands of campaign contributors and to raise money from them "retail" that previously had been raised "wholesale." In short, Congress' post-Watergate effort to reform the campaign finance system led directly to Rove's concentration in political databases and direct mail. The nation's smartest political operative became the beneficiary of Congress' efforts at campaign finance reform. Rove had been saving new databases, new lists of people and contributors, assiduously, ever since.

Chapter 5

VISUALS

The printed word, from its origins, has been used to influence the public and elites. Yet illustrations and other visuals exercise a powerful influence, too. The importance of visuals is adroitly illustrated in the nineteenth century story of New York City's corrupt political boss William Tweed, who was attacked by the cartoonist Thomas Nast. His cartoons in *Harper's Weekly* proved so devastating that Tweed reportedly said: "Stop them damn pictures. I don't care so much about what the papers write about me. My constituents can't read. But, damn it, they can see pictures."[35]

Since then, many scholars argue that visuals have become even more important. The photograph, the moving picture, television and, most recently, the Internet can influence the public through visuals even more vigorously than the printed word. Not everyone finds this change appealing. In reviewing the book *Amusing Ourselves to Death*, journalist Tom Stites observes that its author, Neil Postman, says Marshall McLuhan only came close to getting it right when he said the "medium is the message." Postman corrects McLuhan, saying that the medium is the metaphor — a metaphor for the way we think. Written narrative, Postman adds, is a metaphor for thinking logically. In contrast, electronic media, with their visuals, often bypass reason and impact emotions directly. Image media are NOT a metaphor for thinking logically. Images disable thinking, so unless people read and use their reason, democracy is disabled as well.[36]

But Postman's warning has had little effect on American elections. As Karl Rove demonstrated in class, the importance of conveying information visually applies to whether one is producing name tags, or messages for television, or the background against which a candidate speaks. Pictures are not only worth a thousand words; sometimes they're so powerful that it doesn't matter what the substance of a speech or news story may convey. The right picture can overwhelm or alter the substance of the story itself.[37] Indeed, consider the cases of Tony Schwartz and Willie Horton. Of all the people Rove mentioned in class or out, no one except Ronald Reagan drew more adulation than the late, legendary broadcast advertising man Tony Schwartz. Schwartz was "crazy ... mentally ill ... hospitalized" and didn't travel as a consequence of an illness, Rove said. Yet Schwartz created the most famous ad in American political history.

In 1964, Schwartz worked for the campaign of President Lyndon B. Johnson, who was running against Republican Senator Barry Goldwater of Arizona. Goldwater, a reserve general and member of the Senate Armed Services Committee, was the day's leading conservative. He opposed such social programs as Social Security and Aid to Families with Dependent Children, and supported escalating the War in Vietnam. Ironically, Johnson himself was on track for the same escalation — but not publicly, at least before the 1964 election. Goldwater's reputation for straight talk peaked at the Republican National Convention, when he declared: "Extremism in the defense of liberty is no vice; moderation in the pursuit of justice is no virtue."

In the "daisy commercial," Schwartz tied Goldwater's reputation for shooting from the hip, his threat to use nuclear weapons in Vietnam,[38] and his support for escalating the war directly to Americans' Cold War fears of a nuclear holocaust. The commercial showed a peaceful, colorful scene of a charming little blond girl gently plucking the petals of a daisy, one, two, three, four, five — then froze the frame in reverse black and white, like a negative. With the camera focused tightly on her face, an announcer spoke over her frozen count of the petals with the countdown to a thermonuclear explosion, and a mushroom cloud reflected from the little girl's eyes. As the mushroom cloud then filled the screen, Lyndon Johnson's voice warned: "These are the stakes! To make a world in which all of God's children can live, or to go into the dark. We must either love each other, or we must die." Another voice over then declared, "Vote for President Johnson on November third. The stakes are too high for you to stay home."[39]

The commercial aired as a paid advertisement only once — on the then-dominant CBS television network. It then ran wild, for free, on newscasts and public affairs programs across the country, dominating attention and crystallizing differences in the candidates, even as it misrepresented the candidates' differences. By seizing a few salient knowns about Goldwater and attacking with the projection of Johnson's own developing policy, the commercial elicited a kind of communication *jiu-jitsu,* pulverizing Goldwater's candidacy. The ad's genius lay, first, in taking into account Americans' fears of the Cold War erupting into nuclear war, the potential dangers of such a war exploding from a more aggressive war policy in Vietnam as the hottest battleground for the then-superpowers, and the reality of Goldwater's own words that extolled extremism and questioned moderation. It lay, second, in superimposing those fears and the dangers of policy imbalance on the face of peace, the eyes of a child. By combining those factors, even when an escalation in Vietnam was the precise path Johnson, privately, intended to follow, the ad attacked the challenger for the policy the incumbent himself would carry out.

In the second case, a furloughed African-American Massachusetts penitentiary inmate, Willie Horton, became notorious in 1988, thanks to a flurry of ads by the campaign of Vice President George H. W. Bush targeting Democratic candidate Governor Michael Dukakis. To portray Dukakis as being soft on crime the Bush campaign ran the famous "revolving door" commercial, falsely implying that 268 violent murderers were roaming the streets because of Dukakis' lenient attitude toward parole; in fact, there was only one, Willie Horton.[40]

The "revolving door" commercial was one thing. But another commercial graphically focused on the African-American Horton who, indeed, while briefly furloughed, brutalized a man and raped his wife. That ad, produced by the nominally independent National Security Political Action Committee, capitalized on racial stereotyping and fear. Rove told students the committee had no relation to the Bush campaign.[41] At the time I was in no position to refute this assertion; I only learned later that experts widely believe the PAC group was working with the campaign's knowledge and approval or that the campaign itself supplied them with the ad. That commercial was supplemented by at least two more from a San Antonio, Texas, group, ALAMO PAC. Of those two commercials, one accused Dukakis of being soft on drug legislation; another showed a burglar, apparently free and on furlough, furtively sneaking through someone's dark bedroom.[42] On the campaign trail, in the meantime, Bush reinforced the televised attack on Dukakis by talking in detail about Horton.

What Rove did not mention to students is that, by 1980, communication research (to say nothing of professional experience) had determined that people don't differentiate very well between the sources of materials they read or see, but amalgamate them into a personally coherent picture.[43] Indeed, one tactic in political communication strategy is to take advantage of that human failing, but Rove did not address that issue either. The concerns addressed in the Horton commercial did not involve race, Rove maintained to the class, but criminality and of Dukakis' being soft on crime. Other observers disagree. Robert McClure and Thomas Patterson suggest that the entire point of such commercials is to invoke fears that will drive certain white voters to vote in racially charged ways.[44] In any event, that ad campaign is ranked among the top eight nastiest in American history, and "one of the most famous, or infamous, examples of modern attack campaigning."[45]

As to the "independence" of the ads, Rove — and his friend, the late Lee Atwater, who ran that Bush campaign — made it their business to know every Republican player, to enable deploying their assets most effectively. Indeed, two years later, in Atwater's home state, South Carolina, a mysterious whispering campaign against Senator John McCain materialized after he defeated Governor Bush in the New Hampshire presidential primary. The whispers said that Cindy McCain had drug problems. It turned out she had a back injury and had become addicted to prescription painkillers. Rumors also spread that the McCains had adopted a black child, when, in fact, the child was from Bangladesh.[46]

Rove admired Tony Schwartz's capacity to transform a set of facts 180 degrees, using scare tactics. In discussing the Horton commercials, he appeared to approve the use of scare tactics and altering or fudging issues with respect to race, the republic's longest-standing and most deeply divisive issue, in order to win a campaign. Over the years, Rove has made much of the Republican Party's opportunity to seize the Latino vote and win elections with it for the long term, while by contrast seeming to pay little heed to African Americans. The electoral confirmation of that impression would be reinforced in Florida in November of 2000, when African Americans voted against George W. Bush by 92 to 8 percent. On the other hand, Rove used faith-based initiatives and anti-gay rights initiatives to whittle away at that margin. In Ohio in 2004, for example, partly because the anti-gay-rights measure on the state ballot turned out conservative black voters, 16 percent of African Americans voted for Bush, a margin that helped Bush to win Ohio and retake the presidency.[47]

For the class on political television with Mark McKinnon, Rove included in our reading a chapter from *Going Negative*,[48] in which the authors conclude that Americans exposed to negative ads are less likely to vote, feel less confident in the political process, place less value on their participation, and "infer from negative advertisements that the entire process, not just the targeted candidate, is deeply flawed." In class, Rove declared those findings "bogus" and said they'd never been replicated. Indeed, he was at least partly correct: The academic literature is divided on the effects of those ads.[49] On that issue, *Washington Post* political columnist David Broder, as opposed to Rove, had much to say to our class.[50]

Chapter 6

ADVANCE WORK

Karl Rove had secured David Broder's agreement to lecture to our class for more than an hour by teleconference, another instance in which he was introducing me and others to new information technologies. While I'd done a fair amount of television news work, teleconferences were at this point newer to me and to the University of Texas College of Communication, which had just installed a new system. To set up the session with Broder in a new classroom in the Communication College, I worked over the course of six weeks making arrangements with the operator of our system in Austin, and with contacts at George Washington University. Broder used the university's studio, only a few blocks from his office at the *Washington Post*, to talk to our class.

Asked by one our students what he thought of negative ads, Broder replied, "I take a dim view of [them] ... If, as Thruston Morton suggested, the essence of politics is really constructing a government, then the criticism of [media] campaigns" is that they produce "a climate [directed mainly] at winning." Politicos in Washington "are running scared," Broder said. "We've had smaller and smaller voter turnouts since 1928. If the strength of government rests on trust from people, when fewer give their votes, the government is weaker." The result among voters is an "attitude ... of deep cynicism ... and [an inclination] not to help govern ... for themselves." Comparing the situation to one that physicians face, Broder said, "If your patients distrust you, it's a debilitating thing." The increasing use of negative political advertising, he said, results in "declining participation and declining trust in government. ... When politicians tell other people how rotten everybody else is ... it's not surprising we have the attitudes we do. ... Politicians ... make an effort to reconstruct the record in a way favorable to them ... and so voters get less than they deserve."

The "reconstruction of the record" is facilitated by the overwhelming use of media to wage political campaigns. Campaigns rely on messages divined and assembled with the help of careful polling, then conveyed through carefully selected media to drive voter response. The results undercut the power of party political organization and have the effect of concentrating the power to reach and motivate voters in the campaigns themselves. The result is to dilute not only the power of parties to exert influence in the give-and-take over policy, but to reduce the capacity of journalism to inform and to deprive voters of what they need to make good decisions, Broder said. Once they establish their messages, "Politicians are quite willing to indulge in repetition. But the press ... abhors repetition. So meaningful stories are done only once — and then are forgotten. The result is, there's some dumbing-down of campaigns, and less content in them than in the sixties, when I was covering them."

Broder said the last good presidential debate took place in 1960, when Kennedy and Nixon squared off. In more recent times, debates have increasingly come under the power not of the League of Women Voters or of journalists, as in earlier years — but of the candidates themselves, whose representatives carefully prescribe how the candidates will appear, and under what terms. In the 2004 election, for example, the Bush and Kerry campaigns kept third-party candidate Ralph Nader out of the debate, and restricted the terms and conditions of the debates themselves through a thirty-two-page agreement (crafted in large part by Rove) that minimized the potential for each candidate to look bad. As a consequence, such debates are "more under control and there are conditions, rules, timing, format, that make them less useful." They have "become exercises in manipulation, not in informing people and policy." At party conventions, Broder added, "every single thing is done to evoke a particular emotional response. I call that manipulation. Others say that's just smart politics ... Everything is constructed, designed to produce an effect ... to be positive for your side, negative for the other. Everything that does not is rigidly excluded."

While Broder spoke, Rove was in and out of the room tending to apparently more pressing business, and he missed some of the elements of Broder's speech with which he might have taken issue. Our small, sound-insulated teleconference room was crowded with students, and some became sleepy from the stuffiness of the room, the length of our session with Broder, and our lack of a plan to relieve the tedium of watching a single talking head. Everyone was ready for a break.

A few minutes before Broder concluded, I spotted next hour's lecturers, advance men Fred Shannon and Brian Montgomery, outside in the hallway, and went out to welcome them. The tallish Shannon was a colleague of Mark McKinnon's at Public Strategies Inc. of Austin. Montgomery, a bulkier presence than Shannon, was then communications director at the Texas Department of Housing and Community Affairs and later became Deputy Assistant to the President and Director of Advance at the White House. Rove returned to introduce the two, who reinforced Broder's points from the opposite vantage point: that of specialists working in campaign advance.

Sharp advance work, Shannon said, must recognize that "Society suffers ADD [attention deficit disorder]." In the course of our lives, he said, "We get eighty thousand messages a day." The problem for advance people is to cut through that competition. To do it, "we give a visual background for what the candidate's doing. If you get the right background, there's more appeal." To that end, Montgomery added, advance work must create "visual excitement, an emotional experience ... to get the crowd going." Experts doing good advance work "may spend hours for two to three seconds of media impression," he said.

Montgomery showed a video clip of a Bush campaign rally, a big crowd cheering wildly while a succession of images flashed across the screen, from a smiling and waving Arnold Schwarzenegger, to a young African-American girl sitting on the platform, and to candidate Bush moving around the platform. The visual feel of the scene was of a leader in motion, who gave a sense of freshness, action, and decision. To create the desired impressions requires painstaking advance work, Montgomery said, including great attention to detail. The media are there for the event, he said; the crowd, for the emotion.

It's the advance man's job to set up the event so that nothing goes wrong, Shannon added. The candidate's job is to get out and deliver the speech. The advance men are there, Shannon explained, to make the candidate feel more comfortable, to make sure he looks good on camera, and to pump up both candidate and audience for the event.

The fundamental issue for advance people, Rove added, boils down to one question: "What's the universal picture — the national message" that you wish conveyed? "Good advance," he said, "insures the backdrop to elevate the message."

Backdrops and props can be important in achieving that objective, Montgomery said, even when speed and time constraints may sometimes mean the transgressing of property or an ethical boundary. Sometimes, he said, it's easier to beg forgiveness afterward than to get permission beforehand. Shannon disagreed, arguing, "Good timing, preparation, funding, and good luck should be used instead of staging an event." Rove seemed to side with Shannon. If one tries to be deceptive, he said, you will be caught, especially in a presidential campaign. Sometimes props may be useful to convey a message, but "be careful what you contrive!"

There is some irony to that remark. Five years later, on May 1, 2003, President Bush, dressed in a flight suit, landed on a U.S. aircraft carrier in a tail-hooked jet fighter, then stood before the assembled sailors to declare that major hostilities in Iraq were over. He did so framed by a huge banner that declared "Mission Accomplished." It was the ultimate in the use of backdrops and props. The White House initially claimed the banner had been made by sailors on board, but it had, in fact, been produced by a White House team. As "props," fighter aircraft and an entire aircraft carrier framed the Commander-in-Chief, implicitly portraying him as triumphant warrior.

Questioned by the media after the event, Press Secretary Ari Fleischer first claimed that Bush flew in a plane "Top Gun" style onto the carrier Abraham Lincoln near San Diego because it was too far out in the Pacific Ocean for him to take a safer — and cheaper — helicopter. The claim turned out not to be true.[51] Furthermore, as Cox News columnist Tom Teepen wrote, "We were told at first that Bush ... [the] caring commander that he is ... didn't want to keep the sailors from their waiting honeys by detouring it near shore. It turns out the ship was so close to shore it had to be turned so the president would look on TV as if he were in deep ocean."[52]

At the time of Bush's announcement, 139 Americans had been killed in the fighting.[53] By this writing seven years later, the war had taken 4,700 coalition members, most of them Americans,[54] and at least 31,000 Americans were wounded.[55] Although no one knows for sure, the number of Iraqi war dead are said to range from 100,000 to 1.3 million.[56] And it turned out, according to Democratic Congresswoman Loretta Sanchez of California, that Rove had been on Bush's plane.[57] In the words of David Gergen, an adviser to four presidents, "That speech always will be remembered as a symbol of the mistakes and misjudgments that have characterized this war."[58]

Chapter 7

ELECTION DEBATES

For the class on candidate debates, we planned to hear from James A. Baker III. When Baker couldn't make it, Rove looked for a replacement while I tracked down tapes of presidential debates to show students key moments in television debate history. In the end, the presidential debate expert who appeared was Rove. His grasp of the issues and detail was remarkable. He worked from the list of debate tapes I'd found, yet appeared mainly to wing it, standing before class with few notes and working mainly from memory. His delivery was mostly straight-on at the class, broken only by the showing of the tapes and his occasional pacing, hands moving to punctuate points. Again Rove's approach to the topic, while nominally about the actual debates, focused almost entirely on message and image control. And he spoke as though he were talking to a roomful of fledgling political consultants.[59]

Candidate debates, he said, are subject to innumerable "weird preparations," all of which must be carefully controlled. He talked first about the preparations and then about preparing the candidate, outlining his points and filling them in with vivid examples as he went. "Pick the format that's best for your candidate," he urged, whether town hall meeting, traditional moderator and panelist, or Lincoln-Douglas-like debates with candidates going at each other. Moderators or panels of journalists are used most often in debate because they're least likely to cause problems for candidates, resulting in fewer gaffes, he said. Town meetings can be the best and worst of formats; best, if it goes well, for their apparent spontaneity; worst, if the questions are unexpected, awkward, or hostile.

Challengers almost always want more debates and should ask for more than they want, then use them as bargaining chips for other concessions, as John F. Kennedy did in 1960, Rove said. Then, watch out for these variables:

- Long or short openings and closings?
- What length should questions be, and rebuttals?
- A three-step format — question, answer, rebuttal — or only two?
- How much time is devoted to each step?
- Multiple topics? Or single?
- Domestic and international issues in separate debates, or lumped together?

Incumbents, Rove said, should "fight for fewer debates than you actually want," then get into the details:

- When will it/they be arranged?
- Where will the candidate be before going on the air?
- When and how will the candidates arrive on stage and meet?
- Will they stand at podiums; otherwise, how will they move around?

In 1960, Rove recalled, John F. Kennedy gained an advantage in one debate when Richard Nixon injured a leg as he arrived at the studio. Nixon was disadvantaged not only by the pain, but because he favored his leg all evening as he moved back and forth to the podium, and his handlers had failed to provide a comfortable alternative for him. In contrast, in 1988, the representatives of Governor Michael Dukakis, who was physically shorter than Vice President George H. W. Bush, wanted two podiums, not one. "The image of these two guys standing, and one a little mouse of a guy going to the podium, was not what they [the Dukakis people] wanted on television," Rove said. Instead, Dukakis' people held out for separate podiums, with Dukakis standing on a riser behind his.

- What's the temperature in the room?

- When and how will camera shots be framed, before, during and after the debate? Cameras should be arranged so that your candidate doesn't stand in the background when the other candidate speaks.
- Who's in the audience? What are the rules of behavior for them? When will applause be permitted?

In the 1984 Mondale/ Reagan debates, Rove said, audience members were allowed to clap, but because of the format, it appeared at one point as if everyone were clapping for Mondale, which angered the Reagan team.

- Does the candidate control seats in a direct line of sight?

In a debate between Texas GOP Republican hopefuls Clayton Williams, Tom Luce and Kent Hance, Williams' opponents were seated directly in front of him, which threw Williams off his game. To maintain image control, Rove said, no photo outtakes — meaning shots taken spontaneously and not as part of the regular televised debate — should be permitted. And candidates must pay attention to cutaway (reaction) shots.

In 1992, in a town hall debate between Bill Clinton and H. Ross Perot, George H. W. Bush was caught in a cutaway shot looking down at his watch. The shot gave the impression that Bush felt the appearance wasn't going well and wanted to get out as soon as he could.

- Will notes be permitted, carried in or not? May the notes be taken to the podium?
- May the candidates make notes on the spot?
- How are candidates to be signaled that time is coming to an end? With a light(s)? Flash cards? Time devices?
- Who will be on the panel; who will be the moderator? From what range of possible press candidates will panelists be selected? How will he/she/they be chosen? For example, Rove said, when Republican candidates ask him about Dave McNeely, who once was a staff member to a Democratic state official, being nominated as a panelist, "I, myself, tell them that he is an

honest, capable, fair reporter, but most of the time, I get overridden!" This brought a laugh from his audience.

- What about forms of address? In 1988, he said, there were issues as to whether the candidates should be addressed as Mr. Dukakis and Mr. Bush — or Governor Dukakis and Vice President Bush, as to whom might gain an advantage. In the end, moderators addressed the two by their titles; Dukakis referred to Bush as the "vice president" and "Mr. Bush"; Bush called Dukakis "my opponent."

Rove then rattled off the following list of debate preparation rules, off the cuff, neither numbering them nor putting them up on the board.

- "Lower your expectations of how you'll perform, no matter how good you are." In 1994, when Jeb Bush debated Lawton Chiles in Florida, Chiles was expected to be the better debater. But when Chiles underperformed, Jeb Bush was perceived to have won. On the other hand, in the next debate, Chiles was in better form, and was perceived to have won.
- "Set aside preparation time with a *limited* number of preparers," Rove said. "Don't overwhelm your candidate. Fine-tune messages you've road-tested. But the day before the event, don't overwork him!"

Rove then showed a video clip of Ronald Reagan, who was in his seventies, looking tired in a 1984 debate with Walter Mondale. Rove said Reagan's staff overworked him when preparing him for the debate. "Debate prep that day wiped him out," Rove explained, "and Mondale gave a good performance." Because Reagan appeared tired in that debate, journalists the next day began asking: "Is Reagan too old to serve?" Bad plan, Rove said. Instead:

- "Build up your candidate before the debate." In 1960, Richard Nixon's staff scheduled a speech for him with a hostile audience, the Carpenters Union, just before he debated JFK. Because of that scheduling, Nixon looked tired and bore a sinister-looking five o'clock shadow. That put the GOP ticket two down, Rove said. In a previous vice-presidential debate, Nixon's running mate "[Henry Cabot] Lodge was inept, and Nixon needed to erase the assassin image" he projected through his first debate.

- "Predetermine which questions or points are likely to come up. Identify them weeks before the event to road-test them. Itemize ten weird questions" to help control the unexpected, and prepare the candidate to answer them.
- "What's your theme? The answer to virtually every question should come back to your theme. What's the constant theme?" New versus proven, as in the Bush campaign in 1988? A Bridge to the Future, as in the Clinton campaign?
- "What's the single most memorable line? It should support the theme."

A video clip of Ronald Reagan in his second debate with Mondale showed Reagan primed for the inevitable journalistic question: Are you too old to serve? Reagan replied: "I'm not going to let and I will not use my opponent's youth and inexperience for political gain!" The line, underscoring Reagan's humor and command of communication, brought down the house, made Mondale's rebuttal impossible and effectively buried the issue. How could anyone accuse Reagan of being too old if he could poke fun at himself on the issue and upend the Democrats' nominee, a younger and highly experienced man?

- "Think of what your opponent's saying," he urged. To illustrate the point Rove showed a 1988 debate clip between vice presidential candidates and U.S. Senators Lloyd Bentsen and Dan Quayle. Asked whether he lacked experience, Quayle replied that the length of his political experience equaled or exceeded, at the time, that of John F. Kennedy. Quayle's response set up Bentsen, who turned toward Quayle and delivered in a querulous and condescending tone: "Senator, I knew John Kennedy. John Kennedy was a friend of mine. Senator, you're no John Kennedy." The studio audience for the debate reacted with catcalls and applause at Bentsen's rejoinder. The remark devastated Quayle, who had no response but to show umbrage, and his response reinforced the impression of inexperience.

"Answer the question you want, not the question you're asked," Rove urged. In the process, stay on message.

"Nothing works like repetition," he said. In a 1976 debate, two years after Gerald Ford pardoned Richard Nixon and stained himself in the aftermath of Watergate, Jimmy Carter repeated the line that yoked Ford to the disgraced president: "I will restore trust." The moral, Rove said, is to "return to your principal theme" and repeat it.

"Remember that TV is a hot medium. It exaggerates emotion ... It raises your temperature" — and can lower it, undesirably, in the opposite direction.

In a 1988 debate between Michael Dukakis and George Bush, CNN correspondent Bernard Shaw asked Dukakis what he would do if Kitty Dukakis were attacked and raped. Dukakis, thinking as a candidate rather than as a husband, reacted logically and unemotionally, thereby appearing detached, disengaged and lacking in the compassion needed to be president. "Remember that emotion is a window into your soul." Open the window carefully and with deliberation.

In a first debate, Rove said, it is "better to be on the offense, than the defense. How you look is as important as what you say."

Playing a clip from the Kennedy-Nixon debate of 1960, Rove noted that on television one got the impression that JFK had won; yet on radio, it sounded as if Nixon won. Nixon gave a workmanlike performance, Rove said, but he didn't *look* presidential. The dominant medium helped to determine the debate's outcome.

"You have fifteen to thirty seconds to create an impression." Make the time count, he added.

"Don't commit suicide," Rove said, recalling that Walter Mondale in 1984 declared: "Mr. Reagan will raise taxes, and so will I. He won't tell you. I just did." In that moment, Mondale effectively said that he, too, would raise taxes. This drove voters away from him.

After a debate, Rove said, "someone [in the media or politics] will declare a winner [as] the person who did better than expected." Debates have little to do with either candidates or their major issues. You get 30 to 120 seconds to tell how you'll reorganize the economy, or 30 to 60 seconds to respond. Conflict-oriented coverage focuses on the candidates' shortcomings; gaffes are played up much more than substance; and a bad performance can sometimes discourage voter turnout.

Of course, each side will declare victory, Rove said. A candidate's staff needs to get out and say how and why your candidate won, even if the debate did not go well.[60]

Chapter 8

JOURNALISM

In mid-March, Dave McNeely invited Texas journalists Patricia Kilday Hart, Ross Ramsey and Rich Oppel Jr. to discuss political reporting.[61] As it turned out, the class also got a lesson in how Rove views reporting. While they lectured, Rove, seated at the front of the room facing students, read through and filed papers, doing his work and paying the journalists little mind. But when Oppel mentioned Governor Bush's veto of a health care bill, Rove looked up from his work and turned to object. He attacked Oppel's interpretation and accused the press corps of misreporting the issue to the detriment of Governor Bush.

A month later,[62] Rove would also "correct" television reporter DeDe Feldman, when she was telling the class an anecdote about President George H. W. Bush talking to a grocery store clerk about a check-out scanning machine. In the footage shown on TV, and then widely repeated in the press, it appeared that the scanner was a new wrinkle for the President. Not true, Rove insisted: The President had been talking to the grocery clerk about a "new technology" to replace scanners, but a reporter's account of the event made it seem as though Bush thought the scanning machine itself was a new technology. This suggested that Bush was out of touch with the routines of ordinary people. Challenging reporters' stories is necessary, Rove implied, not only to correct the record, but to correct the public's perception of the event in favor of one's candidate.

Rove had disagreements with Hart, Ramsey and Oppel when the presenters' discussion moved to state legislative politics. Republican Rep. Arlene Wohlgemuth, as *Texas Monthly* later put it, "is enshrined in the legislative hall of infamy as the symbol of wanton, pointless destruction.

It was she who, in a flare of anger over Democratic efforts to kill an anti-abortion bill, perpetrated the Memorial Day "Massacre of 1997," using a parliamentary device to wipe out an entire calendar of bills."[63]

Why, Rove demanded, did journalists not cover the role of Democratic Rep. Debra Danburg in that case?[64] Rove's point was that Danburg had used the same tactic as Wohlgemuth a little earlier, to sink Wohlgemuth's bill requiring parental notification of juveniles seeking an abortion. When House Speaker Pete Laney refused to intervene to keep her measure from dying for the session, Wohlgemuth used Danburg's same parliamentary maneuver to take down Laney's entire legislative calendar. Students' eyes widened as the reporters challenged Rove over what had really happened and which measures were appropriate. They were arguing about yet another round in Texas abortion politics and didn't make it clear to this collegiate audience that the central issue at stake was the Democrats' effort to preserve abortion in Texas as safe and unrestricted.[65]

In contrast to the huffy reception he had given some of our white journalist guest speakers, Rove warmly welcomed African-American John Doggett, a lecturer in business at the University of Texas, who also was hosting a conservative talk show on country radio station KVET. Doggett's political views contrasted sharply to those of most African Americans. Doggett offered a new and attractive, substitute visual frame for African-American backing for Bush and the conservative cause. What neither Rove nor Doggett mentioned in class was that Doggett had become a national news figure a half-dozen years earlier, during the Senate hearings to confirm Justice Clarence Thomas' nomination to the Supreme Court. Doggett was part of the effort to assassinate the character of Thomas' chief accuser, Professor Anita Hill.

Hill worked as Thomas' assistant in Washington, D.C., both when he was Assistant Secretary of Education for Civil Rights and when he became chair of the Equal Employment Opportunity Commission.[66] Late in the hearing process of President George H. W. Bush's nomination of Thomas for the Supreme Court, Hill came forward to accuse Thomas of sexually harassing her while he was her boss in both positions.[67]

Subsequently, in an affidavit introduced as evidence in the hearings on Thomas' nomination but never shared with Hill before it was presented in the hearing,[68] Doggett claimed that Hill, whom he'd met at a party, was "somewhat unstable" and "fantasized about my being interested in her romantically." He implied that the same had happened with Thomas.[69] When Doggett testified in person much later in the hearing, he did not dispute Senator Patrick Leahy's question, "Do you just feel that you have some kind of a natural irresistibility" to women?[70] His testimony and affidavit resulted in NPR reporter Nina Totenberg characterizing Doggett as "the guy who thought he was God's gift to women, and to Anita Hill."[71]

In our class, Doggett was a soft-spoken, tall and effective spokesman for talk radio, which he said had transformed politics. The importance of talk radio was affirmed seven years later by David Keene, president of the American Conservative Union, who said that "conservatives have prospered whenever they've been able to utilize technology to get around established channels. So the first really great surge of conservative grassroots activity came with the development of direct mail, and then cable TV, and radio talk shows — things that allow conservatives to reach their audience without a filter."[72] Here was another example of how conservatives have used technology, albeit more low-tech, to advance their politics.

Doggett described his program as "intelligent conservative, Republican, pro-life ... talk radio." He described for students how he prepared for his show, which aired from 1 to 4 p.m. weekdays, how much he read, what it took to produce the show. "There are no sound bites, scripts, or control" over how the program will run. The length of the program, he said, caused candidates to run out of canned material, so listeners can differentiate between the knowledgeable and the scripted. Doggett said talk radio has among the highest percentage of voters using any medium — some 75 percent who listen also vote.

Once Doggett concluded his presentation to head back for KVET, Rove reviewed the uses of talk radio and noted that it's been considered a source for negativism, as well as a powerful political force. Because it's less regulated, he said, some people say inflammatory things, fueling strong emotions and strong reactions. But, he said, talk radio has few gatekeepers, has a low capital cost compared to other media, and is non-mainstream — for many people, an escape from "the liberal media."

I interjected at that point. Research, I said,[73] shows that mainstream news media as a whole are neither liberal nor conservative, but middle of the road, and generally reflect a social consensus of values.[74] For the second time that semester, I listed some of those values on the blackboard, again, so they'd soak in for students and Rove. At that point, Rove turned in his seat to me at the blackboard and frowned disapprovingly. He seemed not to appreciate the challenge to his contention about "liberal media," but he seemed to pay attention to the research. He concluded the session by saying that radio programs like Doggett's enable "resetting the agenda on a more conservative floor [as to] source and frame."[75]

Chapter 9

ROVE AT HOME

In late March, midway through the semester, Rove invited McNeely, Nona and Andy Sansom (Andy was executive director of the Texas Parks and Wildlife Department) and me to dinner at his home. Rove's home presented a comfortable mixture of bustle and peace. The bustle emanated from Rove's voluminous study, located at the center of the house. The peace came from his gracious wife, Darby. (The Roves have since divorced.) Although she described herself as a moderate liberal from Mississippi, she betrayed no hint of discord with her conservative husband.

Outside, a rambling, railed porch surrounded the gray farmhouse. A white fence framed the entry and flower gardens, which were displaying some early spring blooms. Inside, the rooms were spacious and bright, accented with hardwood floors and tastefully subdued traditional furnishings. From the outside porch on the west, we had a commanding view of the beginnings of the Texas Hill Country, but the home was only twenty minutes from downtown Austin. As the sun went down, the house bathed in the majesty of hill country yellows, reds and violets, an awe-inspiring and spiritual tableau. At one point in the semester I asked Rove about his religious beliefs and he said he was not an atheist, but an agnostic, an unbeliever who wanted to believe, but could not. And so it came as a surprise to me when, a few years later, I heard he had been attending an Episcopal church in Washington.

Shortly after we sat and had drinks, Rove looked through the window behind him and cried, "Andrew Madison Rove!" The Roves' only son marched into the room wearing a Cub Scout uniform. Rove hugged and jostled physically with Andrew for several minutes. Andrew's middle name partly saluted James Madison, who fought for states' rights and drafted the Constitution. But Rove also admired Alexander Hamilton, who, along with Madison, wrote the *Federalist* papers and was the foremost proponent of a strong federal government. Rove, nominally conservative as to government power, seemed equally prepared to invoke greater government power, as pragmatics would argue. Rove invited us on a tour of the house while Darby finished preparing dinner.

At the center of the house stood Rove's study, long and vast. Tall built-in bookcases lined three sides, revealing a book collection impressive in size. Looking for a book relating to our conversation at that moment, Rove positioned the movable ladder attached to the bookcases to the right spot and trotted up, a little ungainly as he picked out a volume. I marveled at his book collection and remembered during the semester how he impressed me by the scope of his reading — recalling, for one, the day he told students that Walter Lippmann's book, *Public Opinion,* provides a foundation for much of political science and journalism theory. Reflecting a point by Plato, Lippmann argued, first, political scientists, not the public, should be entrusted with running politics, and, second, mass media were relatively ineffective in educating the public. Lippmann's ideas seemed to connect to Rove's. This view, however, contrasts sharply with John Locke's and John Dewey's idea: that the public should control public affairs.

On the house tour, Rove pointed to a wall-hanging — a pale green document, perhaps seven by 12 inches, carefully framed and given a place of prominence not far from his study. It was the charter given to his great uncle, in Milwaukee, that made him Norwegian consul to the United States — early evidence of a familial inclination to public service. Rove was clearly proud of it.

After the tour, Rove told me more about how the house had become the Roves' home. They had found the house in a small farming community, about an hour's drive away. Rove said they bought it for about $1,200 and moved it to their hilltop location for $10,000. The transactions confirmed another of Rove's dominant traits — his ability to capitalize on opportunities. A championship-winning debater since high school, he can size up the pros and cons of any given situation, prepare to act quickly and effectively, and then preempt everyone else to seize the advantage — whatever it might be. In the national chaos that followed September 11, 2001, for example, when many investors panicked and the stock market plummeted, Rove bought mutual funds at market lows.[76]

Dinner was delicious. We made short work of the roast of wild pig, which recently had been killed in a hunt. Like many Texans, native or transplanted, Rove enjoyed game hunting, perhaps as much for the camaraderie of talking politics as for the sport. But it also reminded me of one of Rove's heroes, Teddy Roosevelt — hunter, political adventurer, and conservationist. But Rove's similarity to Roosevelt diverged from there. TR started the national forest system and connected to the conservation movement partly through the naturalist John Muir, who introduced the president to Yosemite, an area TR later proclaimed as part of the new National Park System. Muir was the inspiration for the founding of the Sierra Club. Rove and Bush, by contrast, beat back most environmental organizations in Texas when it came to assisting the development and petrochemical industries of the state. Later, they sought to sell off 800,000 acres of federal forests.[77]

As the entrée vanished, Rove asked if there was more, and when Darby said "no," he seemed almost as indignant with her as he did with some of the news people with whom he'd crossed horns in class. Darby was nonplussed, as were the rest of us. We all then affirmed that we had more than enough. None of us was going home hungry.

After dinner, out on the porch, our conversation grew quiet in the beauty of the hill country, as the light drew low and the sky changed. When it came time to leave, Rove, apparently feeling that the vanished entrée had rendered him less than a good host, pulled out generous packages of frozen game sausage to go home with us. Although I'm not a hunter, I enjoyed them. One was very spicy. A few days later, when curiosity got the better of me, I e-mailed Rove to find out what the sausages were.

"The big package is nilgai," he wrote back. "The smaller ones are venison."[78]

"Nilgai?" I replied, after consulting my dictionary. "As in large, slate-blue antelopes of India? Where the heck did you shoot 'em?"[79]

"I got them in Kenedy County, Texas," he replied. "Fewer than two dozen were released by the King Ranch in the 1930s. Now, there are some 60,000 of them in Kenedy and Kleberg counties."[80]

Rove had bagged his game not far from the site of what became a more famous hunting expedition — the one where, in 2006, Vice President Dick Cheney peppered Austin lawyer Harry Whittington with buckshot on the Kenedy County ranch of Tobin Armstrong, an investor in Rove's political consulting firm. Rove's hunting expedition may have been less auspicious than Cheney's, but the Armstrongs were a Republican bulwark in the state, and their ranch was a hunting ground for many conservatives.

Rove may be shrewd in building relationships but he is a generous man. For example, he knew that as a graduate student I had limited resources for escaping the city or vacationing. When the semester was over and my girlfriend was visiting, he and Darby generously loaned me the use of their retreat in the Hill Country 120 miles west of Austin, along the Guadalupe River. From the outside, it was unassuming, but its interior had been transformed into a striking, light and colorfully furnished second home with a lovely and expansive screened-in porch suitable for hosting an event for up to dozens at a time. While I lived in Texas, Rove continued to invite me to use it. I felt what seemed to me then (and still does) the genuine warmth of his friendship, and I reciprocated as best I could, hosting dinner with his family and McNeely at my apartment.

That fall, Rove and Governor Bush demolished another Democratic gubernatorial hopeful, Garry Mauro. The Bush campaign outspent Mauro $25 million to $3 million, an effort that simultaneously fueled the Bush presidential bid. Bush swept the state almost 60-40, even securing the support of some of Mauro's friends. Democratic Lieutenant Governor Bob Bullock, who'd been godfather to two of Mauro's children, not only didn't back Mauro, he publicly supported Bush. The cantankerous Democrat had given Bush the entrée he needed — to be a "uniter, not a divider" — with even the state's top Democrat behind him. Rove used the victory to advance the Bush presidential candidacy nationwide.[81]

I didn't see Rove again until the following spring when I dropped by the "Politics and the Press" class, at his invitation, and then joined Rove, McNeely, and the newest crop of students at Scholz's beer garden for a final draft together. While Rove and Bush were launching the pre-presidential primary campaign, I finished my dissertation and was ready to move on. It dawned on me that, for some non-academic positions, Rove would serve well as a reference — so I wrote him, again, asking if he might be willing. If Bush lost the presidency, "your reference for me could be worth more than my reference for you," he said, then added: "Naturally, I'd be delighted to give a reference. And I hope you'll again use our Guadalupe River place. We've done more work on the two houses and bought the lodge next door, which is now being renovated. Just call Kristen and she'll make arrangements. You're the best."[82]

PART II

PROPAGANDA AND POLITICS

Chapter 10

PROPAGANDA: EARLY HISTORY

Propaganda is the deliberate and systematic attempt to shape perceptions, manipulate cognitions and direct behavior to achieve a response that furthers the intent of the propagandist.[83] Communication scholars Garth Jowett and Victoria O'Donnell, who define it this way, note that propaganda "is almost always in some form of activated ideology" — sometimes agitative, to move an audience to certain ends; sometimes integrative, to make an audience passive, accepting, or non-challenging.

Jowett and O'Donnell classify propaganda as white, gray or black, depending on its source and level of accuracy. *White* is when the source is identified correctly and the information is accurate; *gray* is when the source may or may not be correctly identified and the accuracy of information is not certain; and *black* is when the source is false, lies, fabricates or deceives. When people think of the term *propaganda*, they usually think of *black propaganda*, which means the source and elements of the message are falsely presented, or misleading, deceitful and covert. The propaganda of Adolf Hitler's Nazi Germany is the most recognized example of black propaganda. The goal is to disseminate false news stories to mislead journalists and citizens and to weaken adversaries.[84] Propaganda defined in this way is the enemy of democracy. On the other side of the continuum is white propaganda. Some advertising falls into this category. The goal "is interactive and attempts to satisfy the needs of both persuader and persuadee."[85]

The systematic use of propaganda dates to ancient Greece, when it became embedded in the communication technologies of its time, which included temples, statuary, and buildings that symbolized and idealized the state.[86] The black propaganda of disinformation dates from the Battle of Salamis in 480 BC, when the Athenian commander Themistocles introduced black propaganda to defeat the Persian commander, Xerxes.[87] Once Alexander the Great dominated Greece a century later, he had himself deified as the son of Zeus, his face appearing on coins, statuary, and works of art to remind people of the source of his power.[88]

In Rome three hundred years later, Julius Caesar extended these practices, beginning with "stories of his military exploits, combined with actual terror tactics at home to put fear into the populace."[89] Caesar made lavish use of spectacle, huge triumphal processions hailing his victories in the civil war. The point was to create an image of invincibility. Indeed, his slogan "veni, vidi, vici" — "I came, I saw, I conquered" — became part of the language, inspiring hearers to hail the conquering Caesar, and reinforcing the idea that Caesar descended from the gods.[90]

Only Popes, Napoleon and Hitler rivaled Caesar in his understanding of the uses of symbol and the psychological needs of the governed. Using propaganda to subjugate was less expensive than billeting more legionnaires, and it encouraged obedience through cooperation rather than force. Indeed, the subjected won the right to become Roman citizens under some circumstances, a move intended to increase obeisance to emperor and empire.[91] By creating his own legends and making himself seem supernatural, Caesar set in motion a psychology that led Romans from republicanism to monarchy and empire — a manipulation later used by Charlemagne, Napoleon, Mussolini and Hitler. To this day, images of the "eagle, the armored breastplate, the man-god on the white horse, or the powerful orator" remain as testament to empire, and to Rome.[92]

Jowett and O'Donnell remind us that "not all propaganda messages are negative, but are often aimed at some positive social or political purpose."[93] Christianity was aimed to a large extent at the defeated, the slaves, and the less successful part of the Roman empire. It had to compete with literally hundreds of other similar religions for this audience at the time of the dissolution of the Roman empire, and considering that Christ and his followers did not have control over the existing communications media at the time, the ultimate level of adoption of Christianity must be considered one of the great propaganda campaigns of all time.[94] In fact, the term *propaganda* was borrowed from Roman Catholic Church doctrine, whose goal was to "propagate" (spread) the faith.

Christianity has used stories in the form of parables, dramatic gestures at temple, metaphor — seeds on stony ground, the eye of the camel, the shepherd and his flock, Peter "the Rock," Simon "the Fisherman" — to produce powerful messages. The twelve dedicated disciples helped spread the faith, which was strengthened through rituals of baptism and communion. The cross became the ritualized symbol of Christianity three hundred years after Christ. Believers have also used two curved intersecting lines symbolizing a fish — which they scrawled on walls, trees, in the dust, and elsewhere — demonstrating that powerful propaganda can be generated even through graffiti.[95]

Buddhists, Jews and Muslims also employed propaganda. Although each religion has used different strategies to achieve its goals, all have relied upon the use of charismatic figures, heavy symbolism, a simple and moral philosophy, and an understanding of their audience's needs. In each case, the new religion had to find a way to replace the existing religious beliefs and to win over the minds and hearts of the populace.[96] The Crusades (1095-1291) are a good example. In November 1095, at the Council of Cleremont in southeastern France, Pope Urban II produced a convocation of robed cardinals, bishops, and nobles, while commoners waited outside the church. When the convocation inside ended, Urban moved outside to a large platform erected for the occasion. He warned:

> It is the imminent peril threatening you and all the faithful which has brought us hither. From the confines of Jerusalem and from the city of Constantinople a horrible tale has gone forth ... an accursed race, a race utterly alienated from God ... has invaded the lands of those Christians and has depopulated them by the sword, pillage and fire.[97]

The Pope blamed Muslims for the defiling of churches and Christian altars, the appropriating of their use for Islamic rites, and the rape of Christian women. The Pope urged the faithful to fight in Muslim lands that "floweth with milk and honey ... like another paradise of delights," unlike some poorly producing lands at home. His speech inspired the crowd to hail the Crusade as God's will and to rip their clothing to make two strips forming a cross, a gesture soon repeated by thousands across Europe and encouraged by the clergy. If the vivid imagery of individuals rending their clothes for the cross weren't enough, "woodcuts of a monstrous Turk trampling the cross were circulated from village to village." All these propaganda strategies built on an underlying mood of piety established a century earlier.[98] Ultimately, though the Crusades failed militarily, they helped the Church solidify its grasp as feudalism declined.[99]

Propaganda also helped the Church to overcome Roman power and to foster the Crusades. The invention of movable type and the printing press also propelled challenges not only to feudal authority and monarchy, but to the Church itself.[100] Martin Luther's German Bible provoked schism. Published in vernacular German and made available to anyone who could read, Luther's Bible demystified Scripture and removed it from exclusive use of the Catholic clergy. The new Bible's availability short-circuited the authority of the church by promoting individual literacy and conscience. Its significance was evident four hundred years later, when the German sociologist Max Weber paraphrased Luther:[101] "A man following an ethic of responsibility will arise at a place where he must say, Here I stand; I can do no other."[102] Weber also evoked Luther's words in his famous 1918 lecture, "Politics as a Vocation." It was in that context — discussing politics rather than religion — that Weber hailed the centrality of individual conscience to social welfare. Weber drew a strong connection between individual conscience, moral bearing, collective welfare and leadership.

Once Martin Luther and his adherents claimed the moral high ground during the Protestant Reformation, the Catholic Church struck back. Pope Gregory XV in 1622 created the Church's Congregation for Propagation of the Faith to spread the gospel to the New World and fight the Protestant revolution in Europe. While the means to do so were left to church officials in the field, the goal was to bring the faithful to accept church doctrine voluntarily. According to Jowett and O'Donnell, Pope Gregory's plan "laid the foundation for modern propaganda techniques in that it stressed the control of opinions and through them, the actions of people in the mass," using techniques to change minds and spread the doctrine.[103]

Just as acting on moral conviction is essential to political leadership, so is it essential to waging war. The Prussian strategist Carl von Clausewitz in "On War," first published in 1832, declared that moral elements are necessary to win a war.

They constitute the spirit that permeates war as a whole, and, at an early stage, they establish a close affinity with the will that moves and leads the whole mass of force ... The effects of physical and psychological factors form an organic whole, which, unlike a metal alloy, is inseparable by chemical process. In formulating any rule concerning physical factors, the theorist must bear in mind the part that moral factors may play in it ... Hence most of the matters dealt with in this book are composed in equal parts of physical and of moral causes and effects. One might say that the physical seem little more than the wooden hilt, while the moral factors are the precious metal, the real weapon, the finely honed blade.[104]

In the British colonies of the New World, pamphlets and newspapers became the primary means to distribute British as well as colonial propaganda.[105] Drawings were often used to attack the British. Among the best-known were inflammatory engravings by Paul Revere, one depicting British soldiers firing on a colonial crowd, and Benjamin Franklin's famous snake, cut into eight pieces to depict the separate colonies, and titled "Join, or Die."[106] Franklin's engraving, published May 9, 1754, was the first cartoon to appear in an American newspaper, and within a month nearly every newspaper in the colonies reprinted it.[107]

The American revolution gained power and traction from Thomas Paine's *Common Sense*, which provided logical reasons why the colonies should eliminate British political control.[108] Paine's rhetoric so inspired the cold and dispirited troops of General George Washington at Valley Forge that one week later, they destroyed enemy forces at Trenton, New Jersey. Paine's words, "These are the times that try men's souls," have been evoked by American propagandists ever since, even to raise morale nearly two centuries later, during WWI.[109]

After the defeat of the British and the failure to adopt the Articles of Confederation, the Founders turned propaganda against each other. And once the new Constitution was enacted and Washington became president, the adherents of states' rights, such as Secretary of State Thomas Jefferson, and proponents of strong federalism, like Secretary of the Treasury Alexander Hamilton, launched vilifying personal attacks against each other in the nation's new "partisan" newspapers, sometimes anonymously, sometimes through surrogates. Washington became exasperated as his two most important advisers continued to battle, a conflict that eventually led to the emergence of political parties.

Two hundred years later, in our Politics and the Press class, students asked Karl Rove why vicious attacks still occur in American politics. Rove reviewed the history between Jefferson and Hamilton, noting that personal political attacks like theirs peaked during the Jacksonian era. Rove suggested that *ad hominem* media attacks are simply part of politics.

Chapter 11

PROPAGANDA, WWI AND PR

By the early twentieth century, advances in American business had separated management's responsibility for corporate success from the function of ownership. At that point, while stockholders profited from a company's success, corporate management became the province of a bureaucracy of specialists. Business specialists perfected their command over land, labor, and capital — including assembly-line efficiency, finance, operations management, risk management, purchasing, production and promotion.

In 1906, the Pennsylvania Railroad hired public relations counselor Ivy Lee, a former journalist, to teach management how to manage media coverage of train disasters. When an accident occurred on the railroad's main line near Gap, Pennsylvania, Lee convinced the company to transport news reporters there at its expense. Although railroads traditionally had hushed up such accidents, Lee's plan earned the Pennsylvania Railroad good press. In contrast, the press and public strongly criticized the New York Central Railroad which had a similar accident not long afterward and concealed it.[110] Lee's actions helped institutionalize propaganda in the business world — more commonly known as *public relations.*

About the same time corporate America discovered public relations, the executive branch of government did, too. Theodore Roosevelt became the first president to make himself frequently available to reporters, and to provide a press room in the new executive office wing of the White House.[111] During World War I, President Woodrow Wilson appointed newspaperman George Creel to head the U.S. Committee for Public Information. "Since the morale of the front line derives directly from the morale of the civilian population from which the armed forces are drawn,

the mind of a nation must be mobilized no less than its man-power."[112]
When European and American governments called upon their citizens to
sacrifice for war, they knew the indispensability of public cooperation. To
achieve it, they deployed communication media to bolster public morale,
stir entire populations' sense of patriotism and commitment to the war,
and arouse hatred and fear of the enemy.[113]

Creel's Committee for Public Information (CPI) mailed and
telegraphed thousands of press releases twenty-four hours a day every day
— some six thousand separate releases in its twenty-six-month life.[114] It
published a 115,000-circulation newspaper for public officials and news
organizations, used naval radio transmitters to transmit directly into
foreign channels of information, targeted immigrants through six hundred
foreign language papers published domestically in nineteen languages, and
sent forth 75,000 "Four Minute Men" to speak in movie houses
nationwide. The CPI managed to keep the press from publishing sensitive
war information not by exercising censorship, but by outlining an
eighteen-point list of "What the Government Asks of the Press" and
urging that it practice voluntary restraint.[115]

From this vast exercise in propaganda — including experiments with
"the spoken word, motion pictures, the telegraph, the wireless, posters,
signboards, and every possible media" — Creel deduced that "people do
not live by bread alone; they live mostly by catch phrases."[116] With that
deduction, Creel stumbled upon to persuade that far surpasses the
propaganda of Alexander, Caesar, and Napoleon.[117] This new approach
succeeds by slowly re-shaping values and culture, in order to change
public consciousness. It further succeeds by engineering popular
acceptance of great power as both natural and unchallengeable, then
getting people to adopt these changes into their own common sense.
Achieving change by popular consent can succeed where armies of
coercion or threats from police fail. But, as Carl Boggs argues, to do so
requires mystifying power, public issues and history; it requires citizens
to become fatalistic and passive toward their political system; it requires
deprivation and sacrifice in the name of the system; and it ultimately
achieves people's consent to their own domination. The key is to establish
and maintain a new conventional wisdom[118] — and to channel it into what
people adopt as their own common sense.[119]

To shape the conventional wisdom, Creel, through Wilson, conscripted virtually the entire advertising industry. The Advertising Division of the CPI produced hundreds of advertisements and billboards for the campaign and pressured newspapers across the country to provide free advertising space. The committee published a weekly bulletin sent to 750 newspaper cartoonists, with ideas and captions from which the cartoonists were expected to produce drawings. Painters, sculptors, designers, illustrators, and cartoonists all rallied to the cause. CPI's Division of Films provided story outlines for film executives, resulting in films such as *Pershing's Crusaders, America's Answer*, and *Under Four Flags*. The CPI enlisted academics to write authoritative pamphlets on the war; produced exhibits at state fairs; and produced and distributed 200,000 slides, images, and photos for exhibit in schools, churches, and community centers. The committee emphasized visual media, especially dramatic posters and ads aimed through the eyes at the heart. For example, a Red Cross photo montage poster produced for CPI juxtaposed a giant close-up image of a protective nurse/mother, arms outstretched, seeming to hover over a battlefield littered with bodies. Another depicted a mother carefully cradling her child as they sank below the surface of a dark ocean, victims of a German submarine sinking the Lusitania. In bold letters across the painting was a one-word demand: "Enlist!"[120]

During the war, Creel denied engaging in censorship or quashing dissent. Nevertheless, the Espionage Act of 1917 and the Sedition Act of 1918 gave the Postmaster General and Attorney General the power to censor and restrict dissent, effectively making criticism of the war illegal. Authorities rounded up critics of Wilson and the war, sometimes without warrants, took them to jail, held them without bail, and tried them by a judge who sent people to prison for long terms. Among the victims was an adolescent girl sentenced to twenty years in prison. Throughout, CPI sustained an atmosphere of thought control, warning people to be "vigilant," to keep an eye on their neighbors and to act as government informers.[121]

Creel's work so effectively rallied public support against the Central Powers that toward the end of the war it also helped Wilson launch an eight-thousand-man force to eastern Siberia. The force was sent there to protect a $1 billion American investment in guns and equipment along the eastern end of the Trans-Siberian railroad. American forces, on Russian soil for the first and only time, supported Czech forces and Cossacks against the Red Army. After the war, the Allies prepared to invade Russia to put down the Bolshevik Revolution.[122] Congress, fearing the deployment of Creel-like persuasion at home, forbade spending public funds for its use post-war and shut down the Committee on Public Information June 30, 1919.[123]

Creel insisted that all American propaganda from the Committee for Public Information be fact-based, but some Allied propaganda was not. Both the Allies and the Germans circulated false atrocity stories. British propagandists used them to conscript America into the war. British propagandists in 1915 promoted the story of an English nurse, Edith Cavell, whom the Germans tried and shot for helping British and French troops escape to neutral Holland. The British focused, too, on the sinking of the luxury liner, the Lusitania. Britain's Bryce Commission focused an array of atrocities in a report later attacked for using dubious depositions. Indeed, the Allies in 1917 invented the story of Germans boiling down corpses of their soldiers to be used for fats, a story exposed as false only in 1925 during a debate in the British House of Commons. European propagandists used atrocity stories and other propaganda because they considered them to be quite effective — just as Pope Urban had done to set off the Crusades.[124]

One legacy of Creel and the CPI was the recognition that media could be used to sway public opinion toward almost any point of view, a fact political scientist Harold Lasswell underscored in his book ten years after the war:

> Propaganda is one of the most powerful instrumentalities in the modern world. It has arisen to its present eminence in response to a complex of changed circumstances which have altered the nature of society... .A newer and subtler instrument must weld thousands and even millions of human beings into one amalgamated mass of hate and will and hope. A new flame must burn out the canker of dissent and temper the steel of bellicose enthusiasm. The name of this new hammer and anvil of social solidarity is propaganda."[125]

Among the more effective lessons of the CPI propaganda campaign, however, was its approach to journalism. Wilson chose Creel to head CPI about the same time that a wartime censorship bill came before Congress, and American news organizations presumed that Creel would become the censor. Creel, however, a former journalist, opposed the legislation and delayed accepting his appointment until President Wilson approvingly read Creel's written statement on the issue.[126] As Creel himself said later,

> It was not that I denied the need of some sort of censorship, but deep in my heart was the feeling that the desired results could be obtained without paying the price that a formal law would have demanded ...With the nation in arms, the need was not so much to keep the press from doing the hurtful things as to get it to do the helpful things. ... Better far to have the desired compulsions proceed from within than to apply them from without ... My proposition, in lieu of the proposed law, was a voluntary agreement that would make every paper in the land its own censor, putting it up to the patriotism and common sense of the individual editor to protect purely military information of tangible value to the enemy.[127]

The Allies, who had implemented strong censorship laws and established the bureaucracies to enforce them, expressed anxiety and doubt about the American approach. "Yet the American idea *worked*," Creel wrote later. "And it worked *better* than any European law ... all behind a wall of concealment built upon the honor of the press and the faith of the individual editor."[128] Suasion was more effective than law.

Some journalists saw the results as too effective. Walter Lippmann quoted his colleague Frank Cobb as saying, "For five years there has been no free play of public opinion in the world. Confronted by the inexorable necessities of war, governments conscripted public opinion ... they goosestepped it. It sometimes seems that after the armistice was signed, millions of Americans must have taken a vow that they would never again do any thinking for themselves. They were willing to die for their country, but not willing to think for it."[129]

Nonetheless, under the pressures of war, with power focused not formally, but informally through moral suasion, the boundaries of journalism shifted. Journalists who might have challenged government action before the war seemed to behave less critically, once war came. War seemed to short-circuit Americans' thinking for themselves, free the government from press criticism, and unleash new power to shape public opinion.

The impact of Creel crystallizes through Lippmann, the most influential American journalist of the twentieth century. Sent forth himself to propagandize enemy troops during the war, Lippmann nevertheless seemed confident, for a time, that propaganda's effects at home could be expunged after the war, and that the news might again be an instrument by which citizens self-govern. To strengthen the news post-war and free it from the confines of propaganda, Lippmann prescribed the elements of objectivity.[130]

But only two years later in 1922, Lippmann reversed course, when his belief in objectivity seemed to collide with his understanding of the power unleashed by Creel. CPI's consent-making had been so powerful, Lippmann predicted that "the knowledge of how to create consent will alter every political calculation and modify every political persuasion."[131] Creel's mastery in creating public consent, not least in journalism, altered the balance of power between the executive branch and the Congress, which might never again recoup its place as a co-equal branch of government.

Chapter 12

PROPAGANDA AND GRAMSCI

One casualty of Mussolini's Italian fascism in the 1920s was Antonio Gramsci, a member of parliament who was also general secretary of the Italian Communist Party. Although legislator Gramsci had parliamentary immunity, the fascists arrested and imprisoned him in 1926. On the last day of his trial, the state prosecutor pointed to Gramsci and told his judges: "We must prevent this brain from functioning for twenty years."[132]

In the near term, the fascists seemed to succeed. Gramsci, already in poor health, nearly died in prison in 1931 after suffering a massive stroke. He died of a cerebral hemorrhage in 1937, shortly after release.[133] But unwilling to give in to his captors while imprisoned, Gramsci began a research mission. Why, he asked, do people often fail to act in their own best interests? Confronted with a fascism so clearly detrimental to human rights, why did Italians submit to their own subjugation?

In the course of his work, Gramsci developed *hegemony theory* — the idea that people submit to antidemocratic power partly because they believe such domination to be natural and partly because they may have something to gain from it. The gain may be in terms of vocation, position, financial well-being, sense of family, sense of belonging or fitting in, sense of worth, or some other intangible. Whatever the prospective gain, Gramsci concluded that the genius of capitalism lies in providing a market mechanism through which *individuals* may willingly exchange their consent. Gramsci discovered the key to political motivation: We're all willing to exchange general support for the political system in return for receiving something important to us. The only question is, at what price?

But making the exchange, Gramsci found, also depends on another essential mechanism of persuasion. People consent to their domination not merely because they have something to gain, but because they share a common base of assumptions, a motivating instructional software upon which they base decisions. That software is the *conventional wisdom*. It's a concept similar to that of George Creel: the catchphrases Creel used to couple the public to propaganda during World War I. The conventional wisdom can powerfully reinforce consent to power through mundane expression, such as: "You can't fight city hall," "Better dead than Red," "If you can't beat 'em, join 'em," and so on. In sum, Gramsci discovered that imposing power effectively is not a one-sided question, but at least two: power requires not just authorities to project it, but citizens to accept. To take one classic example:

> We hold these truths to be self-evident, that all men are created equal, that they are endowed by their Creator with certain unalienable Rights, that among these are Life, Liberty and the pursuit of Happiness. — That to secure these rights, Governments are instituted among Men, *deriving their just powers from the consent of the governed.*[134] [emphasis added]

In short, Gramsci defined hegemony as intellectual and moral leadership whose principal elements are consent and persuasion. The social group or class that succeeds in dominating, Gramsci said, is the one that succeeds in pervading society with teachings in culture and ideology that the population accepts, in service to a social order to which it consents (i.e., to which it consents, because of the conventional wisdom).[135] But hegemony is also ensured by what writer Stuart Hall calls "the armour of coercion"[136] — the threat of force.

It is not just ruling economic elites, however, who shape the conventional wisdom. Intellectuals — academics and opinion makers — organize thinking and teach it to others. Although economic elites have great influence, intellectuals are the intermediaries, the producers of culture, who render ideology and produce the conventional wisdom by a process of legitimation. In that process, intellectuals — writers, artists, and journalists — render the existing power structure palatable, and the values and ideals by which others support it, acceptable. As Benedetto Fontana, an interpreter of Gramsci's thought, puts it, the intellectuals' role is "to translate the interests and values of a specific social group into general, common values and interests" that are sustained by most parties concerned.[137] Thus, a stable social-political order is established based on a hegemonic equilibrium, as Gramsci put it, through a "combination of force and consent, which are balanced in varying proportions, without force prevailing too greatly over consent."[138]

One can track hegemony's continuous reinforcement through the everyday workings of government. Gramsci suggested that hegemony exists when "there exists democracy between the leading group and the groups which are led, to the extent that the development of the economy, and, thus, the legislation which expresses such development, favor the molecular passage from the led to the leading group."[139] In other words, the legislative process — the business of compromise and trade-offs — both demonstrates and secures consent in a hegemonic order. The hegemonic structure, in addition, is reinforced daily through regulation, executive action, and judicial decision making — through the tacit exercise of citizen consent. Moreover, as political scientist W. Lance Bennett pointed out, one can track through the interpretive work of journalists how they situate these processes within a system in which a fundamental assumption of journalism is that *the system works*.[140] Consent is negotiated at lower levels of governmental processes and surrendered upward at each step, exchanged for some of what the consenters want. Journalism facilitates that process at the level of ideology, precisely through the everyday workings of its core value, the ethic of objectivity.[141]

Someday, Gramsci suggested, leftist forces may reverse the process and take back the social order, not by armed conflict, but by a "war of position." A war of position begins from the intellectual and cultural bases such forces already hold, Gramsci said. It then adds a regimen of political education on a scale large enough to amalgamate a "historical bloc" of constituencies — a cultural amassing of people and ideology organized, over time, to take power.[142] Doing so requires building institutions — Gramsci had in mind worker councils, cooperatives, cultural associations, and so on — in which new modes of culture, relationships, and allegiances may be built to support an ideology.[143] To build such institutions and to marshal and exercise such forces, he maintained, is to win the war of position decisively. An armed revolution, a "war of movement," is not the decisive phase in achieving a political realignment, Gramsci said, partly because it fails to secure popular consent. Instead, "the only decisive battles are those in the war of position."[144] Winning a war of position requires building institutions and political processes that legitimate the new order, and translate it into the philosophical software — the conventional wisdom — that can mount and organize a revolutionary political challenge.[145] To drive the challenge, a political party is the best vehicle because it can act both to educate politically and to coordinate disparate organizations into a national force.[146]

Thus, Gramsci answered his own question: People fail to act in their own best interests and accept their subjugation because of the workings of hegemony. Fascism succeeded in Italy because influential social classes detached from political parties at the moment of hegemonic crisis. Fascism succeeded when Italy reached that critical stage because the Italian Socialist Party failed to properly organize. In contrast to conventional Marxism, Gramsci separated economics from politics. Politics may lag behind economics, he said, but politics is the means to construct hegemony.[147] Creating an alternative hegemony requires shaping the conventional wisdom through political education, boycotts, propaganda campaigns, counter cultural education, nonviolent protest — all means to wage and win a "war of position." If Marxism generally fails to mobilize *masses* into revolution, capitalism generally wins, in Gramsci's analysis, because of its ability to deliver to *individuals* enough of what they want in exchange for general support of the political system.

While Gramsci explored hegemony from prison, researchers in the United States such as Harold Lasswell focused on the success of propaganda during World War I.[148] Some researchers evaluated propaganda messages; others focused on persuasion, especially how to conceptually define and measure attitudes.[149] Gordon Allport sought to define attitude; L. L. Thurstone and Rensis Likert sought to measure it. Likert's scales asked respondents to specify their attitudes on a given issue from "strongly approve" to "strongly disapprove."[150]

Others approached the issue by studying propaganda's deleterious effects. Clyde R. Miller of Columbia University in October 1937 became chief executive of the new Institute for Propaganda Analysis (IPA). While he was a journalist during World War I, Miller became convinced he'd been hoodwinked by propaganda, and grew concerned that new propaganda would draw the United States into another European war. Through a grant from Boston merchant Edward A. Filene, Miller started IPA, and identified seven common propaganda "devices" outlined in a November 1937 bulletin. As the bulletin noted, "Observe that in all of these devices our emotion is the stuff with which propagandists work. Without it they are helpless; with it, harnessing it to their purposes, they can make us glow with pride or burn with hatred, they can make us zealots in behalf of the program they espouse."[151]

Chapter 13

PROPAGANDA AND ELLUL

The Institute for Propaganda Analysis went out of business in October 1941; propaganda analysis couldn't survive in an environment in which the U.S. government was propagandizing for World War II. The fall of France in June 1940 and the alliance of Germany, Italy, and Japan in September galvanized the United States, making the study of propaganda seem less important than the need to prepare for war. IPA board members — notably Paul Douglas, Charles A. Beard, E. C. Lindeman, and Hadley Cantril — resigned. Cantril had been doing confidential work for President Roosevelt, charting public opinion on the war.

Once war broke out, many researchers undertook government-sponsored research to both improve propaganda and counter propaganda, and to assess how to influence Americans to support the war.[152] New research focused on the nature of German propaganda and on how the American Office of War Information might boost civilian morale and direct commercial media to bolster the war effort.

The mastery of wartime public opinion in the United States echoed abroad in ways that upended advocates of Marxism, who believed World War I manifested the kinds of conflicts they predicted would overturn capitalism. As sociologist Carl Boggs explained in *The Two Revolutions*, his study of the period, classical Marxism held that conflicts between workers and management, socialism and capitalism, would inevitably produce a revolution whose seeds were sewn in Russia in 1917, even if they had been suppressed by the Great War. Yet, post-war, the seeds didn't germinate; in fact, the reverse seemed to be true, as Boggs wrote.

> Instead of the anticipated class polarization, leading to widespread socialist consciousness and insurrectionary politics, the

overwhelming trend was toward stabilization, a fragmented class consciousness, and political reformism. This trend ... actually became more pronounced with capitalist development so that, by the mid-1920s, the traditional crisis schema had lost its credibility ... The task was to understand not only why capitalism seemed to have infinite adaptability, but also why even where cataclysmic crises did occur — as in Germany, Italy, and Hungary — it turned out to be not the left but the *right* which managed to seize the initiative.[153]

While American media underwent the first wave of consolidation in the 1920s, Adolf Hitler's propaganda minister Joseph Goebbels was distilling Hitler's principles of propaganda. Goebbels summarized them as

a carefully built up erection of statements, which whether true or false can be made to undermine quite rigidly held ideas and to construct new ones that will take their place. It would not be impossible to prove with sufficient repetition and psychological understanding of the people concerned that a square is in fact a circle. What after all are a square and a circle? They are mere words and words can be molded until they clothe ideas in disguise.[154]

Hitler's principles for propaganda were: (1) avoid abstract ideas, appeal to the emotions; (2) constantly repeat a few ideas, use stereotyped phrases, avoid objectivity; (3) argue only one side; (4) criticize enemies of the state constantly; and (5) vilify one special enemy.[155] It worked — not only in Germany, but where the fascists also seized power in the 1920s and eventually became Hitler's allies, in Italy.

After World War II, research continued on the effects of mass media versus individual contact in persuasion; the importance of opinion leaders; and how to make broadcast advertising more effective in selling soap to consumers. Researchers identified a two-step, and then a multi-step, process in the flow of information, from high credibility subjects to those of less credibility or stature. It was an area of study, focused on radio advertising at Columbia University and on persuasion at Yale,[156] that improved the efficacy of broadcast advertising and sales personnel. Peacetime boosts to American business and industry resulted from wartime scientific research on propaganda and persuasion, trained first on an enemy and then, modified, on Americans.[157]

Writing after World War II, the French intellectual Jacques Ellul argued that modern propaganda is tied to the growing sophistication and dominance of science and technology. Whether in the hardware of coinage and construction, or in the software of language, Ellul held that "true modern propaganda can only function within the context of the modern scientific system." Furthermore, he said "propaganda is the expression of these branches of science; it moves with them, shares in their successes, and bears witness to their failures."[158]

Gramsci, reflecting from prison on the successes of Italian fascism, charted the theoretical processes by which Italians might find their way beyond fascism. In contrast, by reviewing the scientific pursuit of propaganda during World War II, Ellul concluded that to be effective, propaganda must be total, promoted by every means to permeate and infiltrate every societal niche.[159] Ellul saw propaganda as a technological development, its efficacy based on scientific analyses of psychology and sociology. Propaganda thus establishes, Ellul said, a set of rigorous, tested rules that impose themselves on the propagandist, too. Propaganda requires a precise analysis of the environment and of the individuals targeted for influence; its processes must be measured with precision.[160]

Ellul further differentiated political propaganda from sociological propaganda.[161] Political propaganda, he said, includes "techniques of influence employed by a government, a party, an administration, a pressure group, with a view to changing the behavior of the public. The choice of methods used is deliberate and calculated; the desired goals are clearly distinguished and quite precise, though generally limited."[162] In contrast, he said, "Sociological propaganda is a phenomenon much more difficult to grasp than political propaganda, and is rarely discussed. *Basically it is the penetration of an ideology by means of its sociological context.*" [emphasis in original] The usual approach to propaganda is as an effort to diffuse ideas through the mass media with the aim of getting the public to consent to some identifiable political or economic change in the law or system. Such efforts follow traditional lines of propaganda activity.

In contrast, sociological propaganda is more subtle. Its aim is to make fundamental changes in ideology — in other words, to change the assumptions on which people think and act, to win their consent to still broader change. According to Ellul:

> Such propaganda is ... diffuse ... conveyed [less] by catchwords or expressed intentions. Instead it is based on a general climate, an atmosphere that influences people imperceptibly without having the appearance of propaganda; it gets to man through his customs, through his most unconscious habits. It creates new habits in him; it is a sort of persuasion from within. As a result, man adopts new criteria of judgment and choice ... spontaneously, as if he had chosen them himself. But all these criteria are in conformity with the environment and are essentially of a collective nature. Sociological propaganda produces a progressive adaptation to a certain order of things ... which unconsciously molds individuals and makes them conform to society....the individual in the clutches of such sociological propaganda believes that those who live this way are on the side of the angels, and those who don't are bad; those who have this conception of society are right, and those who have another conception are in error ... such propaganda becomes increasingly effective when those subjected to it accept its doctrines on what is *good* or *bad* (for example, the American Way of Life). There, a whole society actually expresses itself through this propaganda by advertising its kind of life ... By doing that, a society engages in propaganda on the deepest level.

In order for it to be effective, Ellul said such propaganda must act gently, in seemingly harmless ways that act slowly but which penetrate social mores. Such a process conditions citizens and ends by creating "a fully established personality structure" that resonates with the new ideology. Sociological propaganda by itself is not adequate in moments of crisis; but nothing is easier, Ellul said, than to graft a regular propaganda campaign onto a regimen of sociological propaganda that has conditioned a people in a direction that makes it more willing to provide its consent.

Then, by a series of intermediate stages, we not only see one turn into the other [e.g., a propaganda campaign turned into a regimen of sociological propaganda), but we also see a smooth transition from what was merely a spontaneous affirmation of a way of life to the deliberate affirmation of a truth. Public relations consultant Edward L. Bernays called it the "engineering approach," which is tied to a combination of professional research methods through which one gets people to adopt and actively support certain ideas or programs as soon as they become aware of them. This also applies to affairs in the political realm.[163]

In sum, from the time of Alexander the Great in 300 B.C., propaganda has been central to the exercise of power. Propaganda became more important as suffrage widened and as governments depended increasingly on public opinion. As Abraham Lincoln put it, "Public sentiment is everything. With public sentiment nothing can fail; without it nothing can succeed. Consequently, he who moulds public sentiment goes deeper than he who enacts statutes or pronounces decisions."[164]

The development of scientifically based propaganda dates to the specialization and bureaucratization of business in the late nineteenth and early twentieth centuries in the United States and, especially, to business' use of public relations. Improving on the public relations methods of business, the U.S. government deployed the first mass use of propaganda in World War I. George Creel and the Committee on Public Information used new methods "to impregnate the entire fabric of perception with the message of the war"— in the United States and around the world.[165] Underlying Creel's success was a recognition that facts are manipulable by propaganda and persuasion and by technological advances in media that make message delivery instantaneous and effective.

As Gramsci and Ellul outlined, a political minority, harnessing the power of propaganda and technology, can transform itself into a majority by creating new institutions and deploying media and technology to induce an entire people to act against their own best interests, partly by getting people to exchange their political consent for what they want *as individuals*. Central to that effort is the production of a new conventional wisdom, and its translation into common sense. Journalists, as legitimators of ideas and as producers and disseminators of ideology and culture, are integral to that process.

A good historical example of this theory appeared in the United States during the Great Depression, after the political Left rebounded and dominated the political Right. By the mid-1930s, in near panic over the success of Franklin Roosevelt and the Left, the Right in the United States reorganized, drawing in part on the lessons of Creel.

PART III

A Brief History
of the Right

Chapter 14

ROUTING THE RIGHT

The twenties roared after World War I and the media industry prospered. Newspapers hit peak market penetration by the second decade of the twentieth century; commercial radio broadcasts multiplied; and movie-going audiences began watching newsreels and "talkies." Radio filled the air with music, entertainment and news. In 1919 General Electric incorporated the Radio Corporation of America (RCA), and American Telephone and Telegraph (AT&T) and Westinghouse became part owners. In 1926, RCA formed the National Broadcasting Company (NBC) to run radio stations owned by RCA, General Electric, Westinghouse, and AT&T. The vertical integration of broadcasting had begun, with NBC producing programs to fuel the sale of radios (and eventually, televisions).[166] Six years later, the government antitrust division broke up RCA, forcing GE, AT&T and Westinghouse to divest; but not before newspapers, too, faced a first wave of mergers and acquisitions.

The roaring stopped October 24, 1929, after financial speculation spawned Wall Street's collapse. By the time Franklin Roosevelt defeated Herbert Hoover three years later, American industrial output had plummeted, followed by farm production. A third of the nation's able-bodied workers were jobless. Fear — of unemployment, lost life savings, homelessness, and starvation — consumed the nation; a "terror," Roosevelt called it. He fingered business and banking for responsibility in the collapse, and addressed the nation to calm the fear.

This great Nation will endure as it has endured, will revive and will prosper ... let me assert my firm belief that the only thing we have to fear is fear itself ... Only a foolish optimist can deny the dark realities of the moment. Yet our distress comes from no failure of substance... Plenty is at our doorstep, but a generous use of it languishes in the very sight of the supply ... the rulers of the exchange of mankind's goods have failed ... The moneychangers have fled from their high seats in the temple of our civilization ... there must be an end to a conduct in banking and in business which too often has given to a sacred trust the likeness of callous and selfish wrongdoing ... This Nation asks for action, and action now.[167]

It was an epic pivot point. Marx predicted the fall of capitalism eighty years earlier; the Bolshevik Revolution seized Russia twelve years before Wall Street's collapse. By 1932, capitalism lay in ruin in the West, and the president of the United States blamed American capitalists for the destruction. With Roosevelt defining political boundaries in moral terms, business appeared to be in moral bankruptcy, and the nation affirmed the moral compass of its leader. If the Great Depression resulted partly from the playing-out of unregulated markets, Roosevelt deployed government power to reassert economic and moral control and to defeat fear.

In the first hundred days of his administration, FDR set the pace for succeeding administrations.[168] Congress passed a flurry of bills, transforming the role of government in the economy and American life. An Emergency Banking Relief Act stabilized banking and reassured depositors. The federal government became public projects builder, employer of last resort, and guarantor of agricultural markets through an alphabet soup of new agencies: Federal Emergency Relief Administration, the National Recovery Administration, the Agricultural Adjustment Administration, and the Tennessee Valley Authority. New legislation started the Civilian Conservation Corps and the Civil Works Administration, succeeded by the Works Progress Administration. FDR appointed Frances Perkins secretary of labor, the first woman cabinet member in history, and at the urging of Eleanor Roosevelt, he appointed more women to federal posts than any president before. He included black Americans in his new job programs, though segregation remained. In 1935, Congress approved the signature program of the New Deal, the Social Security System.[169]

Although he hadn't detailed his direction for the country, Roosevelt in the 1932 election defeated Herbert Hoover 57 percent to 40 percent.

Once the New Deal reached a high pitch four years later, FDR trounced Alf Landon by 61 percent to 37 percent, carrying every state except Maine and Vermont. The New Deal had not only won the day but prevailed for the era by its political and social success.

Large segments of the business community opposed Roosevelt, but business seemed powerless to stop him. National Association of Manufacturers (NAM) president John Edgerton objected to Social Security, government health care for the infirm, basic welfare assistance for women and children, unemployment insurance for the jobless, and government as employer of last resort. People's loss of savings, shelter, and sustenance, Edgerton said, was not the fault of business; the homeless and the jobless had only themselves to blame.[170] By 1935, the popularity of the New Deal had so backed the corporate right into retreat that the NAM sacked Edgerton as president. Business and the political Right felt a new fear: NAM's new leaders warned that if business failed to advance a corporate welfare state, a government welfare state would supplant it.[171]

By Roosevelt's second election in 1936, the rout of the Right was nearly complete. The wave of New Deal legislation seemed to buoy most Americans. And Roosevelt won over most reporters, if not publishers, with his charm and availability. Journalist James Reston characterized Roosevelt's approach as, "Let me make the news and you can write all the editorials you want against it."[172] If the administration achieved substantial results, however, it did so partly by deploying its own enormous new public relations assets, and overwhelming the opposition. As conservative Harvard political scientist E. Pendleton Herring observed:

> Never before has the Federal Government undertaken on so vast a scale and with such deliberate intent, the task of building a favorable public opinion toward its policies ... News comes out of the Federal bureaus in a flood. Today's mistake is washed away by the plans of tomorrow. Sifting out the news from the mass of prepared official statements is a task which discourages further curiosity for more detail on the part of the busy journalist ... The present system insures that a favorable presentation of all news concerning the Government is available to the newspaper. For the newspaper men, the easy course is that of acceptance without further investigation.[173]

Roosevelt and the New Deal swept the era. Business and the political Right changed battle plans to wage a deeper war.

Chapter 15

RETURN OF THE RIGHT

W orried about the possibility of socialism in America, the National Association of Manufacturers, the U.S. Chamber of Commerce, and an array of business groups combined forces to counterattack. By the mid-thirties, they mounted an "American Way" campaign that was designed to change the terms and focus of national debate.[174] The American Way campaign promoted the idea that a harmony of interests linked corporate America with most Americans. In particular, the campaign sought to undercut progressive income tax and organized labor, and to promote capitalism, not government, as the agent of change.[175]

To advance its campaign, NAM created a new national Special Committee on Public Information (SCPI), composed of business and professional leaders and local CPIs. The local CPIs were established to encourage newspapers to run positive stories about local industry. The campaign provided educational institutions and libraries with materials that presented industry's views and enlisted local representatives to make speeches and presentations to local groups, just as the Four-Minute Men had done in movie theaters during World War I. A national media strategy ensured that radio, movies, slides, newspapers, magazines and even the 1939 World's Fair promoted a pro-business, government-reducing message. One CPI service mailed materials promoting the campaign's message to three thousand weeklies, including a pamphlet called *Believe It or Not Pocketbook of Knowledge*, which outlined the superiority of the American Way. Six nominally independent scholars from Princeton, Vanderbilt, New York University, Stanford, the University of Southern California, and the American Academy of Political and Social Science all wrote articles blaming the Depression on the New Deal and argued that unfettered business was the fastest way to recovery.

Throughout the campaign, NAM kept a low profile. Many newspaper publishers ran the feature stories the CPIs sent them and kept their authorship secret. *You and Industry* booklets appeared in schools, colleges, and public libraries; a *Young America* news weekly for boys and girls began in 1937; and Paramount distributed documentary films for schools and movie theaters which showed an *America Marching On*, which was narrated by CBS newsman Lowell Thomas. Where New Deal photographers emphasized the social forces at issue during the Depression, the American Way campaign's photographers reduced social problems to matters to be decided in family or interpersonally, with individualism focused as a primary virtue. For example, between 1935 and 1943, the Farm Security Administration used the images of such photographers as Walker Evans and Dorothea Lange to depict the social and economic challenges to Americans living in poverty, whether in city slums or rural areas that the FSA sought to improve.[176] Roy Stryker, who directed the photographers, had asked them to highlight the "social forces" they found present in their work.[177]

In contrast, NAM's publicity turned the question inside out, focusing all issues through the lens of individual, family or interpersonal life, removed from business or social influence.[178] Instead of depicting social issues, the new NAM campaign focused on the grandeur of corporate accomplishment, with happy consumers become content by buying products. And though he'd initially refused the idea as unpalatable to a New Dealer, by 1943 Roy Stryker himself accepted a job as head of a special photographic unit in the public relations division of Standard Oil of New Jersey, part of the NAM campaign. As media critic Stuart Ewen explains, the company embraced Stryker's visuals to promote the idea that a company long noted for cold-blooded self-interest had developed a sense of social concern.[179]

Overall, the American Way campaign sought to publicly establish a harmony of interest between corporate America and the majority of Americans, to undercut the progressive income tax and organized labor, and contest the government programs of the New Deal. To do it, the NAM created a different vision of the future. It spent a half-million dollars in

1936 on the campaign, according to Ellul, $3 million in 1945 and $5 million in 1946.[180] As Ellul puts it: "Here we are truly in the domain of propaganda; and we see the multiple methods employed to influence opinion, as well as the strong tie between sociological and direct propaganda."[181]

The American Way campaign took years to kick in, but its impact reflects partly in its focus and ferocity. Campaign surrogates used national security and anticommunism to engender a new climate of fear, to gain political traction to rein in or stop the political Left.

- In 1941, when World War II demanded equal sacrifice between whites and blacks and American racism became plain, FDR named a Fair Employment Practices Commission (FEPC) to investigate complaints by African Americans working in federal war plants in the South. In counterattack, the leader of the South in the Senate, Georgia's Richard Russell, claimed the FEPC was laced with communists, its chairman "a wild-eyed radical lionized by the *Daily Worker*."[182]

- After World War II, the lifting of wage and price controls resulted in strikes at home when organized labor sought to improve reduced take-home pay. But to forestall wage increases, industry accused labor of communist intervention. Indeed, according to Ellul, the American Way campaign paved the way in 1947 to pass the Taft-Hartley Act, to reduce labor's power.[183]

- By summer 1948, Whittaker Chambers, a former Communist spy turned managing editor of *Time* magazine, testified that a Communist spy ring had operated in government since the 1930s. In December, "documents of enormous importance" relating to the investigation were found in a hollowed-out pumpkin on a Maryland farm, just as Chambers claimed.[184] Under pressure from the House Un-American Activities Committee, Hollywood studios blacklisted artists and writers, rather than subject themselves to internal scrutiny. Through 1949, there were trials in New York. Among the accused, former State Department official Alger Hiss, president of the Carnegie Endowment for International Peace, was convicted of perjury, though not of spying. By October 11, leaders of the American Communist Party were convicted of conspiracy to overthrow the government. Within two weeks of Hiss' conviction, Republican Senator Joseph McCarthy declared the State Department packed with Communists.

- In 1950, the anticommunist California PR team of Clem Whitaker and Leone Baxter helped to defeat a Truman administration proposal to enact national health insurance, using dirty tricks and accusations that the measure was a communist trick. (In the same year, Richard Nixon was elected to the U.S. Senate by smearing opponent Rep. Helen Gahagan Douglas as a anticommunist sympathizer.)

- In 1949-1950, the CIO expelled allegedly communist-led labor unions from its ranks. During the Red Scare, the climate of fear grew so pervasive that the later-merged AFL-CIO assumed its own rabid, anticommunist position, effectively defending itself by denying some of its working-class roots.

- In 1949 Senator Lyndon Johnson, D-Texas, a New Dealer, saw an opportunity to curry favor with his patron Senator Russell. Johnson so completely and falsely framed two-term Federal Power Commission Chairman Leland Olds as a communist sympathizer that neither President Truman nor Eleanor Roosevelt could save his re-nomination.[185]

- The FBI's J. Edgar Hoover in 1956 mounted secret and illegal "Cointelpro" operations, conducting surveillance on two thousand domestic citizens,[186] raising fears of communist infiltration in order to wiretap them, and targeting, in particular, the Rev. Martin Luther King.[187]

- Once the Congress with President Johnson passed civil rights, voting rights, and affirmative action measures in the mid-sixties, Richard Nixon fanned racist and communist fears into a "Southern strategy" to win elections in 1968 and 1972 and dampen progress in civil rights.

- The fear of communism from 1947 to the Soviet Union's fall in 1991 resulted in the U.S. propping up right-wing governments in Italy, Greece, and Pakistan; assassinating or assisting in the assassination of political leaders in Iran, Guatemala, South Vietnam, and Chile; and expending enormous sums to undermine communist regimes in North Vietnam, Cuba, and the Soviet Union.[188]

- If the American government's program for fighting communism and the Cold War was ideologically driven, it appears to have been driven equally by the self-interest of the military-industrial complex. As author Melvin Goodman writes in his study of the CIA: "Military intelligence consistently exaggerated Soviet military power, especially the quantity and quality of Soviet strategic forces and the capabilities of key weapons systems. The Air Force in particular exaggerated Soviet missile forces, apparently to gain more resources to deploy more missiles. Indeed, when the CIA sought to create a center to analyze foreign offensive missile systems, senior Air Force generals unsuccessfully tried to stop it."[189] In the meantime, the CIA spent two-thirds of its resources on tracking developments in the primary American adversary, the Soviet Union, yet failed to anticipate the collapse of its government in 1989 — a failure the CIA has never adequately explained.[190]

Chapter 16

THE RIGHT AND THE
NATIONAL SECURITY STATE

In his 1796 farewell address, George Washington warned Americans to "avoid the necessity of those overgrown military establishments which, under any form of government, are inauspicious to liberty, and which are to be regarded as particularly hostile to republican liberty."[191] A century and a half later, during World War II, Senator Harry Truman heeded that call and held hearings on wartime military misspending. At the end of the war, he closed down the Office of Strategic Services, fearing powerful secret government agencies. As the Cold War intensified, President Dwight D. Eisenhower, too, warned against the military-industrial complex and a society dominated by specialists in science and technology:

> We have been compelled to create a permanent armaments industry of vast proportions ... [and] three and a half million men and women are directly engaged in the defense establishment. We annually spend on military security more than the net income of all United States corporations ... We must guard against the acquisition of unwarranted influence, whether sought or unsought, by the military-industrial complex ... [in which] research has become central ... The prospect of domination of the nation's scholars by Federal employment, project allocations, and the power of money is ever present ... we must also be alert to the ... danger that public policy could itself become the captive of a scientific-technological elite.[192]

Eisenhower was fourteen years too late. By July 1947, responding to Soviet Union expansionism, Congress (with Truman's assent) passed the National Security Act, setting up the Central Intelligence Agency and National Security Council (NSC).[193] The NSC's first formal action was to authorize covert action against communists in democratic elections in Italy, the beginning of decades-long CIA subsidies to Italy's Christian Democrats, and of similar interventions in France.

In the meantime, private military contractors began to profitably focus on the communist threat, as well. General Electric used its pitchman Ronald Reagan during the 1950s to decry communism as the enemy and to advance free markets on the weekly televised "General Electric Theater" and on speaking tours across the country. GE and other military contractors won increasing defense spending partly by reinforcing the fear of communism, partly by advancing the military-industrial complex into a three-cornered interest structure nearly impervious to budget cutting: the military, defense contractors, and members of Congress. For the military, the new structure promoted increasing military budgets; for defense contractors, more revenues; for members of Congress, more defense installations and jobs in home districts, if only they'd spend more for national defense.[194]

By 1948, the result was the American "national security state," a term author Daniel Yergin defined as a "unified pattern of attitudes, policies, and institutions by which ... the country had to become organized for perpetual confrontation and for war." He explains:

> The attitudes were derived from the two commanding ideas of American postwar foreign policy — anticommunism and a new doctrine of national security. The policies included containment, confrontation, and intervention, the methods for which U.S. leaders have sought to make the world safe for America. The institutions include those government bureaucracies and private organizations that serve in permanent war preparedness. These developments have helped to increase dramatically the power of the Executive branch of the U.S. government, particularly the presidency. For the national security state required, as Charles Bohlen put it in 1948, "a confidence in the Executive where you give human nature in effect a very large blank check."[195]

The new structure delivered the goods both practically and ideologically. Welding science and technology to national defense made all three ideologically unassailable, for where they led, the social sciences and the humanities would be almost forced to follow. By extending a wartime crisis atmosphere, communication scholar J. Michael Sproule observed, the proponents of the Cold War conscripted intellectuals and shifted even the study of propaganda.

> Beginning in 1941, *propaganda* ... underwent a series of metamorphoses whereby the term first was replaced by *morale* and later by *psychological warfare*. By 1948, *persuasion, communication*, and *information* were the favored locutions for what formerly had been called propaganda ... Between Pearl Harbor and the Tet Offensive, communication science acted as the data-eliciting and data-organizing arm of hot-war and cold-war command decision making. Persuasion science represented a new mode of symbol study based on that tangent of progressivism that stressed production efficiency more than participatory democracy — thereby reversing the emphasis of the propaganda critics ... This new conception of social scholarship found scientists of society rendering service through fealty to America's legitimate, informed and presumably well-intentioned leaders.[196]

In short, the intellectual boundaries of Yergin's national security state expanded beyond confronting Russians in Eastern Europe. Restricted no longer to classified realms of science and engineering, the same set of attitudes, policies, and institutions now reshaped the social sciences and the humanities, undercutting critical thought, and impairing public judgment. Fear of communism appeared to disengage the nation's judgment of anyone, public or private, nominally engaged in national defense. A military-industrial complex with much to gain used Americans own fears against them, with results recalling Edgar Allan Poe's "The Raven." When it came to the national defense, fear made Americans willing to spend: ever more.

Chapter 17

RISE OF THE NEW RIGHT

The early Right placed a great deal of emphasis on publicity. In contrast, the New Right,[197] which began to emerge in the 1960s, was more focused on using the new sciences of persuasion to criticize mainstream news media.[198] The Nixon administration, through Vice President Spiro Agnew, began the attack. In a speech in Des Moines televised live November 13, 1969, Agnew assailed the "instant analysis and querulous criticism" that followed presidential addresses by news people who, he said, did not represent the American people. Agnew blamed television for growing demonstrations against the Vietnam war and declared that it was time "that the networks be made more responsive to the views of the nation." A week later, Agnew extended his attack to the *New York Times* and the *Washington Post*, and reiterated his criticism of network television news. Edward Fouhy, former network news executive and producer for *CBS Evening News with Walter Cronkite*, remembers Agnew's Des Moines speech vividly.

> [I]t was as if he was aiming that speech at what we were doing. He was arguing about the fact that after the President would appear on television, we'd have a panel discussion of a couple of journalists and they would analyze what the President said — a perfectly legitimate journalistic focus. But they wanted their message to appear unsullied, so that only their message would settle in the minds of the viewers. And of course this was, now that I look back on it, essentially a power play. They wanted to have the power to have their message unmediated ... .[199]

William Safire and Pat Buchanan wrote many of Agnew's speeches and often used alliterative jabs. One of the most memorable, written by Safire, characterized the media as "nattering nabobs of negativism."

While Agnew attacked the news media head-on in 1969, a new organization called Accuracy in Media (AIM) began monitoring mainstream news and producing reports to accuse the mainstream media of liberal bias. AIM engaged a widening circle of conservative critics of mainstream news. Agnew's criticisms effectively halted the practice of instant network news commentary, and pressures from the Nixon administration invigorated the conservative critics. The pressures focused on the *Washington Post* after the 1972 Watergate break-in, when *Post* coverage drew little competition. Indeed, the *Post*'s reportage seemed to take the paper out on a limb until CBS News aired its own two-part series on the growing scandal, based on the *Post*'s work. When CBS' program, too, came under Nixon administration attack, CBS producers shortened the second episode by three minutes.[200] But staff members at the *Post* nevertheless called the CBS coverage a "lifesaver," even though no immediate wider press coverage of Watergate seemed to follow.[201]

The state of Maryland eventually brought felony charges against Agnew for malfeasance committed while he served as Baltimore County Executive. Agnew pleaded no contest, resigned the vice presidency, and eventually went to prison, discredited. Meanwhile, evidence in the Watergate scandal mounted as press scrutiny intensified from the *Post* and competitors. In August 1974 Nixon stepped down under threat of impeachment. National news coverage of the Watergate scandal brought mainstream news to its zenith of credibility and influence. AIM's daily monitoring of the news, however, continued, the precursor to a range of conservative critiques, which pushed mainstream media to the right.

Accuracy in Media was but one of several new organizations established on the political right following World War II. In 1943, seeking to restore free-market economics after the New Deal, Lewis H. Brown, chairman of the Johns-Manville Corporation (later bankrupted for its liability in the production of asbestos) founded the American Enterprise Association (AEA), a small-time and little-known business lobby.[202] In 1969, under the direction of former Goldwater aide and U.S. Chamber of Commerce staffer William J. Baroody Sr., AEA became the American

Enterprise Institute (AEI). Two years later, in 1971, the U.S. Chamber of Commerce published a memo warning that the social movements of the time showed the free enterprise system under attack by the media, the academy, the political establishment and the courts. The memo urged a business counterattack, spending money "to inform and enlighten the American people," by creating a "movement" to subsidize "scholars, writers and thinkers" through new, generously supported "national organizations" that would press for "balance" and "equal time" in news coverage — and change public opinion.

That same year Nixon appointed the memo writer, conservative Democrat and former American Bar Association president Lewis Powell, to the Supreme Court. Meanwhile, former Nixon treasury secretary William Simon cautioned conservatives that "business money must flow away from the media which serve as megaphones for anti-capitalist opinion."[203] In 1972, Colorado beer brewer Joe Coors donated $200,000 to found what became AEI's friendly competitor, the Heritage Foundation.[204] Even the Coors contributions were dwarfed by those from right-wing philanthropist Richard Mellon Scaife, who gave millions to Heritage, the Hoover Institution at Stanford University, the Center for Strategic and International Studies, the Free Congress Research and Education Foundation, Accuracy in Media, and the American Enterprise Institute.

The new institutions of the Right grew steadily through the 1970s, but their founding and growth required an intellectual precursor: conservative intellectual William Buckley Jr. and his magazine *National Review*. Buckley, in turn, was part of the founding of Young Americans for Freedom, and, thus, the hiring of a key figure in the New Right: direct mail dean Richard Viguerie. In 1951, fresh out of college, Buckley published *God and Man at Yale*, a critique of his alma mater that attracted the attention of many in the fledgling conservative movement, including attorney William Rusher. Rusher went on to become publisher of the *National Review* in 1957, two years after Buckley launched it.

Buckley openly suggested that if Yale was indeed supposed to be a fundamentally Christian institution and a pillar of the free-enterprise system, its alumni were not, to put it mildly, getting their money's worth. Rusher was present at the creation of another Buckley-inspired institution.

In 1960, when the Republican national convention failed to nominate Senator Barry Goldwater for president, Republican nominee (then Vice President) Richard Nixon nominated the moderately liberal Senator Henry Cabot Lodge of Massachusetts to balance his ticket. The horrified reaction of conservatives led ninety young men and women, some still in college, to gather in early September at Great Elm, the Buckley family estate in Sharon, Connecticut, to found a new national conservative youth organization nominally independent of party called Young Americans for Freedom.

YAF's founding document, The Sharon Statement, focused on "the individual's use of his God-given free will," liberty, and economic freedom, the restriction of government to protection of freedoms "through the preservation of internal order, the provision of national defense, and the administration of justice." It declared that because "the forces of international Communism are, at present, the greatest single threat to these liberties ... the United States should stress victory over, rather than coexistence with, this menace," and said that U.S. foreign policy should be judged by the measure: "Does it serve the just interests of the United States?"[205]

As the sixties began, Richard Viguerie, a law student who chaired the Harris County, Texas, Young Republicans, found himself going downtown to Republican headquarters in the afternoons, rather than following his fellow students to the University of Houston law school library.

> That's why the law professors and I came to a unanimous agreement that I was not cut out for the study of law. Nobody, including myself, knew what I was cut out for, but it was not for the study of law. So I would hear as a youngster, the elders in the GOP talk about media bias. "We put out a press release last week, no coverage, media bias. We called a press conference yesterday, no one came, media bias." And as time went on I began to think to myself, yup, that's true, but where does it get us? How does it advance the ball down the field?[206]

In July 1961, Viguerie flew to New York City to interview for a job as executive secretary of the new Young Americans for Freedom.

I had the interview with Bill Rusher, and then I guess it went well so he takes me over to [YAF co-founder] Marvin Liebman's office. I interviewed with Marvin. And after a while Marvin walks me around his office and he shows me his mailroom, 20 x 30 feet where he has a supply of envelopes, stationery, postage meter, etc. And then he takes me outside the room and there was a cabinet of 3 x 5 drawers, where he had 3x5 index cards where some thousands of names and addresses, where he recorded— "Mrs. Hilda Jones gave $100 on this date and $300 on this date," that type of thing, and he explained to me how he raised money through the mail. And I remember my eyes just getting real big and I said, "My gosh, where's this thing been all my life?" And I just felt like a 2- or 3-year-old duck that had never seen water, but he knew what to do with that water.[207]

When Goldwater lost the presidency in 1964 by a margin exceeded only by FDR's defeat of Alf Landon in 1936, many thought the upset spelled the end of conservatism. Viguerie, nevertheless, went to the clerk of the U.S. House of Representatives and began copying the names of Goldwater donors who were on file. There were so many, he hired helpers, and they copied some 12,500 names and addresses before the clerk began to feel uncomfortable and asked them to leave. With the names, Viguerie began building a computerized mailing list, which Rusher said developed into "the biggest collection of conservative mailing lists in the country. At one time or another he conducted mailings for just about every conservative organization in existence — usually on terms that gave him control of the names and addresses of all who responded." The list enabled Viguerie and allies to bypass mainstream media by reaching audiences directly. Up until then, as Viguerie put it, "we would go up against the microphones in the country and we couldn't get through CBS, the *New York Times*, *Time* magazine, etc. So, with direct mail, we started going around that blockage, right into people's homes." [208]

Viguerie's lists and the computer technology that combed them supported a burgeoning array of conservatives. In a California primary in 1967, Viguerie helped Max Rafferty upset U.S. Senator Thomas Kuchel, the Republican minority leader in the Senate. Two years later in Illinois, Viguerie ran a direct mail campaign for Phil Crane, one of thirteen

Republicans vying for a congressional seat in a special election, and Crane won in an upset.[209] Viguerie then backed conservative Congressman John Ashbrook of Ohio, who challenged President Nixon and pushed him to the right in 1972. Between 1973 and 1976 Viguerie raised seven million dollars for Governor George Wallace.[210] The greatest victor, however, was not a Viguerie client.

Ronald Wilson Reagan had a large following because of his movie career and through his stint as spokesman for General Electric from 1952 to 1964. In 1966, Reagan was elected governor of California, and only ten years later, nearly beat incumbent President Gerald Ford for the GOP presidential nomination. As Viguerie saw it:

> I think I can make a strong case that Ronald Reagan would not have gotten the nomination in '80 or been elected president without direct mail. He wouldn't have been a serious candidate probably in 1976 [against President Gerald Ford] without direct mail. Everyone in politics has to have a base ... [Reagan's] was the conservative movement. ... His 1980 competitors, John Connally, Howard Baker, Bob Dole, George H. W. Bush, were getting $1,000 contributions, and he was getting $15, $25, $50 contributions. [But] he had a quarter of a million small donors ... without the ... new and alternative media — there wouldn't have been a Republican Congress elected in 1994, George Bush wouldn't be in the White House, Reagan wouldn't have been president.[211]

Karl Rove, too, developed a following through his mastery of direct mail, whether by bringing the Virginia Republican Party out of debt or raising money for Texas Governor Bill Clements (chapter 18), or undercutting other candidates for governor and the Congress (chapter 4), and the presidency (chapter 30). Yet, from one standpoint, these were tactical victories, in which direct mail played an important role. Before Rove developed his mastery, his predecessors, partly through direct mail, were amassing strategic victories aimed at gradually changing the politics and journalism of the United States.

Chapter 18

THE RIGHT AND
ITS INSTITUTIONS

P art of the canniness of the New Right lay in latching onto previously *Democratic* constituencies — some of them church-going evangelicals, but more of them Catholics. As Viguerie explained, "Conservatives brought together, as the core of their appeal, two of the strongest motivators in America — religion and patriotism. These two motivators were joined against the threat of communism. In this regard, one of the great political accomplishments of the new conservative movement was its use of the communist threat to bring masses of Catholic voters into the Republican fold and away from their ancestral immigrant home with the Democrats."[212]

If direct mail helped elect conservative office-seekers, it was just as pivotal in building new institutions. By 1973 and 1974, Viguerie began working closely with the other founders of the New Right: Paul Weyrich, Morton Blackwell, Charles Black, Howard Phillips, Bill Richardson, and Woody Jenkins. Phillips wanted to "go to the grassroots"; Weyrich, to organize precincts; Jenkins, a Louisiana Democrat, to organize conservatives beyond the Republican Party; Blackwell, to study how to win and to train young people in the methods. As Viguerie remembered, "I'll never forget Morton telling me how shocked he was when he arrived in Washington as executive director of the College Republicans in the Sixties and discovered that Barry Goldwater, Strom Thurmond and John Tower didn't sit down each week, to plan the conservative strategy for that week."[213] And so the New Right leaders began doing the political organizing and planning themselves.

In 1974, with the financial help of beer magnate Joseph Coors, Weyrich founded the Committee for the Survival of a Free Congress (CSFC). Viguerie's company did the direct mail for CSFC.[214] In 1975, Charles Black, Roger Stone, and Terry Dolan founded the National Conservative Political Action Committee (NCPAC), which not long after became the largest conservative PAC in the country, distributing $2.3 million in cash and in-kind contributions in races in 1980 and millions more in advertising to elect conservatives. NCPAC helped upend Democratic Senators Dick Clark and Floyd Haskell in 1978. Two years later, the group, besides boosting Reagan, helped defeat four more Democratic U.S. Senators: George McGovern, Frank Church, John Culver, and Birch Bayh. Viguerie handled the direct mail for NCPAC.

In 1975, Howard Phillips founded the Conservative Caucus, which three years later had 300,000 contributors and supporters, organizational chairs in 250 congressional districts and an annual budget of nearly $3 million. Viguerie undertook that direct mail campaign, too. Viguerie and Blackwell had worked together since their days in Young Republicans. Viguerie provided direct mail support to Blackwell's efforts in the Committee for Responsible Youth Politics and the Leadership Institute, through which Blackwell recruited and trained thousands of young people — including Dolan, Ralph Reed, Grover Norquist and Karl Rove.[215]

While Viguerie and his colleagues organized the New Right in the early and mid-Seventies, neoconservatives positioned themselves as a new policy establishment. Neoconservatives have held principal positions in such journals as *Commentary* and the *Public Interest* and have played important roles in *Encounter,* the *New Leader, American Scholar,* and *Foreign Policy.* Articles by neoconservatives appear frequently in *TV Guide, Reader's Digest, Fortune, Business Week,* and *U.S. News and World Report.* Their bylines turn up only a little less regularly in *Time* and *Newsweek, Harper's, The Washington Monthly, New York Magazine, Esquire,* the *Wall Street Journal* and the *New York Times.* But it's their research institutes that have been the key to advancing conservatism in the past two generations.

For example, the American Enterprise Institute for Public Policy Research (AEI) as late as 1969 had only two resident scholars, and its ideas had marginal impact. But by the end of Gerald Ford's presidency, members of his administration were becoming part of AEI, thanks partly to Ford's former defense secretary Melvin Laird, who'd been connected to AEI since the Goldwater campaign and raised money for AEI in the 1970s. Several Ford administration officials became affiliated with AEI for a time, including former Federal Reserve Chair Arthur Burns and Ford himself. AEI, from its refurbishing in 1971, had been populated mainly with free-market economists. But AEI head William Baroody began wooing neoconservatives in the late sixties and early seventies. Irving Kristol became a "senior fellow," the first of a number of social scientists to join.[216] "By involving prestigious academics of centrist to mildly liberal views in research and discussion with the AEI's more traditionally conservative spokesmen, the organization was gradually brought out of isolation,"[217] writes Peter Steinfels, author of *The Neoconservatives: The Men Who Are Changing America's Politics.*

> The institute's numerous productions, liberally funded and distributed to the press, gained credibility in the centrist-to-mildly liberal academic community while the center of gravity in policy debates was, in fact, shifted to the right. For this purpose, the neoconservatives were perfect. James Q. Wilson and Robert A. Nisbet joined free-enterprise conservatives like Milton Friedman, Paul W. McCracken, and G. Warren Nutter on the AEI's Council of Academic Advisers ... The institute established a Center for the Study of Government Regulation with an advisory council that included Kristol, Wilson, Paul Weaver, and Aaron Wildavsky. The center, in turn, published *Regulation*, a journal of information useful to business and government officials ... mixed with the AEI's ideological interpretation.[218]

Other fruits of AEI included an article published in the AEI journal, *Public Opinion*, in 1981. It reported that "the media elite" politically were predominantly Democratic, left of center and had no religious affiliation. Sixty-eight percent believed "the government should substantially reduce the income gap between the rich and the poor" and 90 percent believed it is a woman's right to decide whether to have an abortion. The findings caused William Rusher to conclude that "America's media elite are far to the left of American public opinion in general on the great majority of topics." The study echoed in such other conservative publications as *Human Events, National Review,* and *The Public Interest,* and set off discussion and focus on the media.[219] It helped to sell the conservative point of view on media to the public, even as it ignored scholarship that demonstrates media content is not liberal.[220]

Another notable conservative research institute is The Federalist Society for Law and Public Policy Studies, founded by a group of conservative law students in 1982. Since then, it has expanded to include lawyers and academicians who have remade the federal judiciary. At this writing, the society has some five thousand law student members, a lawyers division with twenty thousand members, and a new faculty division, begun in 1999 to "help foster the growth and development of rigorous traditional legal scholarship."[221] The 2005 confirmation of John Roberts as chief justice of the Supreme Court, and of associate justice Samuel Alito, who had been a member of the Federalist Society, in 2006, marked the latest milestones in an effort that began with Reagan attorney general Edwin Meese to identify and recruit judges to render decisions closer to the eighteenth century views prevalent when the country was founded. Both Roberts and Alito worked in the Reagan administration. The Federalist Society and other conservative groups organized support for the nomination and confirmation of Supreme Court Justice Clarence Thomas in 1991, and the consequent vilification of law professor Anita Hill, who testified against him.[222] The society since 1985 has received some $12 million in grants from the right-wing Earhart, Bradley, Simon, Olin, Carthage, Koch and Scaife Foundations. [223]

Many of President George W. Bush's judicial nominees are Federalist Society members; so were most of the members of the staff in Special Prosecutor Kenneth Starr's effort to impeach and try President Clinton. President Bush was responding to a legacy of Federalist Society criticism of the American Bar Association when he sought to limit ABA input on judicial nominations. As Grover Norquist told a reporter, "If Hillary Clinton had wanted to put some meat on her charge of a 'vast right-wing conspiracy,' she should have had a list of Federalist Society members and she could have spun a more convincing story."[224] By 2005, the Federalists' effort to nominate and confirm more conservative judges attracted two older allies on the Right: the National Association of Manufacturers and the U.S. Chamber of Commerce. The chamber already had worked aggressively to change the ideological composition of the judiciary at the state level. NAM head John Engler helped get his organization behind Bush and the G.O.P. in the election of 2004. He then offered NAM's lobbying help to assist the White House in confirming judicial nominees.[225]

The importance of the American Enterprise Institute and the Federal Society to the success of the New Right did not get past Karl Rove. On May 15, 2006, he told an AEI audience:

> As a young man I somehow finagled my way onto the AEI mailing list, and for a decade my mailbox was filled with pamphlets and analyses and reports and books — lots of books, glorious books ... Some of the volumes were devoted to obscure topics like trucking dereg[ulation] and a particular favorite of mine, the Argentine election. But I still have my copy of the essay by Richard John Neuhaus and Michael Novak called "To Empower People." I found "The Moral Basis of Democratic Capitalism" by Irving Kristol, Paul K. Johnson and Michael to be extremely powerful. I was excited — and that may be a strange word — by Michael's book, *Democracy and Mediating Structures*. I still have my copy and occasionally dip into it ... No think-tank in this city can match what AEI does.[226]

Six months earlier, Rove addressed the members of the Federalist Society and also praised its role in helping the Right reclaim power.[227]

> Consider where America stands today versus where we stood when the great William Rehnquist was named to the High Court in 1972. That was right around the time judicial activism was most dominant. Now, the wind and tide are running in our favor — due in large measure to your organization ... One of George W. Bush's greatest contributions as President will be the changes he has brought forth in the courts and our legal culture — and those changes would have been impossible without the Federalist Society. You have thoroughly infiltrated the ranks of the White House ... More than 200 exceptionally well-qualified nominees — many of whom have found intellectual sustenance and encouragement from The

Federalist Society — have been confirmed as Federal judges since 2001 ... the reason we will prevail rests in large measure on the good work of the Federalist Society.[228]

Chapter 19

THE NEW RIGHT TAKES OVER

On the whole, American conservatives as a group have by no means been unified through the decades. As William Rusher noted, conservatism by the 1950s drew from three ideals: classical liberalism, which arose in the eighteenth century to challenge the feudal order (a wing these days more akin to libertarianism); the traditionalism of Edmund Burke, which arose in reaction to liberalism; and anticommunism. Left on their own, the three philosophies would compete. But by the 1950s, representatives from each found a unity in reaction. As Rusher explained,

> By 1950 they all perceived in twentieth-century liberalism the principal threat to their separate purposes. The new liberalism had embraced and vastly extended the Enlightenment's rejection of the traditional bases of social order; it had accepted the socialist concept of the dominant role of the state in human affairs and, both by these concessions and by a conscious, if intermittent, policy of appeasement, was fatally undermining the strength of the West at the moment of its deadliest peril at the hands of communism. Not for the first time in human history, a powerful alliance was hammered together under the pressures of a common foe.[229]

As the New Right developed in the late sixties and early seventies, it welcomed the religious right — Protestant evangelicals and Catholic conservatives who would otherwise have been part of the New Deal constituency. The newest additions made the coalition more unwieldy, as Alan Crawford points out in his book, *Thunder on the Right*. Yet combining the coalition with technology, organizing power, discipline, and mastery of news by alternative means, the disparate groups made common cause, with masterful results.[230]

By 1980, according to journalist David Brock, seventy American Enterprise Institute and Heritage-like institutions were in place, shaping the cultural, media, and government agendas, helping elect President Reagan and a more conservative Congress, and compiling impressive legislative results. By 2000, Brock said, the Right had founded some *five hundred* such institutions, and conservatives became even more bullish. Edward Crane, president of the libertarian Cato Institute, one of the new think tanks, said: "As we grow, I don't want us to shift toward the mainstream. I want the mainstream to shift toward us."[231] According to the liberal non-profit group People for the American Way, the proliferation of these groups has been managed by the Philanthropy Roundtable, which coordinates right-wing foundations to best support the Right to shape the conventional wisdom.

> Right-wing foundations ... provide grants to a broad range of groups ... [and] right-wing media; national "think tanks" and advocacy groups; a budding network of regional and state-based think tanks; conservative university programs; conservative college newspapers; conservative scholars and more... all bent on promoting a far-right-wing agenda ... .Five foundations stand out from the rest: the Lynde and Harry Bradley Foundation; the Koch Family foundations; the John M. Olin Foundation (which William Simon chaired); the Scaife Family foundations and the Adolph Coors Foundation. Each has helped fund a range of far-right programs, including ... the *American Spectator* magazine ... Public debate on a number of issues has been transformed by foundation largesse.[232]

Indeed, William Simon's book that outlined an agenda for developing conservative power, *A Time for Truth*, was written while he chaired the Olin Foundation.

Eventually, the momentum of the conservative initiatives began to change mainstream news even though news people, at first, seemed to miss the change. In the 1970s, convinced that elitist liberal media had long frozen them out,[233] conservatives bypassed conventional journalism and resorted to direct mail as their primary mass medium instead. As a result, the New Right in November 1978 elected to Congress twenty-five conservative Republicans and eighteen conservative Democrats, using direct mail to organize and to aggregate campaign contributions and campaign efforts, partly by focusing politically on the so-called giveaway of the Panama Canal.[234] Two years later, in 1980, with the help of the fundamentalist Moral Majority — who registered two and a half million new voters — they unseated four of six targeted Democratic senators, and elected Ronald Reagan president.[235]

"We had a political earthquake last Tuesday," Godfrey Sperling of the *Christian Science Monitor* said, introducing New Right direct mail figure Viguerie to speak just after that election. "No one saw it coming. What happened?"

Viguerie replied, "Excuse me, sir, you didn't see it coming, but we tried our best to tell you beforehand."[236]

At the same time, in the early eighties, daily newspapers in America underwent significant change. Papers created entire new business sections, business reporters proliferated, and concurrently, labor reporting diminished. An increasing emphasis on profitability produced more corporate news consolidations, and reduced investigative and other reporting. Most independent hometown newspapers were bought out by media chains, which operated them primarily to make money.[237] In television, the networks became corporate takeover targets. General Electric, which the government forced three generations earlier to divest itself of NBC, bought it again. Disney bought ABC. CBS was purchased by Loew's and ultimately by Viacom.

CBS, once considered the "Tiffany Network,"[238] whose *CBS Evening News with Walter Cronkite* set the standard for news in the seventies and eighties, became a corporate casualty. Journalist Charles Lewis described working as a producer at "Sixty Minutes" when the cuts started.

I worked for CBS and watched Edward R. Murrow's producer get early retirement, basically booted out the door. Twenty-five percent of CBS was fired in '83 or '84. Lawrence Tisch [of Loew's], who also owned a tobacco company simultaneously, was the owner of CBS. And they just started gutting the news division. Now, I'd like to tell you that it just happened once in '83 or '84. But, of course, what was once a two or three thousand person operation got reduced to a few hundred. And, you know, to walk into the Washington bureau of CBS today is depressing in the extreme. I mean, you have a lot of empty offices. You've got one person out on the desk instead of ten. You know, everything is skeletal. And you're watching, well, you've just seen the evisceration of an entire industry and, as we both know, a profession, actually.[239]

The cuts at CBS ultimately echoed in massive cuts in news personnel across the networks, and the re-direction of financial resources that had been dedicated to news. In the meantime, new newspapers such as the *Washington Times* and the *Weekly Standard* started up, often funded, according to Brock, by right-wing philanthropies coordinated by the Philanthropy Roundtable.

By 1987, the Reagan administration succeeded in overturning the Fairness Doctrine — the Federal Communication Commission regulation that once required stations to present controversial issues in a fair and balanced manner, including the granting of equal time to opposing views. The end of the Fairness Doctrine ignited right-wing talk radio. According to one estimate, the top two audience-drawing commentators on the air today are conservatives Rush Limbaugh (fourteen million listeners per week) and Sean Hannity (almost twelve million).[240] Of some four thousand talk radio hosts, almost all are conservatives,[241] such as Ann Coulter, Laura Ingraham, Brit Hume, and Bill O'Reilly.[242] Partly because of the growth of cable television, from 1980 to 2005 the audience for network television news was halved, from 53 million to about 27 million viewers.[243] Cable television now exceeds network television as the public's prime source of national and international news.[244] The right-leaning Fox News Channel, which competes closely with CNN, draws double the CNN audience during daytime hours.[245]

According to Brock: "Today, the most important sectors of the political media — most of cable TV news, the majority of popular op-ed columns, almost all of talk radio, a substantial chunk of the book market, and many of the most highly trafficked Web sites — reflect more closely the political and journalistic values of the *Washington Times* than those of the *New York Times*."[246] Indeed, by 2004, eighty percent of commentators on political television came from the conservative movement, according to linguist and political communication scholar George Lakoff.[247] How could such a shift occur in mainstream news? Washington Post columnist E. J. Dionne tackled the question in 2002:

> Because the drumbeat of conservative press criticism has been so steady, the establishment press has internalized it. Editors and network executives are far more likely to hear complaints from the right than from the left ... ..[Rush] Limbaugh's new respectability is the surest sign that the conservative talk network is now bleeding into what passes for the mainstream media, just as the unapologetic conservatism of the Fox News Channel is now affecting programming on the other cable networks ... It took conservatives a lot of hard and steady work to push the media rightward ... The media world now includes (1) talk radio, (2) cable television, and (3) the traditional news sources (newspapers, news magazines and the old broadcast networks). Two of these three major institutions tilt well to the right, and the third is under constant pressure to avoid even the pale hint of liberalism ... What it adds up to is a media heavily biased toward conservative politics and conservative politicians.[248]

By mid-2005, even these insights seemed outdated. The political right took to the Internet, using blogging as effectively as talk radio.[249]

Chapter 20

AN ABOUT FACE AT THE POST

One sign of the New Right's power today can be seen in the changing political coverage of *The Washington Post*.

In the mid-1970s, the *Post* relentlessly pursued allegations of wrongdoing during the Richard Nixon administration, including Watergate and the Pentagon Papers. After Nixon's resignation, journalist Theodore White reported his interview with speech-writer Ray Price, who drafted Nixon's resignation speech. Nixon and Chief of Staff Alexander Haig directed that the speech include no confession of guilt, a position with which Price agreed. As Price put it, "The *Washington Post* would have loved a guilty statement. But even a guilty statement wouldn't have satisfied them. What they wanted was a ceremony on the South Lawn, with the President incinerating himself, and [*Post* editor] Ben Bradlee toasting marshmallows in the flames."[250]

In contrast, three decades later, the *Post* apologized to the public for allowing itself to be misled by the Bush administration in its coverage of Iraq, but then defended the Bush administration's leaks in the case of former CIA operative Valerie Plame. Her covert status was "outed" by administration officials after her husband, former Ambassador Joseph C. Wilson IV, charged that the White House manipulated intelligence to make a case for the invasion of Iraq.

The introduction to the *Post*'s editorial on the subject states, "President Bush declassified some of the intelligence he used to decide on war in Iraq. Is that a scandal?"[251]

In short, the *Post* seemed to perform something of an about face. In 1974, from both its news and editorial pages, it strongly assaulted a Republican president for the array of abuses of presidential power. Yet in

2006, the *Post* pulled its punches in news coverage of another Republican president whose abuses started war in Iraq, and then it editorially supported his leaking classified evidence to justify it. As former editor-turned-professor Ben Bagdikian wrote in 2004:

> In the years since 1980, the political spectrum of the United States has shifted radically to the far right. What was once the center has been pushed to the left, and what was the far right is now the center. What was considered the eccentric right wing of American politics is now considered the normal conservative outlook. What was the left is now at the far edge, barely holding its precarious position and treated in the news as a sometimes amusing oddity ...
>
> This shift has ... muffled social justice as a governing principle in government agencies. It has granted advantages to the wealthy and to large corporations at the expense of the middle and working classes. It has reversed earlier reforms by starving agencies like the Securities and Exchange Commission and tried to privatize Social Security. It has cut back conservation and environmental laws first enacted by President Theodore Roosevelt, a Republican, at the turn of the twentieth century. These changes have presented to American voters the narrowest range of political and ideological choices among all industrial democracies in the world.[252]

Political observer David Brock echoes Bagdikian's position. The "creation of right-wing media, and of the strategies by which the right wing has penetrated, pressured, co-opted, and subdued the mainstream media into accommodating conservatism, was not an accident," Brock wrote in 2004. "Toward this end, a deliberate, well-financed and expressly acknowledged communications and deregulatory plan was pursued by the right wing for more than thirty years — in close coordination with Republican Party headquarters — to subvert and subsume journalism and reshape the national consciousness through the media, with the intention of skewing American politics sharply to the right. The plan has succeeded spectacularly."[253]

To mainstream politicians and voters, the rise of the Right *was* nearly imperceptible. With Goldwater's humiliating defeat in 1964, the Right appeared to cook itself. Ten years later, despite an enormous election victory in 1972, it seemed to happen again: the Republican Party post-Watergate lay in ruin for the second time in a decade. The ruin was so complete that new campaign finance legislation passed in 1974 to stop the wealthy from hijacking American politics. The legislation came as the corrective to Watergate, which proved so fatal that the head of the Republican National Committee told a reporter that the GOP considered changing the party's name, just as a disgraced corporation might in the business world, to break free from the albatross of the scandal.[254] And yet, Republicans came roaring back. By the end of the first decade of the twenty-first century, the GOP occupied the White House for twenty of the previous twenty-eight years, 1978 to 2008.

How did this happen?

Liberals seem to have assumed that the progressive government institutions they founded during the New Deal and the Great Society had become permanent fixtures, to be left safely to operate.[255] Yet, at the moment that liberals declared mission accomplished, the Right was building, Gramsci-like, under the radar and beyond the capacity of mainstream observers to apprehend. By 1966, Young Republicans were being fenced in by Young Americans for Freedom, and Ronald Reagan was about to become governor of California. YAF, a minor institution of the Right, was joined and surpassed by hundreds of other institutions devised to dominate American politics. Mainstream journalism caught a whiff of things to come when Reagan challenged President Gerald Ford for the Republican presidential nomination in 1976.

At this writing, conservative foundations coordinate strategic philanthropy through the Philanthropy Roundtable, a group of top conservative leaders; and corporate contributions and activities are coordinated through a student of Antonio Gramsci: Grover Norquist, of Americans for Tax Reform.[256] Norquist spearheaded the "K Street Project," an effort to force *all* Washington lobbying to run through Republican-friendly firms which, in turn, amassed money for GOP candidates and friendly advocates.[257] The irony, as E. J. Dionne puts it, is that "conservatives were much more attuned to what Gramsci's theory of intellectual hegemony is about than liberals of the Left ever were. They read their Gramsci more closely."[258]

And at the apex of the burgeoning conservative structure in the 1990s and 2000s was Karl Rove, the man who would end up coordinating people, ideas, resources and strategy and would convert conservative politics and policy into federal and business power.

PART IV

A Brief History of Karl Rove

Chapter 21

ROVE'S EARLY YEARS

K̲arl Rove often surprised me with the extent to which he'd either worked with, or at least known, most of the leading figures in the Republican Party. He began working for former President George H. W. Bush when the elder Bush chaired the Republican National Committee. Rove had worked with former Secretary of State and Secretary of the Treasury James A. Baker, and with the late Lee Atwater, who'd campaigned for Rove to become president of College Republicans in 1973, beating out Terry Dolan of NCPAC fame. Political consultant Mary Matalin had worked with Rove and, later, became his publisher. Ralph Reed also worked with Rove before Reed organized evangelicals into the Christian Coalition. The names of Republican or conservative celebrities rolled off Rove's tongue, and he seemed to stay in touch with all of them. At one point, Atwater, whose slash-and-burn campaign against Michael Dukakis elected George H. W. Bush president in 1988, told Rove: "You know, you should be doing this. You can do it as well as I can." Of course, Atwater was right.

In our "Politics and the Press" class, Rove mentioned that one great advantage of direct mail is that it affords a comfortable distance between the candidate and any negative "hit" the campaign uses against an opponent. Such hits can quickly turn voters against one's opponent and toward one's own candidate, especially when popped as a surprise just before election day, when rejoinder becomes both difficult and crucial. Narrowcasting such hits through Christian radio, for example, can reach target audiences effectively, but direct mail is even better, Rove told our class, because it's nearly "immune from press coverage." Indeed, he developed his business and reputation by specializing in direct mail. But before becoming well known, Rove first went through basic training.

In 1970, Morton Blackwell, later a founder of the New Right, dispatched nineteen-year-old Rove to Illinois to organize student support for conservative Senator Ralph Smith. Smith, appointed to the U.S. Senate after the death of Everett Dirksen, was running against Adlai Stevenson III. Rove struck up an alliance with Young Americans for Freedom to help the cause.[259] While he was there, he also pulled a dirty trick: bollixing the campaign opening of Alan Dixon, the Democratic candidate for state treasurer.

Dirty tricks were nothing new. Rove noted that at the Republic's founding, Thomas Jefferson and Alexander Hamilton, his nemesis, frequently published false statements about each other. In the next century in Illinois, Chicago mayor Richard Daley long relied on the votes of the dead; John F. Kennedy's narrow win over Richard Nixon in 1960 remains suspect because of Daley manipulations. In that election, Nixon took the high road by conceding defeat. But Nixon and political handler Murray Chotiner used their own dirty tricks in 1950, which included accusing opponent Helen Gahagan Douglas of being a communist sympathizer and calling her "the Pink Lady" to make it stick. In South Texas, John Connally resurrected the votes of the dead to elect Lyndon Johnson to the Senate the same year. There has never been a shortage of dirty tricks or character assassinations in American politics, as Rove pointed out in class.

As Rove, in his late teens and early twenties, tried his own political tricks, Nixon's appointments secretary, Dwight Chapin, in September 1971 recruited Donald Segretti to conduct a campaign of dirty tricks against Nixon opponents for which Segretti and Chapin ultimately did jail time. At a point during that campaign, Rove worked with Segretti. That included, according to the *Village Voice*, a moment when Rove, who didn't serve in the military, labeled a World War II veteran and former B-24 bomber pilot a "left-wing peacenik." He was referring to Democratic presidential nominee Senator George McGovern.[260]

For dirty tricks during the 1972 campaign, Segretti went to prison for four-and-a-half months after pleading guilty to three counts of distributing forged campaign literature. One was a faked letter on the stationery of the then Democratic presidential front-runner, Edmund Muskie. The letter alleged that his fellow Democrat, Senator Henry "Scoop" Jackson of Washington, had fathered an illegitimate child with a seventeen-year-old girl. A second letter, published two weeks before the New Hampshire primary in the Manchester, N.H., *Union-Leader*, alleged that Muskie was prejudiced against French-Canadian Americans, who constitute an important minority in New Hampshire. That, and the newspaper's published insult to Muskie's wife, precipitated Muskie's "crying speech" outside the newspaper three days before the primary. Muskie's campaign never recovered and he withdrew from the race. Nixon aide Chapin denied knowledge of Segretti's activities against Democrats, but he, too, was convicted and served eight months in prison for his role in the crimes.

Of course, the most famous dirty trick by the Nixon campaign (in which Segretti and Chapin apparently were not involved) was the Watergate break-in on June 17, 1972, perpetrated by five men, each of them connected to the CIA, and, through G. Gordon Liddy and E. Howard Hunt, tied to the Nixon re-election campaign and the White House. The burglars were trying to repair bugs they'd planted three weeks earlier in the office of the Democratic National Committee in the Watergate Hotel in the Foggy Bottom area of Washington, D.C. In addition, Hunt also had hired one Thomas Gregory in February 1972 to infiltrate the campaign of frontrunner Muskie. Gregory worked in the Muskie campaign headquarters and provided Hunt with weekly, typed memoranda. By mid-April, once Muskie's campaign was faltering, Hunt directed Gregory to move to the campaign of the ultimate nominee, Senator McGovern.[261]

In all, nineteen Nixon administration officials or associates went to prison in the scandal, including former attorney general John Mitchell, chief of staff H. R. Haldeman, and domestic policy adviser John Ehrlichman. A second Nixon attorney general, Richard Kleindienst, resigned and pleaded guilty to a charge of perjury in a Watergate-related matter. Nixon administration officials were prosecuted or shooed from office for burglary, bribery, extortion, wiretapping, conspiracy, obstructing justice and destroying evidence, tax fraud, illegal campaign contributions, and abuse or illegal use of the CIA, the FBI, and the IRS.

None of this seems to have involved Rove. But according to the *Washington Post*, he drew press attention during the height of public outcry over Watergate for teaching dirty tricks during weekend seminars to College Republicans.[262] As it turned out, that accusation resulted from a dirty trick played on Rove. The source of the *Post* story about him evidently was Terry Dolan, Rove's opponent in the 1973 campaign to head College Republicans. Dolan seems to have gone to reporters with tapes and transcripts of the dirty tricks seminars. The seminars conducted were instructing young Republicans to go through a rival's garbage to obtain inside memos and lists of contributors.[263] The ensuing stink prompted Bush Sr., then RNC head and Rove's boss, to send an FBI agent to question Rove.[264] According to former Nixon counsel John Dean, the incident also won brief attention from a Watergate special prosecutor, although no action came of it.[265] After a month's internal review, the GOP cleared Rove and he became chairman of College Republicans.[266]

Testimony before the Senate Watergate Committee, however, did implicate Rove in a Watergate-related instance of political spying a year *earlier*. In January 1972 — a month *before* E. Howard Hunt hired Thomas Gregory to spy on the Muskie campaign — "Carl Rove" (sic) instructed a staff member of the Republican National Committee, a "Mr. Friedman" (the hearing record does not record his full name), to collect political intelligence about Muskie, too. Friedman, attending under an assumed name, went to a youth leadership conference for the Muskie campaign and sent information back to Rove and others about speakers who attended. Friedman's effort, directed by Rove, is listed as one of a dozen and a half operations directed by Donald Segretti against the Democratic presidential candidates — Muskie, then Senator Hubert H. Humphrey, and McGovern — from March 1971 through November 1972.

Segretti's dirty tricks operation was the largest of those outlined by Senate investigators. But E. Howard Hunt's activities had code names: one called "Gemstone," employed Gregory and a "John Buckley" to spy on the Muskie campaign from July 1, 1971 to July 1, 1972. The other, named "Crystal," was the bugging of the Democratic National Committee Headquarters in the Watergate Hotel in early June 1972. In addition to the operations of Segretti and Hunt, the committee staff found that Nixon political operative Murray Chotiner had hired two former newspaper reporters to travel with the press corps covering the Democratic presidential candidates. And Jeb Magruder and Herbert L. "Bart" Porter, two other members of the Committee to Re-Elect the President (known as "CReeP"), hired two more operatives to tail the Democratic candidates.

In short, the Senate Watergate Committee report implicates Rove in the dirty tricks operation supervised by Donald Segretti, who served time while Rove worked for Republican National Committee Chairman George H. W. Bush as executive director of College Republicans.[267]

Chapter 22

ROVE AND DIRTY TRICKS

Although Karl Rove had no particular background in raising money, he was directed by the national party in 1976 to go to Richmond as finance director of the Virginia Republican Party. His goal was to raise funds to get the state party out of debt. Rove was given magnetic tape with the names of 30,000 previous party contributors. Working from it, largely through direct mail appeals, Rove was able to raise $400,000 in one year and got the party solvent again.[268]

By 1979, Rove was working as an independent consultant, when he took a call from Texas oil millionaire Bum Bright, who offered him a job raising money for Governor Bill Clements' next campaign. Bright wanted to raise $200,000 in two years from direct mail; Clements had 5,000 donors in the first campaign. By the end of the first year, Rove expanded the list to 44,000 names and had raised $1 million for Clements.[269] In the process, Rove compiled perhaps the most important list for the future of Republicans in Texas, cementing one foundation of his political consulting business.

Two years later, Rove set up his own firm, Karl Rove + Co., with Clements as his first client. Clements lost the election that time, but the lists got better — and Rove began using them not only for candidates but for other business pursuits.[270] His main focus remained politics, however, and wherever Rove pursued politics, dirty tricks seemed to appear.

Sometime after winning election as Texas Land Commissioner in 1983, Democrat Garry Mauro had a visit from State Comptroller Bob Bullock, who'd been his boss. Bullock, one of Texas' toughest politicians, was too spooked to talk on the phone. Bullock said, "Garry, Karl Rove is in league with a guy in the U.S. attorney's office in San Antonio. He's an

FBI agent named Greg Rampton. Their sole job right now — their mission in life — is to figure out a way to indict you, me, Jim Mattox, Jim Hightower, and Ann Richards. They're out to get us all."[271]

By June 1984, Mauro was hearing both from veterans for whom the land commissioner's office offered benefits — and from his campaign contributors — that agent Rampton was calling them. Mauro told his general counsel to contact Rampton and offer to provide any documents he wanted. But as Mauro prepared to make a speech to a state Democratic convention in Houston, he received a call from a reporter who'd received leaked information: Would Mauro comment on the FBI subpoena Mauro had received a half an hour earlier about turning over 70,000 land office documents? No charges were ever filed in that case but neither was Mauro ever cleared.[272] Mauro won re-election repeatedly as Texas Land Commissioner and in 1998 ran for governor against Bush but lost. In short, a once bright political future had been short-stopped. (In his memoir, Rove denies working with agent Rampton in this instance or others, and brushes off the dirty trick next described here as not his, but as the work of another consultant).

In 1986, four years after his first loss to Governor Mark White, Clements was making another run against White for the governor's office when late that summer Rove purportedly produced a mock newspaper distributed by direct mail. The newspaper, filled with stories and photos that applauded Clements and denigrated White, included one story that intimated White had recently been stopped for drinking and driving. The story was partly true: White had been drinking and driving and was cited, but the incident occurred 25 years earlier, when White was a student at Baylor University.[273]

Clements took the lead in the race but just before a scheduled debate appeared to be the underdog again. On that same day, a security service purportedly doing a routine sweep found an electronic bug behind a picture frame above Rove's desk. FBI agent Rampton was on hand; he took the bug from Rove, who was Clements' campaign consultant, and turned the bug over to an FBI lab for analysis. The same afternoon Rove called a news conference, in which he noted that such a bug could benefit only the political opposition. The 6 o'clock news led with the story, which took focus away from the debate that followed and rattled White, who learned of the incident just before the debate. Clements won the election. An FBI source later said Rove was at the top of their list of suspects in the case — for bugging his own office to tip the election Clements' way. In any event, the FBI source told journalists Jim Moore and Wayne Slater that the federal prosecutor, a Republican appointee, then closed down the investigation for fear it might implicate the Clements team.[274] At dinner at the Roves a year later, a guest recalled, Rove acted as if he wanted to take credit for the "bugging."[275]

Yet another timely appearance by Rampton furthered Rove's interests three years later. In 1989, Democratic Texas Agriculture Commissioner Jim Hightower, being touted for greater political opportunity nationally, was preparing to run for re-election the following year. Rove, who raised $3 million for Hightower opponent Rick Perry, fed information to several reporters about an alleged kickback scheme involving Hightower.[276] State and federal agriculture auditors' reports later cleared Hightower and his assistants. But then FBI Agent Rampton turned up and began scrutinizing Hightower. Meanwhile, Rove, attending a fund-raiser 1,300 miles away in Washington, announced not only that Hightower was under investigation, but that indictments would soon be handed down.[277] Indeed, Rampton's investigation ultimately led to three of Hightower's aides serving time on federal charges, although the judge gave them light sentences and said a corrupt system was in place long before Hightower arrived.[278]

Agent Rampton later transferred to Boise, Idaho, after a filing with the FBI suggested his actions had been partisan. Rampton eventually was implicated in evidence tampering in the jury trial of Ruby Ridge, Idaho, defendant Randy Weaver, who was subsequently acquitted.[279] But in Texas, the political damage had been done. Rove's candidate, Perry, defeated Hightower in the next election, knocking Hightower from his official platform and sidelining his elective future, too.

In 1992, Rove called a newspaper reporter with the information that Lena Guerrero, a protégée of Governor Ann Richards and her appointee to the Texas Railroad Commission, had lied about graduating from the University of Texas. In the ensuing days, Guerrero and her election campaign imploded, and the aftershocks weakened Richards. Rove, meanwhile, targeted two more women appointees of the governor in efforts that further damaged Richards' re-election prospects. Finally, in an effort to undercut Richards' campaign consultant George Shipley, Rove called an influential member of the Texas Medical Association Board of Directors to get the TMA to drop Shipley as paid adviser to their political action committee.[280]

During George Bush's first run for governor in 1994, his campaign was accused of spreading rumors in East Texas about Governor Richards' tolerance for gays, after Bush's regional chairman, state Senator Bill Ratliff, criticized the governor for "appointing avowed homosexual activists" to state positions.[281] According to Moore and Slater, "Bush surrogates, operating at arm's length, undermined Richards on the issues of guns and gays, including a vicious whisper campaign about lesbianism that ran with an evangelical fervor through the coffee shops and church parlors of East Texas."[282] Indeed, *Dallas Morning News* reporter Anne Marie Kilday told Melinda Henneberger of the *New York Times* that Rove called her one day during the '94 race. Rove said he was reviewing the telephone records of a state official and reputed lesbian. He added that he found it interesting that the official made repeated calls to Kilday "'at your residence' ... He said, 'You've just got to be careful about your reputation and what people might think.'" Rove later denied that such a conversation took place.[283]

In 1996, Rove was consulting for tobacco giant Phillip Morris when he helped guide a push poll that targeted Texas Attorney General Dan Morales, who had announced plans to sue the tobacco industry. A push poll is intended not to measure public opinion, but to dispense information that may be damaging and feed it to voters in ways calculated to undermine an opponent (Chapter 2). In this case, the push poll sponsored by the tobacco companies sought to defeat Big Tobacco-fighter Morales' re-election by linking him with Louis Farrakhan and the Nation of Islam — links that were false. In the meantime, the five trial lawyers Morales had hired to sue Big Tobacco won a $15.3 billion settlement for the state.[284] Rove worked for the tobacco firm from 1991 to1996.[285] He severed his connection, however, once it became clear that he had delivered the results of the push poll against Morales to Joe Allbaugh, executive assistant to Governor Bush, about the same time that Bush was considering running for president.

The legal fees generated from the huge tobacco settlement gave the five Democratic trial lawyers the financial capacity to outflank Republican candidates. In response, Rove, with heavy backing from the tobacco industry, promoted the candidacy for attorney general of conservative judge John Cornyn, who supported limiting the amount of awards in cases of corporate liability, thereby reducing the amounts that victorious trial lawyers might contribute to Democratic candidates. Morales, who stepped out of the race in 1997, was himself sentenced in 2003 to four years in prison for seeking to include Marc Murr, a friend and another lawyer, as a recipient of attorney fees in the tobacco case.[286]

According to former Texas Republican Party chair Tom Pauken, who ran for attorney general at the same time (along with former Railroad Commissioner Barry Williamson, whose campaign was led by a Rove ally, David Carney), Rove worked for Cornyn partly to defeat Pauken as well. Pauken had backed Senator Bob Dole for president in 1988, rather than Vice President George Bush, and George W. Bush, offended at the slight by a fellow Texas Republican, never forgot.[287] Cornyn's candidacy not only enabled Rove to eliminate Pauken in the primary but, in the general election, also another Democrat: former Attorney General Jim Mattox. Although Rove had failed to knock Pauken from his chairmanship of the Republican Party, once he lost the primary for attorney general, Pauken dropped out of state politics.

Cornyn went on to become the first Republican Texas attorney general since Reconstruction. Four years later Rove helped Cornyn win election to the U.S. Senate, and Cornyn reciprocated. On March 31, 2006, when former Nixon White House counsel John Dean was summoned before the Senate Judiciary Committee to testify why the domestic spying of President George W. Bush was worse than Watergate,[288] Cornyn got in a preemptive strike."When I was looking this morning at one of the witnesses that's going to be testifying, that's selling a book and that is a convicted felon, it strikes me as very odd that the Judiciary Committee is giving ... an opportunity to somebody under those circumstances as part of their marketing efforts." As soon as he made the hit, and before anyone could respond, Cornyn left the hearing.[289]

Guided by Rove, Republicans, who eight years earlier had held no statewide offices in Texas, held nearly every statewide post. With the extraordinary backing of the Democratic lieutenant governor, Bob Bullock, Rove re-elected Governor Bush over Mauro in a two-to-one rout that sealed the campaign theme for Bush 2000: "A uniter, not a divider."

Rove was uniting the GOP behind Bush's bid for the presidency until Senator John McCain clobbered Bush by eighteen points in the New Hampshire primary. Soon thereafter, a brutal whispering campaign, similar to that mounted against Governor Richards in Texas in 1994, alleged that McCain, who was in South Carolina campaigning, was weak on military defense issues. James B. Stockdale, a former prisoner of war in Vietnam, received a call from a friend close to the Bush campaign soliciting comments on McCain's "weakness." The caller implied that McCain was somehow psychologically unstable as a result of being tortured in Vietnam.[290]

Candidates Gary Bauer and Steve Forbes identified the Bush campaign as responsible for the whispering campaign.[291] But there were more rumors: that McCain had had an illegitimate child with a North Vietnamese woman, which is why he got special treatment from the Viet Cong; that McCain had a black child; that McCain voted for the biggest tax increase ever; that his wife stole prescription drugs from a charity and abused them; that McCain was pro-abortion; that he left his crippled first wife; that he was a liar, cheat, and fraud.

In fact, McCain's wife did have trouble with prescription drugs, and the McCains did have a dark-skinned child whom they'd adopted from Bangladesh. But the rest of the charges were false. The Bush campaign supporters had engineered a character assassination against McCain and promoted it through handbills, phone calls, push polls, radio, and personal conversation.[292] The attacks worked. McCain lost South Carolina, partly because he resorted to negative campaigning to defend himself, which ironically made him look worse.

That November, Bush lost the election by a half-million votes but won the presidency a month later when the Supreme Court voted five to four to stop the recount in Florida, thereby awarding Bush the twenty-five electoral votes he needed to win. Rove's "uniter" had divided the country but still ascended to the presidency — it simply took more political hits to win. For example, in the month the election was at stalemate, "Brooks Brothers Riots" — protests at the Miami-Dade County polling offices where county officials were re-counting ballots — looked spontaneous. As it turned out, the Bush campaign and the Republican National Committee organized and supported the riots to hamper recounting of the Miami-Dade popular vote. According to documents released post-election to the Internal Revenue Service, the Bush team, using corporate jets from Enron and Halliburton, spent more than two million dollars to fly in Republican operatives to stop the recount. The Brooks Brothers Rioters, many of them GOP Capitol Hill staffers, went on to positions of more responsibility; four of them to the White House.[293]

During the midterm elections of 2002, after September 11, Rove recognized that a highly emotional appeal for national unity was also an effective way to frame Democrats as soft on national defense.[294] Rove pushed Bush out onto the road to campaign for Republicans, which left a trail of Democratic bodies behind. They included Senator Max Cleland of Georgia, the Silver-Star winning amputee who nearly died in Vietnam.

Cleland lost to Saxby Chambliss, who was heavily backed by Bush. Chambliss never served in the military, but his commercials painted war veteran Cleland as being in league with Osama bin Laden and Saddam Hussein. They demolished Cleland's candidacy. The attacks, reminiscent of those on George McGovern in 1972 and more that came in the 2004 presidential campaign, were especially ironic, given the facts that have emerged about the administration's foreknowledge of 9/11. Two months before September 11, CIA Director George Tenet and Tenet's counter terrorism chief, Cofer Black, held an emergency meeting with National Security Adviser Condoleezza Rice, because intelligence indicated an impending attack, and they requested resources to prevent it.[295] CIA officials briefed Bush himself on intelligence about imminent attack while he was on vacation in August 2001 at his ranch in Crawford, Texas. He took no immediate action.[296]

During the Plamegate scandal in 2003, Bush's administration denied that Rove played any role in outing Plame. Despite the denials, it became clear that Rove did talk to reporters about Plame and her husband, Ambassador Wilson (pp. 151-153), and Rove appeared five times before a grand jury before the prosecutor decided against indicting him.

In 2004, when a previously unknown group called "Swift Boat Veterans for Truth" attacked Democratic presidential candidate John

Kerry as unfit for office, the Bush campaign again denied any connection. However, 70 percent of "Swift Boat Veterans" assets came from three wealthy Texans whom Rove had cultivated beginning in the 1980s to finance the state's Republican takeover. The group's lawyer was Bush campaign counsel Ben Ginsberg, who also was counsel to another major pro-Bush group, Progress for America. "Swift Boat Veterans" strategist Chris LaCivita had been a previous executive director of Progress for America. Progress for America spent $35 million itself to defeat Kerry; the following year it was one of the front groups used to attack Social Security. [297]

Rove managed to dodge responsibility for a time for most, if not all, of these political hits. But, as Bush said, Rove was "the architect" of his presidential campaign, responsible for its success, as he has been for most of Bush's political career. Put another way, as Don Sipple, a GOP consultant who worked on Bush campaigns observed, "If I had a nickel for all the things that Rove said he had nothing to do with, I'd be a wealthy man." [298]

By May of 2001, the Bush administration won tax breaks in Congress. The same week, the House passed its version of the No Child Left Behind Act. But the administration's hardball political course resulted in Vermont Senator Jim Jeffords' switching parties, shifting the Senate to Democratic control. I e-mailed Rove. [299]

Ten hours later, putting the best face on it, Rove responded, "Jeffords departs and we get a big tax cut ... it balances out." [300]

Chapter 23

CAMPAIGNING FOR WAR

Although the outgoing Clinton administration had warned the new
Bush administration about al Qaeda, foreign policy didn't figure high on
the Bush agenda. During the second presidential debate with Vice
President Al Gore, Bush said he wanted to "avoid nation-building," a
logical tack for a Texas governor without foreign policy experience
beyond the Rio Grande. His approach made even more sense for an
administration that lost the popular vote in 2000 and took office by only
a single vote in the Supreme Court. To buttress its domestic legitimacy,
the administration sought to cut taxes and pass the "No Child Left
Behind" education law to win congressional support. But it showed no
interest in taking on Israel's get-tough stance toward the Palestinians that
produced a second Intifada that killed more than 7,000.[301]

On the other hand, in January 2001, Vice President Dick Cheney,
who'd been secretary of defense during the first Gulf War, had "a deep
sense of unfinished business about Iraq," and asked outgoing Secretary of
Defense William S. Cohen for briefings for Bush on Iraq as Topic A.[302]
The president didn't seem to respond vigorously, even after he received
a CIA warning about imminent terrorist attack in August 2001, while he
vacationed for a month in Texas.[303]

Reacting four days after 9/11, Bush and his national security experts
met at Camp David, where Secretary of Defense Donald Rumsfeld and
Undersecretary of Defense Paul Wolfowitz suggested three targets: al
Qaeda, Afghanistan's Taliban, and Iraq. That day, only Wolfowitz, with
the same foresight that led him to underestimate the strength of the Iraqi
insurgency, pressed to attack Iraq.[304] Two months later, on Nov. 21, 2001,
Bush took Rumsfeld aside and asked him to secretly begin building war

plans for Iraq. By January, in his state of the Union speech, Bush declared Iraq, Iran, and North Korea an "axis of evil." By June, at West Point, he declared preemptive attack suitable to "confront the worst threats before they emerge."[305]

Former national Security Adviser Brent Scowcroft opposed the Iraq initiative, and in the *Wall Street Journal* argued there was no evidence of an Iraqi arms build-up. But the government's apparent "victory" in Afghanistan, its planning for an Iraq war, and the positioning of U.S. troops circling the Persian Gulf led to a sense of inevitability even before Congress voted its assent.

In the meantime, the administration changed the nation's intelligence structure to get the answers it wanted. In August 2002, the Pentagon formally established the Office of Special Plans, a separate intelligence and strategy unit led by Douglas Feith.[306] Feith and his subordinates, especially Bill Luti, a former Navy officer and former aide to Cheney who was allied with administration hawks, "were essentially an extra-governmental organization, because many of their sources of information and much of their work were in the shadows," according to Marine General Gregory Newbold. The general, who was then operations director for the Joint Chiefs of Staff, opposed the invasion of Iraq, and quietly retired when he couldn't support it. He later told journalist Thomas E. Ricks, "It was also my sense that they cherry-picked obscure, unconfirmed information to reinforce their own philosophies and ideologies."[307] Former Lieutenant Colonel Karen Kwiatkoski told journalist Jim Moore that the process was like "picking the rotten cherries, the absolutely rotten stuff that the CIA had pulled out and thrown away. I mean these were the nasty cherries that were down on the floor, and they picked them up and used them because they fit what they wanted to hear."[308]

Cheney made repeated trips to the CIA to frame the intelligence-gathering, sometimes alone, sometimes with national security aide I. Lewis "Scooter" Libby. Ultimately, CIA Director George Tenet produced the rushed National Intelligence Estimate that the administration wanted, declaring Iraq possessed chemical and biological weapons, had made strides in the weaponizing and delivery of biological weapons, and was reassembling its nuclear program. The NIE undercut the best advice of the intelligence apparatus that had been set up to guide foreign policy.[309]

The same month, chief of staff Andrew Card announced formation of the White House Iraq Group, whose members included Rove, long-time Bush adviser Karen Hughes, political operative Mary Matalin, Deputy National Security Adviser Jim Wilkinson, speech writer Michael Gerson, legislative liaison Nicholas Calio, National Security Adviser Rice, her then-assistant Stephen Hadley, and Libby.[310] Heavy with political operatives, the group met frequently in the White House Situation Room,[311] underscoring the reality that in the Bush White House, politics and national security policy became indivisible.

By August 26, Cheney declared there was no doubt Iraq had weapons of mass destruction (WMDs), and that the administration had the intelligence to prove it.[312] The administration marginalized the formal intelligence community by constructing its new operation in Feith's office, while Feith's office and administration policy adviser and hawk Richard Perle attacked those who didn't fall into line. In a *Wall Street Journal* op-ed article on September 4th, Rove associate Michael Ledeen suggested that, in addition to Iraq's, the governments of Iran, Syria, and Saudi Arabia should be overthrown. But the main push was timed to commemorate the one-year anniversary of September 11.

On September 8, on NBC's *Meet the Press* with Tim Russert, Cheney trumped the intelligence community by declaring that those who doubted the threat of Iraq hadn't "seen all the intelligence that we have seen."[313] The same day on CNN, National Security Adviser Condoleezza Rice said, "There will always be some uncertainty about how quickly [Saddam] can acquire nuclear weapons. But we don't want the smoking gun to be a mushroom cloud." [314]

The same words appeared in the *New York Times'* lead story the same day.[315]

The impact of the White House Iraq Group in constructing the story became clearer two years later when the *Times* and the *Post* publicly deconstructed their coverage in the run-up to the war. The *Times* "found a number of instances of coverage that was not as rigorous as it should have been."[316] It recounted a series of articles it ran that:

> depended at least in part on information from a circle of Iraqi
> informants, defectors and exiles bent on "regime change" in Iraq,

people whose credibility has come under increasing public debate in recent weeks. (The most prominent of the anti-Saddam campaigners, Ahmad Chalabi, has been named as an occasional source in *Times* articles since at least 1991, and has introduced reporters to other exiles. He became a favorite of hard-liners within the Bush administration and a paid broker of information from Iraqi exiles, until his payments were cut off last week.) Complicating matters for journalists, the accounts of these exiles were often eagerly confirmed by United States officials convinced of the need to intervene in Iraq. Administration officials now acknowledge that they sometimes fell for misinformation from these exile sources. So did many news organizations — in particular, this one.

The *Times* said its page one articles on October 26 and November 8, 2001 cited Iraqi defectors describing a secret Iraqi camp where Islamic terrorists were trained and biological weapons produced. The problem, the *Times* reported, was that "These accounts have never been independently verified." Another front page story on December 20, 2001, cited an ''An Iraqi defector who described himself as a civil engineer'' who "said he personally worked on renovations of secret facilities for biological, chemical and nuclear weapons in underground wells, private villas and under the Saddam Hussein Hospital in Baghdad as recently as a year ago.'' The article continued:

> Knight Ridder Newspapers reported last week that American officials took that defector — his name is Adnan Ihsan Saeed al-Haideri — to Iraq earlier this year to point out the sites where he claimed to have worked, and that the officials failed to find evidence of their use for weapons programs. It is still possible that chemical or biological weapons will be unearthed in Iraq, but in this case it looks as if we, along with the administration, were taken in. And until now we have not reported that to our readers.[317]

Its September 8, 2002, lead story, the article said, concerned aluminum tubes the administration identified as components for the manufacture of nuclear weapons, claims supposedly supported by American intelligence. Cautions about the claims were "buried deep,

1,700 words into a 3,600-word article." Administration officials were allowed to expound at length on why this evidence demanded that Saddam Hussein be dislodged from power: "The first sign of a 'smoking gun,' they argue, may be a mushroom cloud." The article continued:

> Five days later, the *Times* reporters learned that the tubes were in fact a subject of debate among intelligence agencies. The misgivings appeared deep in an article on Page A13, under a headline that gave no inkling that we were revising our earlier view ("White House Lists Iraq Steps to Build Banned Weapons"). The *Times* gave voice to skeptics of the tubes on January 9, when the key piece of evidence was challenged by the International Atomic Energy Agency. That challenge was reported on Page A10; it might well have belonged on Page A1.

Another story April 21, 2003, cited an Iraqi scientist who claimed Iraq destroyed chemical weapons just before the war began, or sent them to Syria, and had been cooperating with al Qaeda. The Iraqi official turned out to be in military intelligence. "The *Times* never followed up on the veracity of this source or the attempts to verify his claims."[318]

Related concerns had been raised at the *Washington Post*, as it reported from its front page less than three months after the *Times*' reconsideration.[319] Shortly before the war began, reporter Walter Pincus wrote a story questioning whether the Bush administration had proof that Saddam Hussein was hiding weapons of mass destruction. But the editors resisted using Pincus' story, and ran it only after assistant managing editor Bob Woodward intervened. "Even so, the article was relegated to Page A17."[320] The article continued:

> Given the *Post*'s reputation for helping topple the Nixon administration, some of those involved in the prewar coverage felt compelled to say the paper's shortcomings did not reflect any reticence about taking on the Bush White House. [National Security reporter Dana] Priest noted, however, that skeptical stories usually triggered hate mail "questioning your patriotism and suggesting that you somehow be delivered into the hands of the terrorists."

An examination of the paper's coverage, and interviews with more than a dozen of the editors and reporters involved, shows that the *Post* published a number of pieces challenging the White House, but rarely on the front page. Some reporters who were lobbying for greater prominence for stories that questioned the administration's evidence complained to senior editors who, in the view of those reporters, were unenthusiastic about such pieces. The result was coverage that, despite flashes of groundbreaking reporting, in hindsight looks strikingly one-sided at times.

"The paper was not front-paging stuff," said Pentagon correspondent Thomas Ricks. "Administration assertions were on the front page. Things that challenged the administration were on A18 on Sunday or A24 on Monday. There was an attitude among editors: Look, we're going to war, why do we even worry about all this contrary stuff?"

In retrospect, said Executive Editor Leonard Downie Jr., "We were so focused on trying to figure out what the administration was doing that we were not giving the same play to people who said it wouldn't be a good idea to go to war and were questioning the administration's rationale. Not enough of those stories were put on the front page. That was a mistake on my part."

Across the country, "the voices raising questions about the war were lonely ones," Downie said. "We didn't pay enough attention to the minority ... "

Such decisions coincided with the *Post* editorial page's strong support for the war, such as its declaration the day after [Defense Secretary] Powell's presentation [to the United Nations] that "it is hard to imagine how anyone could doubt that Iraq possesses weapons of mass destruction."[321]

Between them, here were the nation's two top newspapers for political intelligence, even-handedly and unequivocally outlining that they had been utterly misled, and had utterly misled their readers. Key editors and reporters from both publications described how they acquiesced in that misleading with an administration determined to go to war in Iraq—and publicly acknowledged the extent to which they had been misled only much later.

Chapter 24

THE 9/11 COMMENTARY

On Tuesday, September 11, 2001, like millions of Americans, I writhed in horror at the sight of American and United Airlines jets being used as bombs to attack the symbols of American commercial and military power, and killing thousands of innocent civilians. Groping for a constructive response, I turned to writing. Hoping that my knowledge of the administration's political operation might offer perspective to students and colleagues, I wrote an article suggesting that the attacks were the predictable outcome of an American foreign policy produced by a President who lacked understanding of the tensions of the Middle East. Political organizations directly reflect their leaders, I'd learned in my years of political staff work. When the planes hit the World Trade Center with one of my colleagues on board,[322] Bush had been campaigning for brother Jeb, to stanch the political blood loss from the presidential election in Florida. Then, Bush flew Air Force One to the safety of bases in Louisiana and Nebraska, leaving press secretary Karen Hughes before the cameras at the White House and his wife, Laura, in a basement bunker. I finished the editorial, sent it to our campus newspaper[323] and the *Boston Globe*,[324] and shared it with an e-mail list of friends, including Rove.

The editorial was published the next day in the *Massachusetts Daily Collegian* and two days later in the *Globe* (as a letter to the editor). The *Collegian* headline: "A Policy of Neglect and Cowardice, a Pay-off of Death." I argued that Bush had "ignored the suffering of the Palestinians in the Middle East, then urged Israelis and Palestinians to settle their differences by leaving Ariel Sharon to pursue a policy of non-negotiation and state assassinations. ... The result is predictable. ... How can we fail to see our policy has created zealots and suicide bombers, willing to attack us in our own skies, on our own soil?"[325]

On September 13, a right-wing talk radio show snapped up my commentary as fodder to generate telephone responses. Just after noon, an anonymous caller left a bizarre message on my office phone. "Hi, Mr. Israel. I'm an alumni of University of Massachusetts at Amherst. And I was listening to a radio program in which they read I believe a letter that you sent to the editor ... I just want to let you know that it sickens me that you would, in a time where we need to unite, suggest such a thing, and to be so unpatriotic. And I am embarrassed to be affiliated with you and the University of Massachusetts, and I will be writing a letter to the president. Have a good day."

Within minutes, there were two more messages, both anonymous, on my home answering machine. "Bill, you're the worst type of despicable scum." A minute later came another: "I assume you're the Bill Israel that wrote that letter to the *Globe* that was in the paper today. What a piece of garbage that is! Don't you have the common decency to at least wait a few days before you spew out this kind of garbage, at least in deference to the survivors who're left behind? I can't believe an individual like you. Who do you think you are?"

An hour later: "Hi, Mr. Israel. As a person who loves my country, I hope — I'm calling about your article in the paper — and I hope your neighbors do to you what you're doing to the American people right now, you moron. You belong over there with the terrorists."

I got the impression that the first three calls, and perhaps the fourth, were reactions to the radio program. The next two callers appeared to be disgruntled Jews, believing they were chastising one of their own. (In fact, despite my last name, I was raised Presbyterian). So did another caller that evening who did give his name: "Hello, Bill, ... you blame the attack on Israel, essentially. It's all it boils down to. You're a very strange self-hating Jew ... Of course, you will deny this. I just wanted to let you know one reaction to your idiotic, casuistic, sophistic, self-deceptive, wrong-headed, silly letter. Bye-bye."

An hour later: "Yeah, this is Phil in Brookline Heights. And I assume this is Bill Israel, the same guy who wrote the letter to the *Globe* today, the featured letter. If it is, all I can say is, Bill, you're a piece of shit. A fucking little traitor. And you deserve to be, somebody needs to meet you in a dark alley so you can get your fuckin' teeth knocked out ... " and so on.

A few calls were supportive. A caller from Newton Center, Massachusetts, said: "I just wish the political leaders of this country were reflecting some of the thoughtfulness that you showed the other people on that page today. So, just many thanks from a fellow citizen. Take care." Another called to ask permission to reprint my letter. A third, two days later, said, "I'm very proud of you ... It takes a lot of courage, and I hope you didn't get any bad repercussions."

A few days later a threatening call came to the office, but it was not prompted by talk radio. "Yeah, I just read your article, 'A policy of neglect and cowardice, a payoff of death.' *I just read that on the Internet.* And I wanted to let you know that I think you're a complete, fucking fool. If I'd been in that class and you'da said something like that, I would have attacked you and it woulda took about ten people to pull me off you. You are such a fucking idiot I can't believe you're teaching in a university in the United States of America. You just make me want to puke, you vomit motherfucker. That's all I have to say, Sweetheart. Bye."

Even though I sent the commentary to Karl Rove, I doubted that it would influence Rove's handling of the 9/11 aftermath. But I was intrigued to note in the three days after September 11, the administration's response to the tragedy partly reflected what I'd written. By Thursday, William Safire of the *New York Times*, a former Nixon administration speech writer, suggested in his column that a "mole" in the White House had threatened the president's safety, requiring that he flee — a story that even White House spokesman Ari Fleischer later denied. And by Friday, both Bush and Secretary Colin Powell finally were on the phone to Israel's Sharon, directing him to show restraint.

I e-mailed Rove again about 9:30 Friday night, September 14, referring to those developments as "learning from the opposition?"[326] Again, he didn't respond. Early the next afternoon, I felt uneasy when, after I logged on, my computer began downloading a river of e-mail, not from Rove, but from scores of strangers. Someone without my knowledge had posted my e-mail address on a right-wing Web site, Lucianne.com. There, at the top, right-hand side of Lucianne.com's front page was a link to my editorial — but this version was edited down, its logic snipped in order to make people see red. It had been posted at 12:13 p.m. Saturday, less than fifteen hours after my e-mail to Rove, by "Thor" — the Scandinavian god who used his hammer to destroy the enemies of the gods. In a single sentence, the style Rove often used in e-mail, Thor wrote: "This editorial is disgusting."[327]

Lucianne.com is the web site of Lucianne Goldberg, the Republican operative who infiltrated the presidential campaign of former U.S. Senator George McGovern, and who later convinced Linda Tripp to tape her conversations with Monica Lewinsky about her relationship with President Clinton. In reading the Norwegian "Thor," I couldn't help but think of Rove, who at home had shown such pride in his great uncle's charter to be the consul to Norway.[328]

As did the radio program, the Lucianne.com post seemed instantly to activate a network. Within four minutes of the post, a dozen respondents were on it like starving dogs on raw flesh. One of them posted my title and e-mail address and sixty others chimed in within the next three hours. Three hours after that, someone named "2nd amendment mama" posted the editorial on another right-wing site, FreeRepublic.com, including my e-address and office phone, with the note: "With journalism being taught by left-wing, socialist, terrorist-loving scum like this, it's no wonder all the media is like it is. This person is a traitor in my book and should be treated as such..........Have at him Freepers!" ("Freepers" is slang for those who frequent the FreeRepublic.com site.)[329] About the same time, someone else posted my name and home phone on USENET, drawing the wrath of two patrolling civil libertarians who gave the poster a hard time. The next day, the online *Wall Street Journal,* evidently connecting to one of the right-wing web sites, continued the attack, listing me as one of two "Journalism Profs Against America." The other "prof," in an irony, was my master's thesis adviser, Robert Jensen, with whom I frequently disagree, but who had independently written a piece more vociferous than mine.[330]

Meanwhile, on the web site of the *Daily Collegian,* some two hundred respondents, directed from Lucianne.com and FreeRepublic.com, wrote comments, two or three expressing support, most expressing hatred; a few demanding I be fired; one promising, "I'm going to hurt this guy."[331] A university official called me, urging me to pull in and re-group to speak up another day. University officials also asked campus police to check on my safety. But, faced with a political tempest, university officials didn't relish defending my free speech rights and the contribution it could make to a robust discussion of public policy.[332]

As time passed, the responses to my commentary seemed better organized and more calculated. First came a warning from the *Daily Collegian* photographer who had taken my picture to accompany the op-ed piece. He called to apologize. Someone at the *Minuteman*, the right-wing university student newspaper, obtained the photo of me, and the photographer wanted me to know he'd had nothing to do with it. Sure enough, the photo showed up in the next issue of the *Minuteman*, which named me "Jackass of the Month," covering its front and back pages with attacks on me. Only later did I learn that the *Minuteman* is one of eighty campus student newspapers around the United States funded by right-wing foundations coordinated through the Philanthropy Roundtable (Chapter 20).[333] The *Minuteman,* like the other student newspapers, received subventions funneled through the right-wing Collegiate Network, now a subsidiary of another right-wing group, the Intercollegiate Studies Institute.[334] The Collegiate Network has received some $5.8 million in funding[335] to build the network of right-wing campus newspapers. Its president is, among other things, a counselor to the Federalist Society.[336]

If this was the beginning of efforts to vilify me in an organized way, I seemed to be in excellent company. The *National Interest*, a journal founded by the neoconservative Irving Kristol, cited my editorial and lumped it with others in a story asserting that those who had looked for reasons underlying the 9/11 attacks were part of "the American adversary culture" and a "durable reservoir of discontent." Such labels seemed intended to discourage criticism or to blunt independent thinking[337] — just as the Nixon administration used "outside agitator" to denigrate anyone who opposed its war policy in Vietnam. Accuracy in Academe, the conservative correlate in higher education to Accuracy in Media in journalism, cited me and other academics, as well.[338] Another right-wing site attacked my editorial and others as anti-American and anti-West.[339]

An attack posted in yet another right-wing website, cross-listed at Freerepublic.com, castigated MIT Professor Noam Chomsky, me, and several others.[340] And a few months later as my wife and I were flying cross-country, browsing in a bookstore at the Dallas-Fort Worth airport I found myself listed in a new book entitled *Why the Left Hates America: Exposing the Lies That Have Obscured Our Nation's Greatness*, by one Daniel J. Flynn. Flynn never tried to contact me; but, again, I found myself in good company, with the likes of Jensen, my thesis adviser, and Professors Howard Zinn and Chalmers Johnson, among others. That seemed a lot of mileage from one small op-ed page piece.

When I contacted him a year and a half later, Rove denied orchestrating the attack — in fact, he denied even reading my article until then — and I wanted to believe him. When I described the episode to him, Wayne Slater, co-author of *Bush's Brain*, called it "vintage Rove." He and co-author Jim Moore included an account of it in their book.[341]

Yet, the attack on me reflected a different kind of direct mail. Like others discussed in class (chapter 4), this one, too, was largely "immune from press coverage." It, too, enabled a smear from a comfortable distance. But this one occurred, not through a campaign, but through a larger, organized structure. It targeted not a group of potential voters, but an audience of one. This effort was focused not by carefully culled computer lists through a mass mailing. It was directed through right-wing talk radio and Web sites *calculated* to inflame *individual* telephone calls and e-mails. Wallstreetjournal.com and Flynn's book reinforced these messages. Their point was not to debate, but to intimidate.

Direct mail, as Rove noted in class (chapter 4), is usually intended for surprise attack, and for concealing the identity of the attacker. In this case, while the attacks appeared to come mostly from anonymous individuals, they were focused and launched through new structures developed by the political Right. The structures developed gradually and their potency often less visible to my colleagues or the news media. Yet their power can be overwhelming, especially when focused on individuals. Such attacks may make some people and news organizations afraid to speak out, thereby undercutting the freedoms of speech and press guaranteed by the First Amendment. When American news media are harassed, bypassed, diminished in scope, or disabled, how can we expect them to adequately articulate public business. And how, then, can we expect our system to work?

Chapter 25

THE POLITICS OF WAR NEWS

The White House Iraq Group pushed the attack on Iraq with a zeal that discovered new opportunities once the war was underway. Sam Gardiner counted 50 different examples of disinformation or misinformation. Among the more notable: fabrication of heroine and heroic rescue, where none existed; and attacks on challengers and opponents, especially when they were right.[342]

On April 3, 2003, fourteen days into the Iraq War, the *Washington Post* reported that Private Jessica Lynch had "sustained multiple gunshot wounds" and also was stabbed while she "fought fiercely and shot several enemy soldiers ... firing her weapon until she ran out of ammunition." The *Post* quoted an unnamed U.S. military official saying that "she was fighting to the death." The *New York Times* also reported that she had gunshot wounds. The same day, Secretary of Defense Rumsfeld told reporters, "We are certainly grateful for the brilliant and courageous rescue of ... Pfc. [Private First Class] Jessica Lynch, who was being held by Iraqi forces in what they called a 'hospital.'" An April 5 Central Command briefing reported that air support "in coordination with conventional forces from the Marine Corps and the Air Force and the Army were able to successfully rescue Private First Class Jenifer[sic] Lynch out of a hospital and irregular military headquarters facility that was being used by these death squads in Nasiriyah and successfully return her to U.S. hands." That day, Brigadier General Brooks added, "There was not a fire fight inside of the building, I will tell you, but there were fire fights outside of the building, getting in and getting out."

On April 6, the *Washington Times* reported, "The hospital where Pfc. Lynch was held was reported to be a stronghold of the Fedayeen Saddam, a guerrilla force sworn to martyrdom for Iraqi dictator Saddam Hussein. The rescuers arrived by helicopter, secured the building by gunfire and forced their way inside, CNN reported." As late as April 14, *Time* magazine was reporting that, "According to the *Washington Post*, Lynch, an Army supply clerk with only minimal combat training, shot several advancing Iraqi soldiers, emptying her weapon of ammunition and possibly incurring a series of gunshot wounds."

In fact, Jim Wilkinson — the White House Iraq Group member assigned as the top civilian communication aide to Gen. Tommy Franks, head of the U.S. Central Command — was phoned as soon as the rescue helicopters were in the air. "This is very strange for a military operation," Gardiner wrote in his study. "When I tell military friends, they often respond, 'Do you suppose they staged it?'... The information given to the *Washington Post* would have been very highly classified, with special handling, limited only to those who had a need to know. This was a major pattern from the beginning of the marketing campaign throughout the war. It was okay to release classified information if it supported the message. By the afternoon of April 3, when Rumsfeld and General Myers gave their press briefing, the story on the street was that she was America's new Rambo."[343]

In contrast, the BBC online described the Lynch tale as "one of the most stunning pieces of news management ever conceived."[344]Lynch, then a nineteen-year-old army clerk from Palestine, West Virginia, was captured when her company took a wrong turn just outside Nasiriya and was ambushed. Nine of her comrades were killed; Lynch was taken to the local hospital, at the time full of Fedayeen. Eight days later, after the Fedayeen left, U.S. special forces stormed the hospital, capturing the events on a night vision camera.

Dr. Harith a-Houssona, who looked after Lynch, later reported, "I examined her, I saw she had a broken arm, a broken thigh and a dislocated ankle. There was no [sign of] shooting, no bullet inside her body, no stab wound — only road traffic accident. They want to distort the picture. I don't know why they think there is some benefit in saying she has a bullet injury." Witnesses told the BBC that the U.S. Special Forces knew that the Iraqi military had fled a day before the Americans swooped on the hospital.

According to Dr. Anmar Uday, who worked at the hospital, "We were surprised. Why do this? There was no military, there were no soldiers in the hospital. It was like a Hollywood film. They cried 'go, go, go,' with guns and blanks without bullets, blanks and the sound of explosions. They made a show for the American attack on the hospital — action movies like Sylvester Stallone or Jackie Chan."

Moreover, two days before the snatch squad arrived, Harith had arranged to deliver Lynch to the Americans in an ambulance. But as the ambulance carrying her approached a checkpoint, American troops opened fire, forcing it to flee back to the hospital. The Americans had almost killed their prize catch. Yet when footage of the rescue was released, General Vincent Brooks, U.S. spokesman in Doha, said: "Some brave souls put their lives on the line to make this happen, loyal to a creed that they know that they'll never leave a fallen comrade."

The American strategy, as the BBC perceived, was to produce the right television footage by using embedded reporters, images from their own cameras, and even editing the film themselves. The Pentagon was influenced by Hollywood producers, notably Jerry Bruckheimer, the man behind *Black Hawk Down*, who advised the Pentagon on the prime time television series *Profiles from the Front Line*, which followed US forces in Afghanistan in 2001, an approach adopted and developed in Iraq.[345]

Punishing the French. When the French government decided against supporting the United States and the United Kingdom in an intervention against Iraq on the part of the United Nations, the French themselves became a target. At least eight times false or engineered stories aimed at the French ran in the media, the majority appearing after they failed to support actions by the United States and the United Kingdom before the U.N. Among them:

- In September, the *New York Times* reported that the French (and Germans) sold high-precision switches to Iraq that could be used for nuclear weapons;[346] the same story appeared in the UK press. The fact is that although Iraq had requested the switches, the switches were never supplied.[347]
- "American intelligence sources" leaked to the *Washington Post* the incorrect story that the French possessed prohibited strains

of smallpox virus. Moreover, "US intelligence sources" told the *Washington Times* that two French companies sold spare parts for aircraft and helicopters to Iraq. The companies declared they did not, and no proof to the contrary has surfaced.[348]

- "Someone created a story that French Roland missiles were being used to shoot down American aircraft, and that these missiles were new. It turned out the story was not very well put together. The production line for the Roland 2 shut down in 1993."[349]

- On May 6 through 8, the *Washington Times* (and other outlets) reported, "An unknown number of Iraqis who worked for Saddam Hussein's government were given passports by French officials in Syria, U.S. intelligence officials said."[350] Said Fox News: "The reports add fuel to the fire that Paris had been colluding with Baghdad before and during the coalition invasion of Iraq."[351]

By the following week, in the *Washington Post*, France accused the United States of a smear campaign, questions about which White House Press Secretary Scott McClellan dodged. Gardiner wrote, "I've been told from sources in the press that most of the leaks during the 'armed conflict' that appeared in the *Washington Times* came from the Special Plans Office in the Pentagon...The Secretary of Defense told us before the war he was going to do strategic influence. It appears as if the French were a target."[352]

Execution of Prisoners. On March 27, 2003, British Prime Minister Tony Blair at a joint news conference with Bush at Camp David alleged that there had been executions of coalition prisoners. He began his statement with the phrase: "If anyone needs any further evidence of the depravity ... " On CNN's *Larry King Show* the same day, General Peter Pace declared, "They have executed prisoners of war." By March 28, according to Gardiner, "The UK press began attacking the story as not true. One of the soldier's sisters reported his colonel had said he was not executed." The U.K. finally pulled away from the story, but the U.S. side stayed with it through April 7. When Rumsfeld was questioned on the 7th, the story began to change; the pattern of non-answer surfaced. "Again, the pattern was that the story was more important than the facts," Gardiner observed.[353]

Disinformation Attacking Dissent.

- In his January 2003 State of the Union Message, the president declared that the British government had information that Iraq was getting uranium from Africa. In February, Ambassador Joseph Wilson was sent to Niger to investigate the reports, and found them groundless. By March 7, before the launch of the war, the International Atomic Energy Agency (IAEA) revealed that documents on which the allegations were based were forged.
- In April, the London *Daily Telegraph* and the *Christian Science Monitor* reported payoffs to British member of parliament George Galloway, a longtime critic of a hard line against Saddam Hussein. The papers claimed he had received payoffs from Hussein, as much as $10 million over eleven years. By May, the British paper the *Mail*, and by June 20, the *Christian Science Monitor*, reported that those documents, too, were forgeries. The retired general who first leaked the documents to the *Christian Science Monitor* had also claimed he had documents proving that six of the 9/11 hijackers learned to fly in Iraq.
- Ambassador Joseph Wilson was targeted after publicly challenging the administration's claims about Iraqi weapons of mass destruction, after the IAEA declared the Niger documents to be forgeries. According to the *New York Daily News*, the job of the White House Iraq Group was "to make the case that Saddam Hussein had nuclear and biochemical weapons." But so determined was the White House Iraq Group to win its argument, *News* reporters wrote two years later, "that it morphed into a virtual hit squad that took aim at critics who questioned its claims ... One of those critics was former Ambassador Joseph Wilson ... His punishment was the media outing of his wife, CIA undercover intelligence officer Valerie Plame." [354]

Wilson, a retired career diplomat and U.S. ambassador to Gabon from 1992 to 1995, is the former chargé d'affaires at the U.S. Embassy in Iraq. He was sent by the Central Intelligence Agency to the Republic of Niger in late February 2002 to determine whether Iraq had purchased uranium for the production of nuclear weapons. In the course of that trip, Wilson consulted with the resident American ambassador and dozens of local officials. He concluded, as had the U.S. ambassador in residence there, that Iraq had not done so. Wilson reported to that effect upon his return in March 2002.

Nevertheless, in January 2003, despite Wilson's fact-finding, President Bush declared in his State of the Union speech that "The British government has learned that Saddam Hussein recently sought significant quantities of uranium from Africa." Wilson tried behind the scenes to correct the record — and when he could not, on July 6, 2002, he published an op-ed in the *New York Times* laying out concern that "If ... the information [he compiled] was ignored because it did not fit certain preconceptions about Iraq, then a legitimate argument can be made that we went to war under false pretenses."

White House press secretary Scott McClellan denied White House involvement in the attack on Wilson, and when the FBI Sept. 26, 2003 launched an investigation, President Bush declared any White House staffer involved in it would be fired. Then, on October 7, Bush said, "I don't know if we're going to find out the senior administration official," he said. "Now, this is a large administration, and there's a lot of senior officials."[355]

Three days later, White House spokesman Scott McClellan told reporters he had talked to three officials — Libby, Rove and Elliot Abrams — and "those individuals assured me they were not involved in this."[356] However, according to Wilson, MSNBC's Chris Matthews told him off camera: "I just got off the phone with Karl Rove, who said your wife was 'fair game.'" And around the same time, an angry Bush rebuked Rove for his role in the Valerie Plame affair, sources told the New York *Daily News*. "He made his displeasure known to Rove," a presidential counselor told the *News*. "He made his life miserable about this." [357]

On June 23, at a meeting in his office with Judith Miller of the *Times*, Libby said Wilson's wife might be a CIA employee. Wilson then emerged from anonymity with a splash on July 6, telling his story in the *New York Times* column, in a lengthy on-the-record interview with the *Post*, and in an appearance on NBC's *Meet the Press*. Libby met Judith Miller again on July 8 for breakfast at the St. Regis Hotel. Asking that she attribute the information to a "former Hill staffer" (he had once been legal adviser to a House select committee), Libby criticized CIA reporting of Wilson's trip. According to the grand jury indictment brought against Libby through the work of Special Counsel Patrick Fitzgerald, Libby then "advised Miller of his belief that Wilson's wife worked for the CIA."[358]

On July 12, the vice president reportedly instructed Libby to alert reporters of an attack launched that morning on Wilson's credibility by Bush's Press Secretary Ari Fleischer. Libby then talked to Miller and another reporter, Matthew Cooper of *Time*. That same day, another administration official who has not been identified publicly returned a call from Walter Pincus of the *Washington Post*. He "veered off the precise matter we were discussing" and told him that Wilson's Africa trip was a "boondoggle" set up by Plame, Pincus wrote in *Nieman Reports*.[359]

That week Rove and another unidentified source confirmed the information for Novak as well. That unknown source was eventually identified as Secretary Powell's undersecretary, Richard Armitage. And once that source was out, a concerted campaign from the Right sought to discredit the prosecution of Libby for perjury and obstruction of justice by Special Prosecutor Patrick Fitzgerald, the news media, and others who had attacked Rove, in particular, as a source.

However, Cooper and associates reported on *Time* magazine's web site shortly afterward — based on sources he has since identified as Rove and Libby — that "some government officials have noted to *Time* in interviews . . . that Wilson's wife, Valerie Plame, is a CIA official who monitors the proliferation of weapons of mass destruction."[360] Until the CIA leak investigation (and even, at this writing, after it), there seemed little limit to the White House Iraq Group's ability to master the story line and the conventional wisdom.

And until two leading news organizations re-analyzed their own work, it wasn't clear how effectively the White House Iraq Group had misled them into publishing content that effectively supported the war and marginalized those who sought to challenge it.

Chapter 26

CONFESSIONS OF THE PRESS

In the summer of 2004, the soul-searching self-reports by the *New York Times* and the *Washington Post* summarized journalistic shortcomings that misled the American people and the world. They did not, however, note that the problem is not isolated, but a recurring, structural defect inherent in the ties between American journalism and politics.

The same phenomenon occurred during the early years of the war in Vietnam. Then, too, the front pages of the *New York Times* and other newspapers reflected the Johnson administration message: that American naval vessels had been attacked in the Gulf of Tonkin, providing the artifice by which President Johnson secured Congressional approval to escalate the war. In Vietnam the *Times* confined dissenting views to its inside pages—just as it did in the run-up to and during the early stages of the war in Iraq. In the Vietnam war, American television largely reflected the administration line, until forces inside the government itself framed a dissident view.[361] In short, official sources prevailed — not only in escalating the war, *but even as the necessary precondition for framing its opposition* — in Vietnam, and in Iraq. As Tom Rosenstiel of the Project for Excellence in Journalism has said, the media are no substitute for an effective political opposition party; and without an effective opposition party, journalism is crippled.

During the Vietnam war, Pentagon officials offered a daily body count of enemy combatants as an indicator the United States was winning. Nevertheless, by the later sixties a relatively invigorated U.S. news media, encouraged by a vigorous anti-war effort, penetrated the story when the CBS News Saigon bureau and others began to report that the United States was stuck in a quagmire. Journalism evolved, from supporting the war in the wake of Johnson's 1964 electoral victory and his framing of the Tonkin Gulf incident, to a deeper reporting of quagmire only a few years later. Irrespective, even with a relatively unfettered press, the American war in Vietnam killed 58,000 Americans and 2 million Vietnamese.

Forty years later, canny handling by the Bush administration of a crippled media limited vigorous reporting about unproved threats of terrorism from Iraq, and about administration lies concerning Saddam Hussein and weapons of mass destruction. The administration controlled media access, prohibiting even photographs of caskets of American war dead as they arrived at the U.S. airbase in Dover, Delaware, and refusing to calculate enemy war dead. Moreover, by making a political hash of the Democratic opposition in the elections of 2002 and 2004, the Bush administration demolished some of the alternative sources journalists required to tell the larger story. Not until three years later — the election of 2006 — did Americans turn against the administration. By then, 3,000 Americans had died, and an estimated 600,000 Iraqis.[362]

Journalism does not bear sole responsibility for dismantling the lies of war, but it does bear a strong responsibility to uncover them. The great journalist I.F. Stone once warned that all governments lie. The question is: can journalism in wartime *ever* truly see the lies in time, before the loss of life on a vast scale? On that point, history is not sanguine. In wartime, government always has the upper hand.

Just after World War I, reflecting on American journalism's capacity to mislead, Walter Lippmann wrote: "If I lie in a lawsuit involving the fate of my neighbor's cow, I can go to jail. But if I lie to a million readers in a matter involving war and peace, I can lie my head off, and, if I choose the right series of lies, be entirely irresponsible. Nobody will punish me."[363] That this remains the case in the Iraq war, nearly a century later, suggests that American journalism retains the deepest structural flaw.

The *Times* and *Post mea culpas* in 2004, if helpful, in no way contradict a conclusion that misleading American media remains an active and continuing function of the U.S. government. Less than a year *after* the two newspapers outlined their errors, three political communication researchers studying the Abu Ghraib prison torture and murder scandal found that "even when provided with considerable photographic and documentary evidence and the critical statement of governmental and nongovernmental actors, the nation's leading media proved unable or unwilling to construct a coherent challenge to the administration's claims about its policies on torturing detainees. As it turned out in this case, the photos may have driven the story, but the White House communication staff ultimately wrote the captions."[364]

Perhaps, for the sake of political advantage, as suggested in another setting, it doesn't matter what the story is, if you can promote the right picture.[365] Yet the evidence suggests that in the case of Iraq, the Bush administration, through the White House Iraq Group, misled Americans and American journalism into needless war and mass carnage. Furthermore, the United States subsequently inserted secret forces on the ground in Iran, and threatened yet another U.S. invasion, despite official denials, with the addition of a carrier group in the Persian Gulf. The cumulative evidence led Rutgers University journalism and media studies researcher Deepa Kumar to declare that American media themselves have become complicit in a "military-industrial-media complex in preparing the grounds for another war."[366]

Many of the journalists interviewed for this book seem vividly aware of influences that have limited their effectiveness. While several noted that journalism has improved in some ways, many of them affirm that in confronting power, journalism has been outflanked. As a check on parts I through IV of this work, we next ask those journalists to compare what they've seen.

PART V

HOW JOURNALISTS VIEW ROVE, BUSH AND THE NEW RIGHT

Chapter 27

A Study of Journalists: Background and Methods

The human and political disaster of the United States war in Iraq, the failure of congressional oversight before its launch, and the failure of two of the nation's leading newspapers to vigorously report the run-up to the war (Chapter 23) suggest that something is out of balance in American politics and journalism. Although the Bush administration, including Karl Rove, have had a substantial role, the imbalance did not begin with them; they are the latest chapter in a tale that begins with the dawn of propaganda, and accelerates with the methods of George Creel in World War I later applied to the American Way campaign. Those methods became increasingly powerful in the reorganization of the Right in the 1960s and 1970s. One must account for these developments, to evaluate the imbalance, and to determine how journalism changed.

One way to diagnose the changes is to compare media content from earlier eras to that published more recently, studying across media and decades to look for changes in journalism and politics, beyond the single example of the *Washington Post*'s treatment of two different Republican administrations. Yet, because the extent and nature of this metamorphosis is complex, it seems useful, first, to ask journalists themselves what happened, gathering qualitative data from those who experienced the changes.

This book began by asking: How could Karl Rove be so effective? To answer, I outlined answers Rove gave himself, as he taught, and others I gleaned through our interaction. Those answers, in turn, required situating Rove's work in the history of propaganda and the rise of the American political Right. The changes the Right produced by constructing new institutions and ideology with the help of technology changed the structure of American life, captured the culture and — through the vulnerabilities of reality and journalism — the news.

What is missing are specific data on how the political Right, the Bush administration, and Rove have influenced journalism and its practitioners. To gather such data, I questioned journalists, asking: What changes did they see in themselves or in journalism over a thirty- to forty-year period? Did they attribute those changes to the rise of the Right, to the Bush administration, or to other factors?

I selected thirty-two respondents: journalists, former journalists, journalism academics, and two partisans in journalism — one conservative, one liberal. I chose sixteen respondents of the thirty-two from a national conference for journalism professionals and academics at the University of Massachusetts Amherst in late June, 2006; the remaining sixteen, principally from among Washington, D.C. area journalists. I conducted as many of the interviews as possible in person and the remainder by telephone, from June to September 2006; one, in January 2007. For the names of the respondents, see Table 1.

Several earlier studies traced the work, behavior, and inclinations of journalists in various eras. The studies include those by Leo Rosten; Stephen Hess; John W. C. Johnstone *et al.*; and David Weaver and Cleve Wilhoit. These studies sought primarily to gain quantitative or qualitative data on the attributes of journalists, what concerned them, and how they went about reporting the nation's business. None of these studies focused principally on whether a broader scheme of reality construction and control influenced journalism. To address that possibility, this sample includes journalism academics who might have considered the question, and journalists who might have experienced it.

Although Washington journalists had to be a focus of this work, I also included journalists outside the District of Columbia to obtain some regional differences and outside-the-Beltway thinking. Earlier studies tended to focus on men, as journalism was once a male profession. In this study, nine of the thirty-two respondents are women (28 percent). Two African-Americans (one man, one woman) chose not to participate, leaving one Asian-American male as the only minority. The sample includes older and younger journalists.

Table 1
JOURNALISTS INTERVIEWED*

Name and Affiliation	Employment Period
Bhatia, Peter, *Oregonian*	1970s–present
Broder, David, *Washington Post*	1950s–present
Brodeur, Scott, Masslive.com/Advance Media	1980s–present
Daly, Chris, Boston University; formerly Associated Press	1970s–present
Dionne, E.J., *Washington Post* Syndicate	1970s–present
Donley, Jon, Editor NOLA.com (New Orleans)	1980s–present
Edsall, Tom, *Washington Post* (retired 2006); *The New Republic*	1960s–present
Fouhy, Ed, news executive at ABC, NBC, CBS; founder, stateline.org (formerly Walter Cronkite's producer)	1950s–2006
Fox, Steve, U. of Massachusetts, Amherst; formerly Washingtonpost.com	1980s–present
Froomkin, Dan, formerly Washingtonpost.com	1980s–present
Green, Frank, independent filmmaker/editor; formerly NBC News	1970s–present
Houston, Brant, director of Investigative Reporters and Editors, U. of Missouri	1970s–present
Hume, Ellen, U. of Massachusetts, Boston; formerly *L.A. Times*, *Wall St. Journal*	1970s–present
Jarvis, Jeff, C.U.N.Y., formerly Advance.net, *New York Daily News, San Francisco Examiner, Entertainment Weekly*	1970s–present
Judd, Jackie, formerly ABC News	1970s–present
Kornblut, Anne, *Washington Post*; formerly *New York Times, Boston Globe New York Daily News*	1990s–present
Lenert, Ed, U. of Nevada, Reno	1970s–present
Lewis, Charles, president, Fund for Independence in Journalism, formerly of Center for Public Integrity, and CBS' *Sixty Minutes*	1970s–present
Matusow, Barbara, CBS Radio, WNBC, WRC, *Washington Journalism Review*	1970s–2004
McManus, Doyle, Washington bureau chief, *L.A. Times*	1970s–present
Meyer, Phil, U. of North Carolina, formerly Knight-Ridder, Inc.	1950s–present
Nelson, Jack, *L.A. Times* (retired)	1950s–2003
Pincus, Walter, *Washington Post*	1950s–present
Porter, Vikki, Knight Digital Media Center, U. of Southern California formerly Gannett newspapers	1970s–present
Press, Bill, political commentator, "The Bill Press Show," Sirius Satellite Radio; Formerly CNN, MSNBC; KABC; aide to former Calif. Governor Jerry Brown; former chair, California Democratic Party	1960s–present
Rosenstiel, Tom, director, Project for Excellence in Journalism, formerly *Los Angeles Times, Newsweek*	1980s–present
Sussman, Barry, editor, *Nieman Watchdog Report*; formerly *Washington Post* city editor and special Watergate editor	1960s–present
Thomas, Helen, Hearst newspapers; formerly United Press International	1940s–2010
Tumulty, Karen, *Time Magazine*	1970s–present
Viguerie, Richard, American Target Advertising; a founder of political direct mail; founder, *Conservative Digest*	1960s–present
Walter, Amy, *Cook Political Report*	1990s–present
Wertheimer, Linda, National Public Radio	1960s–present

*Interviews (31) conducted June-September, 2006; 32d interview added January 2007.
  Affiliations listed are not conclusive, but current at the time of the interview or indicative of work with which the interviewee may be easily identified.

One focus of the study needed to be the *Washington Post,* for its importance in reporting the Watergate scandal, a high point in American journalism. I therefore sought out *Post* personnel, present and former, to situate current *Post* practice as compared to its Watergate performance. A selection of journalists helped to do so (representing a Watergate-era sensibility: Broder, Dionne, Pincus, Sussman, and Edsall; and a younger sensibility: Froomkin, Fox, and Kornblut, who was interviewed while she worked in the Washington bureau of the *New York Times,* before she went to work for the *Post*).

For each of the 32 respondents, I used the interview protocol depicted in Table 2. The protocol's questions were constructed, first, to elicit a spontaneous overall impression of the most important changes in journalism or journalists over the past thirty to forty years, partly to see to whether, without specific prompting, I might elicit the answers I sought more directly in question 2. Questions two through four were intended to more directly elicit respondents' views of the impact of the Right in the past thirty to forty years; and to determine to what extent respondents discerned an impact on journalism from the Bush administration, or from Rove.

To pose Question 2, I produced a prompt sheet, reproduced in Table 3.

When dramatic changes occur, historical context and theoretical models sometimes help to make sense of the changes. Two such models are employed here, to interpret the answers of the journalists.

According to Professor Donald Shaw of the University of North Carolina, the rise and fall of media can be understood as an evolutionary, and largely economic, phenomenon. Newspapers, which started in the United States in the 1700s, reached peak market penetration around World War I, then successively lost market ground to competition from magazines, film (newsreels), and news delivered by radio, television, cable television, and most recently, the Internet. According to Shaw, each succeeding medium builds on the strengths of previous media, and audiences and advertisers move to the media which best deliver the services their users seek. An ensuing, continuous rise and fall of media thereby occurs, according to Shaw. Shaw says this occurs because a relatively constant proportion of dollars are available for individuals to

Table 2
INTERVIEW PROTOCOL
(Questions for Interviewees)

1. I'm looking at changes in the news over a 30-40 year period. Talk just a minute about your vantage points in looking at these changes – where you've been over that period, or the relevant parts of it. What's been your position in observing these changes ... and what have you seen? Establish context for how you've seen these changes, and what you've seen.

2. Read the brief article. (one-page prompt – Table 3)
   -have you experienced a similar phenomenon?
   -explain
   -what have **you** seen of this phenomenon? What pieces stand out, as clear examples to you, in your mind?
   -what specifics?

3. Coming more to current times, to what extent have you seen these changes as a function of the Bush administration?

4. To what extent, in particular, as a function of the work of Karl Rove? Again, specifics are important here.

5. Any things you'd like to add?

6. Best ways to reach you, in case of need to clarify?

7. Any problem with staying on the record?

   Thank you!

devote to media, as demonstrated by Shaw's long-time research partner, Maxwell McCombs of the University of Texas.

The continuous, changing mix of how individuals spend their fixed proportion of dollars on media, in turn, determines each medium's successive rise and fall, in an evolutionary way. The more effectively a medium delivers an audience, the deeper its market penetration, the greater its rise, and the deeper the fall-off of its competitors. The losers may never fully come back, but may secure market niches that help them to maintain certain audiences. Although Shaw wrote in 1991,[367] before the Internet phenomenon, one could argue that the World Wide Web is merely the latest in the succession of media that Shaw outlines, and is part of a media evolution.

Table 3
INTERVIEW PROMPT SHEET FOR QUESTION 2

"Today, the most important sectors of the political media – most of cable TV news, the majority of popular op-ed columns, almost all of talk radio, a substantial chunk of the book market, and many of the most highly trafficked Web sites – reflect more closely the political and journalistic values of the Washington Times than those of the New York Times." [1]

By 2004, 80 percent of commentators on political television came from the conservative movement. [2] According to Ben H. Bagdikian: "In the years since 1980, the political spectrum of the United States has shifted radically to the far right. What was once the center has been pushed to the left, and what was the far right is now the center ... The major mass media have played a central role in this shift to the right." [3]

According to E. J. Dionne:

> Because the drumbeat of conservative press criticism has been so steady, the establishment press has internalized it. Editors and network executives are far more likely to hear complaints from the right than from the left ... [Rush] Limbaugh's new respectability is the surest sign that the conservative talk network is now bleeding into what passes for the mainstream media, just as the unapologetic conservatism of the Fox News Channel is now affecting programming on the other cable networks ... It took conservatives a lot of hard and steady work to push the media rightward ... The media world now includes (1) talk radio, (2) cable television, and (3) the traditional news sources (newspapers, newsmagazines and the old broadcast networks). Two of these three major institutions tilt well to the right, and the third is under constant pressure to avoid even the pale hint of liberalism... What it adds up to is a media heavily biased toward conservative politics and conservative politicians." [4]

By mid-2005, the political right had begun using webblogs and blogging, as effectively as talk radio. [5]

One benchmark of change appears in comparing the attitude of the *Washington Post* in its treatment of two different Republican administrations. In the first, the journalist Theodore White quotes former Richard Nixon speechwriter Ray Price, who was charged with drafting Nixon's resignation speech, but directed that there be no confession of guilt. As Price put it, "The *Washington Post* would have loved a guilty statement. But even a guilty statement wouldn't have satisfied them. What they wanted was a ceremony on the South Lawn, with the President incinerating himself, and Ben Bradlee toasting marshmallows in the flames." [6] In contrast, little more than 30 years later, the *Post*, which participated in the publishing of the Pentagon Papers in 1971, and in 2004 in effect apologized for being misled by the administration in its coverage of Iraq, defended the Bush administration's selective leak in the Valerie Plame case as "A Good Leak." The introduction to its editorial reads, "President Bush declassified some of the intelligence he used to decide on war in Iraq. Is that a scandal?" [7]

---

[1] David Brock, *The Republican Noise Machine*. New York: Crown Publishers, 2004, 2.

[2] George Lakoff, *Don't Think of an Elephant! Know your Values and Frame the Debate*. White River Junction, VT.: Chelsea Green Publishing, 2004, 16.

[3] Ben H. Bagdikian, *The New Media Monopoly*. Boston: Beacon Press, 2004, 1-2.

[4] E. J. Dionne, "A New Bias in the Media." *Boston Globe*, Dec. 9, 2002, A17.

[5] Andrea Seabrook, "Republicans Turn to Blogs to Deliver a Message," *All Things Considered, National Public Radio*, February 18, 2005, available at:
http://www.npr.org/templates/story/story.php?storyId=4504846

[6] Theodore H. White, *Breach of Faith: the Fall of Richard Nixon*. New York: Atheneum, 1975, 25-26.

[7] "A Good Leak," *Washington Post*, editorial page, April 9, 2006, B6.

In contrast, Professor Barry Vacker of Temple University argues that the Web and the Internet are not evolutionary, but revolutionary. A media revolution occurs, according to Vacker, when a new technology exponentially amplifies the power and reach of previous technologies, which then produces the substance of an information revolution that challenges the prevailing world views and forms of the existing culture.[368]

The changes that journalists in this study describe seem both evolutionary, in some respects, and revolutionary, in others. But the speed with which they are occurring, the sense of bottom dropping out of the newspaper market, for example, and the drastic terms in which journalists such as Charles Lewis and David Broder describe their impact suggest that if the changes are evolutionary in nature, they are revolutionary in scope — possibly on par with the changes set off by the invention of the printing press and movable type.

Interviews for this study took place in the summer and fall of 2006, before midterm elections when Democrats took control of the Congress. Continuing to follow the outline in Table 2, the next chapter itemizes respondents' views on the influences on journalism from the political Right. The chapter after that examines respondents' views on the administration of President George W. Bush, and Karl Rove.

Chapter 28

JOURNALISTS REFLECT ON
THE POLITICAL RIGHT

Unprompted, most respondents cited technology or financial markets as the most important influences on journalism and journalists over the past thirty to forty years. Four of them, in contrast, identified a move to the right as important. But, once prompted, nearly all the journalists agreed that (Question 2) the Right had substantially influenced journalism. Both partisan respondents — one from the Right, one from the Left — affirmed the finding. Altogether, the respondents suggested that the influence of the Right has been substantial (Table 4, p. 214). As one put it: "It's called working the referee. If you boo the decisions against you enough, it changes the referee's behavior. And the right-wingers are not at all reluctant to do that." Asked if he recalled specific stories or moments, the respondent thought a moment and said, "No. Well, maybe it has, and I just haven't been conscious of it. That's the beauty of that technique: that it affects you unconsciously. If you were conscious of it, it wouldn't affect you."[369] But several respondents said recent pressures from the Left, especially in the blogosphere, now equal or exceed those from the Right.

A decided influence. On the political Right, after reviewing Table 3, direct mail expert Richard Viguerie laughed quietly, then responded: "This stuff here is *all* valid … but it didn't happen because of a sense of fairness by the mainstream media. We forced ourselves forward. We literally just pushed our way through." Although conservative syndicated columnists now dominate mainstream newspapers, Viguerie said, in the early 1960s mainstream news organizations ignored conservatives. "And when they did pay attention to us in stories like a cover story in *Newsweek* — 'Thunder on the Right' — we're kooks, we're nuts, we're neo-Nazis, we're fascists, racists, bigots, whatever it might be. And we had to live with all of that."

Journalism is changing, Viguerie said: More journalists, at least in private conversations with him, "are coming closer to just expressing their real views." His observation connects with the suggestion of Jeff Jarvis of City University of New York, that journalists espouse not objectivity, but intellectual honesty. Newswoman Helen Thomas affirmed that approach, as a columnist.[370] According to Viguerie, "The old Walter Cronkites of the world, in their heyday, would have gone to great lengths to claim their objectivity ... They still have a fig leaf out there, but Helen [Thomas] has taken her fig leaf off[371] ... It's interesting how being impotent does that to you. When you feel impotent, you begin to lash out and thrash about. I think that if this goes on much longer where the Republicans are in power, I think you are going to see the level of intensity in the mainstream media increase, because they're feeling that impotence more and more, and it's going to continue." Media will likely become more specialized, Viguerie predicted, with specialized documentary assuming a larger role.[372]

From the political Left, Bill Press declared the impact of the Right to be even greater.

> I think conservatives ought to just declare victory and stop making this ... argument about the liberal media ... the fact is that they not only control the White House and the Congress and the Supreme Court, but they also control the media today. The most extreme are the *Washington Times* and Fox News, which are nothing but megaphones for the Bush administration ... and you add the *Wall Street Journal* editorial page to that, and there is nothing comparable on the Left. Nothing — except Air America [now defunct] and other progressive shows like mine. But nothing on television and nothing in print. I mean, the *Washington Post* supported the war in Iraq. And the *New York Times* printed all the lies about the war in Iraq on the front page and didn't even question Judy Miller's reporting. So you either have the extremes of those who are totally in the tank for the conservative Republican agenda, or you then have the mainstream

media which are ... just repeating the lies, reporting lies, not questioning ... whoever is in the White House ... the one thing that this administration has really succeeded in doing is putting the fear of God into managing editors, program directors, and also working press, that they're afraid to publish or to broadcast anything critical of the administration because they know they will take flak if they do.[373]

Press's own syndicated column has been the target of right-wing letter-writing campaigns to pull it from newspapers in which it runs "simply because it is a different point of view. I don't know of any liberals who would ever do that ... what I find appalling is that managing editors, op-ed page editors, program directors, respond to that ... they don't recognize it for what it is, which is just a bunch of intolerant yahoos who you ought to tell, 'Hey, this is America. You don't like Bill Press today? Well, read Cal Thomas tomorrow. But read Cal Thomas on the same page.' Why does everybody have to be singing from the same hymn book?"

Conservatives' advantages in syndicating newspaper columns and talk radio, Press said, also extend to the production of books.

My agent has been told by publishers in New York: "Liberals don't buy books. So we won't give Bill a contract because Bill's a liberal..." What do you mean, liberals don't buy books?! I mean, liberals read, they support libraries, they have open minds ... [But conservatives] have conquered the book world. They know how to do it. They know how to make an instant best seller. They know the bookstores that report to the *New York Times*. And they will do bulk sales for those bookstores in order to get an Ann Coulter on the *New York Times* best seller list ... Then they add to that all the conservative talk radio shows and the Drudge Report website, and you get instant best sellers. And you do it over and over and over again. There is no such network for a progressive.

Silencing mainstream news. Just as former *Wall Street Journal* reporter Ellen Hume became a target in 1988 for raising questions unwelcome to the Bush-Quayle campaign, so journalist Charles Lewis described similar, deeper effects on journalism in the late 1980s and early '90s. "Something went silent," he said, "where people began to develop laryngitis or something.

> The journalists began to be less enterprising. I mean, the most aggressive story we did about the Clinton administration was the sex scandal, which was entirely orchestrated by the Republican Right. So you'll notice there's no investigation right now [2006] of the Republicans who are in power. They're not issuing subpoenas, they're not holding hearings. There was no hearing about Iraq, about Halliburton or no-bid contracts for one year after the invasion of Iraq, conveniently. So, were there things to investigate? Of course. Did the Republicans have any interest in investigating them? No. Why? Because they know it will generate news coverage. It will help feed the beast in terms of information with subpoenas and witnesses and conflict and all those wonderful things journalists love. They're very, very smart. [During the Clinton administration] they were suddenly deeply, deeply interested in truth, and information, and the nation: "We're at a crossroads. We have to know this and we have to know that." And suddenly, "we don't have to know anything," starting in 2001.

What occurred after September 11, 2001 resembled what newspaperman Frank Cobb saw after George Creel's propaganda campaign of World War I: independent thought became unwelcome. Yet that development related not just to war, but to the business needs of news organizations, which reduced journalism's capacity to be independent. Journalists, Lewis said,

> began to fear that ... they had to be more responsive to [the administration's] concerns, if they wanted to be included in exclusive moments of coverage, if they wanted access as a bureau chief or as an anchor ... And I think the polls terrified them. Reagan was a phenomenally popular president, just as George W. Bush, for a two- or three-year period right after 9/11, was ... I've noticed that the strength of backbone in most journalists about what subjects they want to investigate, and their level of defensiveness or

their level of ambition as journalists is directly proportional to poll numbers. If a president's at 80 or 90 percent, you're going to be a little less likely, not just because they're popular, it's because of what it represents.

The calculus for coverage then clarifies, Lewis said. "The journalist ... says, 'Wait a minute, the whole country thinks this. How can we do something that's going to alienate the entire nation? Do we want to continue to exist as a news organization? As a corporation, selling our product?' They're getting pressure from upstairs, internally. And they're going to be a little reluctant about taking on somebody. It's like if you're going to take a shot at the dragon, you better kill him. If you've got information, it better be really, really well-developed, multi-sourced — so that the bar is so high, you don't even attempt it. You start self-censoring because you don't want to go there." The cumulative impact of these effects on daily journalism, according to Lewis, have been "awesome," and have been seized by the Bush administration.

> They have used every potential lever of power and government imaginable to promote their message, to keep all of their people in line, on message, creating an impenetrable din. And they've managed to put all the journalists on the defensive. We're living through the biggest assault on the news media in my lifetime, and certainly in the last half century. We have not seen this many journalists prosecuted, subpoenaed; we have not seen the number of documents being classified double in three years, as we have just seen. Rollbacks, hundreds and hundreds, more than a thousand rollbacks of freedom of information laws, a tectonic shift. All of this is limiting the public sphere, and to the extent possible, placing the media on the defensive institutionally. And it is a systematic, across-the-board strategy ... to control information. It's cold-blooded, and they happen to be dead right. They get it. [374]

Dominating technology and communication. The dominance of the Right and the weakening of journalism and the Left relate partly to the Right's command of technology, Lewis said. Under Republican National Committee chairman Bill Brock, Republicans invested millions in direct mail, computers, mailing lists, and donor profiles, and assembled a massive grassroots operation covering the nation. Democrats, in contrast, didn't see technology as a priority until the chairmanship of Terry McAuliffe, and as a result are ten to twenty years behind Republicans. As a result, by 2008, Republicans occupied the White House for twenty of the previous twenty-eight years, "and so their domination electorally was not unrelated to their domination technologically, which is related to their communications domination, because it was reaching the public and ... going around the media."

Republicans have dominated the news by controlling technology and communication to influence it, Lewis said. For example, seeing that network news needed a visual image each day, Reagan aide Michael Deaver made sure they got the right one by setting up daily "photo ops," for pictures-only access to the president. If John F. Kennedy was the first president to use television effectively, Reagan was the first to grasp mass appeal and grassroots appeal, Lewis said, and Karl Rove mastered not just television, but the political setting.

> So, by the time you get to Rove in the '90s, they had eight years of the Clintons to raise millions by demonizing Clinton at every turn, having five independent counsel investigations, stoking the base, keeping the base active, being against things, not for things, which is a great way to rally your base. You're not actually getting into policy choices, you're just railing. By the time 2000 comes, and they have a marquee name: from '76 to 2000 there was never a different name on the ballot than Bush or Dole. In twenty-four years, all those presidential elections, they had one or the other. They had a presidential son with spectacular name recognition running for president of the United States, who'd been governor for just a few years ... And you can see how there was a confluence of all these factors, and so that it was, for a guy like Karl Rove, I hate to use words like this, but it's a little bit of a wet dream.[375]

Former network news executive Edward Fouhy noted a similar Republican communication grasp, but a dozen years earlier. Fouhy recalled talking to Richard Nixon aide H.R. Haldeman in the 1968 Oregon primary campaign, as journalists staked out candidates at Portland's

Benson Hotel. Reporters covering Senator Robert F. Kennedy "were gone from 7 a.m. 'til midnight, and he was doing ten to twenty events a day," Fouhy remembers. "And I was covering Nixon and we were doing one event a day, and I said to Bob Haldeman, 'How come you only do one event a day?' And he said, 'Because you guys have only one television broadcast a day.' And, it took me awhile to figure out what that meant, but it's always stayed with me. The Republicans figured out how to use the technology long before the Democrats did, and I think that's still true." Haldeman, Fouhy said, was showing that a politician who attends ten or twenty events a day may be reported tired, off message, or out of control. But a politician who does but a single event better controls both message, and its reporting.

A graver concern, Fouhy said, is the danger that journalists may self-censor. "The Right has figured out that if they relentlessly attack the press, sooner or later they will have an impact. It's kind of like water dripping on a rock ... whether it's Rush Limbaugh or any of the right-wing political commentators, the relentless attack on the press continues." [376]

Such behavior has substantial impact, Meyer said, especially when "looking back at things that should have gotten covered and didn't, I can see how that might be the cause. For example, I'm still worried that nobody is going after the problem of potentially rigging electronic voting systems. I'm just amazed that there is no discussion on them ... that ought to be a scandal. And nobody starts a fuss about it."

That there's less fuss may also be partly a function of resources, Meyer said. The budget cutting at news organizations in the 1980s diminished their capacity to report. The debacle at CBS in 2004, in which Dan Rather reported evidence that George W. Bush received preferential treatment in the Texas Air National Guard during Vietnam — and through which Rather and producer Mary Mapes ultimately lost their jobs — may have had less to do with unsubstantiated evidence, than with diminished resources with which to report. [377]

A journalism of fear, and shift to the right. The result of the cumulative pressures, according to former Gannett journalist Vikki Porter, is that more journalists have become afraid to do their jobs, "And I've become frightened, in a way, by the silence." Even though 2005 and 2006 saw journalism disclosing CIA kidnaping of terror suspects for torture abroad, the torture of prisoners at Abu Ghraib prison, the wire tapping of Americans, and the administration tracking private financial transactions (SWIFT) — still, among journalists, "There is a fear, but I don't know where that fear is coming from." At the same time, she said, "I think we're in danger because we've got journalists being threatened with espionage charges. Those kinds of things are very real, and yet we've lost voices that can motivate a citizenry to react with this right now. The general population could care less about what happens to us [journalists]." When she worked at Gannett, Porter said she felt pressure "not to lose the franchise ... So, I would probably say in total retrospect, and feeling I would have denied [it] at the time, that ... I'd second-guess myself, probably more, sometimes. But at the same time I always considered myself to be a hard news person who pushed. ... I feel I kind of accepted the fact that my publisher was a young Republican kind..." [378]

The pressure Porter described has influenced the quality of reporting, and coincides with a change in political cant, according to Boston University journalism professor Chris Daly, "There's been a dramatic change in the media landscape. For one thing, the papers I worked on are no longer independent; they're now part of ... pretty big-sized corporations." The mergers have resulted in the hiring of fewer reporters who know less, Daly said. In turn, "I think there's been a rightward shift in our politics, and I think that has left the mainstream media looking at a different point on the political spectrum ... The deregulation of radio has unleashed talk radio to be one-sided. That used to be grounds for losing your license. But not any more. The Fairness Doctrine has been repealed. And so a news medium that was once mainly factual is now mainly ideological." Radio stations no longer have a public interest obligation to present news, Daly noted. "So, even the small number that had independent news gathering organizations or capability, when I was a young guy, don't have it anymore, absolutely not. There's one station in Boston, WBZ, that has any significant news gathering capability. AM radio has almost completely lost the ability to report anything. Otherwise it's NPR. And the whole, a huge chunk of the rest of radio is now a big megaphone for the Republican Party. I hear Republican talking points all day long on the radio."

People interested in journalism in the Boston area "regret the loss of news gathering jobs," Daly said. "I think there are far fewer people who actually have the job *reporter*, across all media. But radio has just been eviscerated. Even Boston TV, although it has more outlets, I don't believe the number of reporters has actually increased over the last twenty years. What I see ... on my local TV is a very small number of reporters very often illustrating what was in the *Boston Globe* that morning."[379]

Media scholar Ben Bagdikian is "right that the political spectrum of the United States has shifted radically, or at least, significantly, to the right," according to *LA Times* bureau chief Doyle McManus. "All you have to do is watch a videotape of Lyndon Johnson's 'We Shall Overcome' speech on the Civil Rights Act, and reflect that no president since could have delivered a speech of that kind, to realize that the center of gravity has moved ... So, is the tenor of what you see in the media the cause, or the effect, or part of both?" McManus offered no answer.[380]

Blogs tilt left; mainstream news, right. Tom Edsall, who retired from the *Washington Post* in July 2006, said that while mainstream media have leaned to the right, "the blogosphere ... has begun to tilt to the left ... " Although he warned against conflating the attitude in the news pages of the *Post* with its editorial pages, he said "the points are well-taken about the different attitude at the *Post*, from the Watergate period to the present." Editorial page editors Fred Hiatt and Jackson Diehl "have been much more consistently conservative ... they have been pretty hard line."[381]

Indeed, as the *Post* reported the administration outing former CIA operative Valerie Plame, its editorial page produced four op-ed pieces that objected to prosecuting I. Lewis "Scooter" Libby for that offense — and none supporting his prosecution.[382]

Former *LA Times* bureau chief Jack Nelson underscored the observations in Table 3. "All this is so true ... I've said these very same things myself, many times ... I agree with everything in here, everything, including the last part there about the *Washington Post* and its treatment of two different Republican administrations ... But look at the *Post* [editorial page]. You've got [Charles] Krauthammer, you've got [now the late Robert] Novak. These are people who are not just conservatives. I mean they carry the water. And they are predictable, totally predictable. Novak carried the water for the administration. So does Krauthammer. Krauthammer is unbelievable ... he defends the administration on everything it does on wiretapping, on accusing the press of having damaged national security. I mean, it's unbelievable."

The most poignant example of the influence of the Right, Nelson said, "is the failure of the press, and I mean abject failure of the press, to really cover the lead up to the Iraqi war. They just didn't do it. There was no real challenging of Bush when he would make these statements prior to the war. I guess you've heard Helen Thomas sound off on this ... She's tough. And she's right. She's totally right. But I think that's the clearest example that I know of, the Valerie Plame case. The press really didn't press that issue very much, either ... the press didn't do a lot on it."[383]

Like journalist Charles Lewis, former journalist and media critic Barbara Matusow remarked that Republicans are faster to apply technology and to master organization than Democrats.

> I think politics is a business to Republicans, and so they were
> always much faster to grasp the potential for things such as satellites
> and direct mail appeals ... my theory was that Democrats ran mom
> and pop shops, while Republicans approached it like a business.
> Take the conventions. Every four years, the Republicans turned to
> a slick PR guy ... Bill Timmons, to stage the convention for them
> ... Timmons and his folks knew how to do things — how many
> passes they'd need, what kind of arrangements they had to make to
> accommodate armies of reporters, etc. So the GOP hired the same
> experienced guy every time. Meanwhile, the Democrats would re-
> invent the wheel each time, picking someone who knew absolutely
> nothing about it. And they would piss the press off because there
> weren't enough seats in the press gallery, that kind of thing.

Something similar happened, Matusow said, when the House and Senate press galleries installed a satellite television operation for members, and Democrats seemed loath to use it, almost as if it were beneath them.

Matusow said she had long admired the leadership of the *Washington Post*. "I mean, it took a lot of guts to publish the Pentagon Papers. And I think with [publisher] Don Graham, who I admire, and [executive editor] Len Downie, I think there's no question that the paper has moved right as the town seems to have moved right ... I don't really know why."[384]

Ideology the wrong target? Columnist David Broder agreed that talk radio and Fox News have boosted the Right and blogs are tilting to the left — but he's unsure how much this has washed into mainstream news. Broder's convinced it's not ideology but values that are at issue in this discussion: news institutions develop values and blinders, he said, and the best example is how news people deal with politics and faith.

> We have a hell of a hard time dealing with the religious side of politics. I saw it when George Romney was running ... I saw it with Jimmy Carter. It's not an ideological thing, but for people who orient their lives seriously in terms of religious values, reporters, I think, often really stumble in trying to understand that motivation and getting it right...
>
> When it comes to ideology, which is what everybody focuses on, I think they are just finding they are on the wrong target there. The example that I have used over and over again is, more Americans for a generation got their political news from Walter Mears [of the Associated Press] than from anybody else, whether they knew his name or not. I covered ... six or seven national campaigns and a lot of state campaigns with Walter. We drank in the bars, I don't know how many nights there. I have no idea how he voted in any of those elections and I think if he was sitting here he would say, "I don't know how Broder voted." Because when we get together, that's not what we talk about. It's certainly not what we argue about. And that sense that we're there basically to watch, because we're voyeurs more than anything else, is what I think the critics who're looking for ideological bias in the press miss most of the time.[385]

However, when it comes to another portion of the media, senior correspondent Linda Wertheimer of National Public Radio said, "I think there's no question segments of cable television and what not have turned to the right," perhaps with an influence on votes.[386]

"Drudged." Scott Brodeur of masslive.com, the online arm of the *Springfield, Massachusetts Republican* (Advance Communications), recalled an Internet maelstrom begun in the college town of Amherst, Massachusetts over how often to display the American flag. On September 10, 2001, the town select board voted four to one to limit municipal flag-flying to six holidays. Yet once that vote became conflated with the 9/11 attacks the following day, the story was snapped up by a web news service and CNN, then went into overdrive after hitting the web site that launched the President Clinton-Monica Lewinsky story: the Drudge Report. Brodeur recalled:

> It's almost a verb — we were "Drudged," which means, our traffic has gone through the roof. So I thought, at the time, I had a great idea, which was: let us, for all those people coming in and reading that one story, let's build out some teasers that push them to carry the conversation over in [an online] forum. So we made it, "How do you feel about this?" ... And for the next four years that forum was dominated by right-wing, conservative Drudge people that would just go in there, had no local ties whatsoever, but would bait the people ... It became unusable for Amherst residents that wanted to go in and have regular conversations, because they were constantly being yelled at or just called names. It denigrated the forum and made it unusable ... if [Drudge] picked up a story it would triple our daily numbers or maybe quadruple it ... we would have our top five days ever and invariably ... when Drudge picked up whatever story and pushed it. After that first time, we didn't make the mistake of then taking advantage of that temporary traffic. Because it was disruptive to the normal ebb and flow and really ruined an opportunity. We are finally, four or five years later, getting back to normal.[387]

Corrosive, or intense? Some journalists, like Steve Fox, formerly of Washingtonpost.com, worry that the way some consumers use the blogosphere has corroded civic discourse. "There have always been advocates for either side. What's really been corrosive, I think, has been the misuse of the blogosphere, that more so than TV, than the growth of Fox News ... What worries me is that in the last election cycle you saw many news consumers going to blogs that perpetuated their own point of view, rather than seeking out information from both sides of the argument and then drawing conclusions.   This possibility of going away from seeing both sides is what is corrosive — but it is the consumer's actions, not that of blogs, that is troubling. What bothers me is that you have a public that doesn't seem interested in getting contrarian points of view, and that you have people going to these sources basically to support their own point of view."Anne Kornblut noted a new intensity in the blogosphere. "There are entire organizations devoted to tracking what everyone writes now," she said ... "But it just feels to me much more personalized than I would have expected ... I guess since the 2000 election, it has felt like the sort of personalized nature of it has come from the Left, as opposed to the Right. Just sort of this intensity of purpose has come from the Left ... over time, the Left aggressiveness has felt built up in a way that the Right does not. They've sort of stagnated over the last few years."

The Left began to prevail in the blogosphere with the debut of the liberal group MoveOn.org, she said. "It makes sense that in the eight years since then, the Left has picked up steam as the Right has consolidated its power ... I guess what surprised me are the tactics ... letter-writing campaigns. The Internet makes it very easy to do that and to create sort of a siege mentality for reporters." [388]

Syndicated columnist EJ Dionne agreed that left-wing media criticism has begun to match that from the Right. "For a long time, editors and producers were more likely to look over their right shoulders rather than their left shoulders, because that's where the criticism was coming from. I think the rise of left-wing criticism has made them look over both shoulders, which I think in the long run, whether one agrees with any particular line of criticism, is a very useful thing."

On the other hand, for example, where the blog attack on Dan Rather succeeded partly because he used documents he shouldn't have, it "created an opening to kind of stop the whole story," Dionne said. Dionne's observation recalled Rove's attack in class on two of us who challenged his approach and weathered his counterattack — then let the matter drop (Chapter 1). In both instances, the counterattack did not merely win the "debate;" it eliminated the topic, and its challengers, from discussion.

A question of values? Some of the hostility of the Right toward news people is misguided, said Tom Rosenstiel, who doesn't see in mainstream media "what the right wing sometimes imagines is the case: a manifest, conscious attempt to help Democrats and hurt Republicans." On the other hand, he recalled when Vice President George H.W. Bush, trying to jump-start a faltering campaign, visited Detroit to roll out a new economic plan, slickly produced, if not heavy on new ideas or policies. Rosenstiel said the late Ann Devroy, then chief White House correspondent of the *Washington Post*, "looked at this thing and said, rather loudly, 'There's nothing here!' And I read it and I thought, 'You know, it is a very succinct and rather clear exposition of a conservative philosophy to shrink government and get it out of the way. Yes, there are not a lot of programs here; that's not what he wants to do.' And, in her mind, it was evidence that this was a steward president who didn't want to do anything. She didn't think she was being a liberal. But I thought, 'This is exactly what Dole and Bush and others back then who were fairly mainstream Republicans, complain about.'"[389]

At the same time, the country's broadcast media have become more right-leaning, according to former NBC Newsman, now independent filmmaker Frank Green,

> This year an independent production company contacted me to purchase footage of amphibians for a series of TV shows they were producing for the Discovery Channel on spring. I offered them some beautiful footage of some endangered species of frogs, including never before filmed mating behavior. The producer liked the footage but said that Discovery Channel policy forbid them from using footage of animals mating. She was clearly frustrated, and I was appalled at this intrusion of misguided religious zealotry into science journalism. How do you make an honest film about animals in spring without showing them mating?

Mating scenes would easily have been shown on a similar program a few years earlier, Green said — perhaps not overly graphic shots of animal reproductive organs, but certainly footage of animals mounting. A rightward shift in media became more apparent in the days following 9/11, when "TV broadcasters were tripping over themselves to see who could fly a bigger U.S. flag in their station IDs." The matter is important, Green said, because it "brought their independence into question. In my view, they should be journalists first, and Americans second — but clearly they saw it the other way around — and that's deeply disturbing ... because journalists need to be able to distance themselves from political authority. Flying flags means they're taking sides. It makes objectivity impossible."

Broadcast news years ago abandoned advancing the public interest in favor of using empty symbols, Green said. He recalled being stuck in traffic in San Francisco in 1994 when California State Treasurer Kathleen Brown debated Governor Pete Wilson in a live broadcast.

> Traffic was so heavy I heard the entire debate. The only topic of discussion was the death penalty. Among the thousands of people around me stuck in their cars listening to this debate, very few if any would ever in their lives be affected by the death penalty. And yet, every one of our lives was affected by the choking traffic, caused by urban sprawl and poor urban planning. Not a word about these or other environmental issues in the debate. It was a clear example of the irrelevance of American political debate ... Politics these days is about symbolism, and the moderators of the debate, who feed the questions, are squandering the opportunity to get real about the issues. No wonder our voter turnout is so low. [390]

A new fourth branch of government. Green's discouragement over broadcast news is amplified by Walter Pincus of the *Washington Post*, who believes journalists have ceded their role to political consultants. The press has responded to Republican criticism, Pincus said, then promotes consultants who undermine journalism, while editors become more reluctant to get out in front of the conventional wisdom. "The press is living in an echo chamber," Pincus said. "It talks to itself, and it's considered itself much too important ... CNN and FOX are on in every newspaper, that's really what their big circulation is. Jim Lehrer has a bigger circulation, but people don't recognize it ... both of them have tiny audiences. But media powers itself. I mean its self-concern is against what its role really is. And it responds to complaints, and the Republicans have learned that ... The press now has fallen in love with themselves. At the same time they are fearful of any criticism." Because presidential handlers and consultants have seduced the press, Pincus said. "It doesn't take a genius to know what it takes to take care of the threat. Anybody who travels with the President, you get your luggage taken care of, you get free meals, you get all this stuff. I used to travel and I couldn't believe it. I mean guys are drinking themselves silly. And then the political press, they spend the evenings with the handlers and with the Roves of this world. We, the press, made all these political consultants famous, to a degree that politicians think they can't do without them ... they are the Fourth Branch of Government." [391]

According to Helen Thomas, Republican consultants have been so effective because they wiped out all the liberals.

> It's rare to hear a liberal any more. The so-called think tanks, and Accuracy in Media and all that jazz. Deliberate, day after day after day, drumming away against the "liberal press." Reagan hissing the word. Bush hissing it, not saying it. I mean, demonization of liberal, where people no longer knew what liberal meant. It was likened to the devil himself... They know no limits. They will stoop to anything. And politicians have had to bow to them. In my opinion, they dominate, I think, by equating liberalism with communism ... When they have command and total domination of the airwaves, and they do, you can't turn on radio in the afternoon without getting that drum beat. I think it's so frightening. You know, when Sinclair Lewis wrote "It Can't Happen Here"? It *has* happened. It has happened ... when people don't even understand their rights are being taken, the basic Bill of Rights, when the government no longer needs a warrant to invade your privacy. And I do think now that you think twice before you say something publicly.[392]

Polarization stains journalism. By the mid-1990s, as she turned out ninety-second packages for the evening news, former ABC News journalist Jackie Judd noticed she began hearing the phrase: "You need to have more edge."

> I didn't know what it meant in the beginning, and what I came to believe that it meant was, it wasn't enough any longer to tell listeners or

viewers what you knew. You also needed to tell them what to think about what you had just reported. I think that happened because everything in the news media business had become so polarized ... all part of the political polarization that we've seen generally in the country and how it obviously has seeped into the media ... The Republicans swept into town [in 1994]. They had a very clear agenda, and I think that they had a sophisticated understanding of how the media could be used to convey ideas about that agenda. When one party, whether it's the Democrats or the Republicans, whether it's Left or Right ... goes farther out to the edge, then the other almost by necessity has to, as well. And the gulf in the middle becomes wider. The stridency that developed in the political debate and dialogue of the nation at the time, I think there was an expectation, and I don't necessarily disagree with this, that that needed to be reflected in our reporting ... The 24/7 news channels have an insatiable appetite and politicians are there to satisfy. And it is sometimes a circus environment. The more strident somebody is, the better.

Pressure came for more "character-driven" reporting, she said, telling the story through an individual. That approach, intended to make a story more real, in fact, made it less so. Even in treating broad social or policy issues, she said, "The issue had to be told through the story of an individual." That requirement seems to echo in the effort by the Right, beginning in the 1930s, to define social issues in individual terms (Chapter 15).

The focus on the individual, the organization of the Right, and the sophisticated uses of technology the Right applied in framing stories became clearer for Judd as she covered Monica Lewinsky's relationship with President Clinton.

Part of it, looking back, I think, really was fueled by access to the web and the kind of careening-around of information and insinuation and criticism that amplified and sometimes distorted everything we were doing. And it made it very difficult to keep reporting it in as traditional a way as I tried to: collect the facts, collect information from sources, and have the reports evaluated and taken for how we presented them ... It was certainly my first experience realizing how OUT OF CONTROL the tornado can be.

Once you get in the vortex and you're spinning there in the middle of that tornado, you don't know where things are going to land or where things are going to take you … Everything I said was put under a microscope and frequently distorted … . And the hatred of the Right of Bill Clinton certainly helped fuel it, undeniably.

The atmosphere surrounding the Lewinsky story was so polarizing that Judd said she found her own reporting under attack, even though its accuracy required no correction. Nevertheless, public faith in journalism took a beating as a result of the story, she said — "Not so much because of the reporting that was being done, but because of the climate in which it was being done." The story accelerated partly because "MSNBC was on the air, CNN, all of these 24/7 news operations with all of these talking heads who knew little or nothing about the story, but they were more than happy to talk about it." Celebrity — individual focus — prevailed in a polarized atmosphere, she said, staining not only the participants, but journalism.[393]

That stain also reflected prevailing media values — and not the conservative values of the *Washington Times* (Table 2), but the values of *People* magazine: the "triumph of consumerism … in our collective American psyche," according to communication professor Ed Lenert. Although he does not dispute Bagdikian's observation of a political shift in the country, Lenert believes the shift speaks less to the success of the Right than to the failure of the Left. "Whereas the Right is able to articulate freedom, individual responsibility, small government, non-adventurism in foreign policy … I'm not aware of where that's coming from, from my side … Al Gore and Dukakis and Kerry — these people had an army of invalids for their political communication consultants. They were simply not up to the job of explaining anything to anyone in a consistent and engaged manner."

In contrast, Lenert found himself impressed in spending forty-five minutes with conservative leader Richard Viguerie. "I find it difficult to identify any similarly situated democratic thinker (with small "d" democrat), who impressed me as having the same integrity. Although I may disagree with the conclusions, the process of his reasoning struck me as being so profound and engaged. So I would say that what has happened has been a default of the Left. It has not been so much the success of the Right."[394]

According to EJ Dionne, conservatives have dominated the media "because conservatives were much more attuned to Gramsci's theory about what intellectual hegemony is about than liberals or the Left ever were." Conservatives

> read their Gramsci more closely ... the category of fairness was redefined in a way that the main thing the media had to worry about was whether they were being fair to conservatives ... it was in a way a deeper triumph than simply intimidation or, you know, pressure, although there was certainly some of that ... Over a very long period of time the main question that occurred within the news business was, "Are we being fair to conservatives?" Once that's the main question, then it becomes much easier for conservatives to raise all kinds of questions. It's only in the last three or four years that that question itself has been challenged.

Conservatives won their definition by two means, Dionne said.

> First, they focused on poll data suggesting that journalists vote primarily for Democrats. Second, I think there's a kind of, if you will, postmodernism of the Right, where conservatives have actually picked up from the postmodernist Left the idea that there is no such thing as objective information, and, therefore, all information should be viewed as biased in one way or another. And, again, just as the Right paid attention to Gramsci, so they've also become more postmodern than liberals are. And so once you undermine the idea that there is such a thing as a reasonably fair rendition of events, and instead always look for the hidden bias, and when the people asking that question are almost uniformly on the Right, it just changes the nature of discourse about journalism.[395]

In summary, respondents reported that the Right over the thirty- to forty-year study period, through a variety of means, has substantially changed journalism.

Chapter 29

JOURNALISTS ON THE BUSH ADMINISTRATION

Asked if the Bush administration has influenced journalism, respondents answered affirmatively and seemed to situate their answers in three categories: secrecy, control, and certain other effects both professional and personal. A few of the answers bridged both the administration and Rove, drawing little distinction between them.

Secrecy. Four of the respondents declared that the administration of President George W. Bush has been the most secretive in their experience. Journalism historian Chris Daly called it

> the most secretive administration in history. They have put more things off limits and generated more fresh material that is off limits than any administration in history. And they begin with a very hostile stance toward news gathering. It's "Catch us if you can," and especially since September 11th. I think that was the most important thing that has happened, basically, since the creation of the web ... the most important thing in shaping the relationship between the news media in general and the federal government, in particular, because I think it emboldened Bush and Cheney to try to withhold information and try to really change the perception of the news media as a special interest, rather than the guardian of the general interest, or the public interest ... this is one of the most dangerous things that I see going on right now.[396]

Former network news executive Ed Fouhy said the Bush administration is the most secretive administration in his memory.

> I see a White House that is more dedicated to stopping leaks, pursuing leakers, and getting a unified message out every day than any I can recall, with the possible exception of the Reagan administration when Mike Deaver was orchestrating the visuals ... I've never seen the White House as difficult to cover, so few people willing to talk to journalists on background. It is impossible to cover Washington and not have sources who are willing to ... go beyond the bare bones of what's in the press release to tell you why something happened or when it's going to happen or what the politics are. And I've never seen a White House that was as closed as this one is. And it has nothing to do with who's the press secretary. It has everything to do with what the policy is.[397]

Under Bush administration pressure, sources became less willing to talk. This was reflected in the day-to-day practice of journalism, according to *LA Times* bureau chief Doyle McManus. Beginning in about 1985, *Washington Post* journalist Jay Mathews began advocating that journalists permit sources to preview, before publication, the stories that journalists wrote with their help.[398] That practice "guarantees more accuracy...which is where Jay started," McManus said, and it doesn't necessarily mean providing a [an interview] transcript. "The most common form of this transaction these days ... is that officials in the national security bureaucracy ask for it. They'll say: 'Let's talk on background, and if you need something on the record, come back to me.' Or: 'Let's talk off the record, and if you need something you can use, come back to me.'" But the practice has mushroomed, McManus said.

> Why is this happening more frequently now? I'd suggest two reasons. First, the Bush Administration is unusually secretive. It has chosen to share less information with the media, Congress, and the public than most of its predecessors. It has warned its employees that they jeopardize their careers if they talk; that's something all administrations do, but this one has been more draconian than most.

So I'd date the current atmosphere from 2001, not 1995 or any other earlier date.[399]

McManus expects this new journalistic practice of going off the record with sources and coming back to them for permission to go on the record to grow.

Former *LA Times* bureau chief Nelson was more blunt: "This is the most secretive administration that I know anything about. They refuse, in many instances refused to even deal with the press. Listen, back during the Carter administration, you could come out of a White House office, walk down the hallway and pass another reporter going into another office. You won't see any of that in this administration. I mean, it's almost like they're off limits. They're confined to that White House pressroom. And in most cases don't return telephone calls, or if they return telephone calls, they have to have somebody listening in. I mean it's unbelievable, the kind of control they keep over the press."

Asked whether previous administrations, specifically those of Reagan and Nixon, exercised a similar level of control, Nelson declared: "Not to that extent, neither one, no, neither one, I guarantee you. They were more available, and the officials in their administration were more available, much more available. And I covered all of those administrations. I could call over and talk to people, I could get people on the telephone without a hell of a lot of problem. I could get them to come to my bureau for breakfast sessions, which we had frequently."[400]

Control. Where the four respondents (above) focused on administration secrecy, eight others said the Bush administration has exerted a greater degree of control over journalists and journalism.

In Massachusetts, Scott Brodeur said he saw that control in the forums and e-mails generated to his web site, Masslive.com.

We definitely see orchestrated campaigns ... there are very salient talking points with people entering forums or writing emails, but mainly in forums, where you're seeing the same phrases used ... trickling down all the way from a Rove kind of style of talking points, all the way into our local forums where people are going in and having political conversations, you do see more of that. You see people wanting to go across and spread messages — the same messages — in as many places as they can. The left-leaning causes, in my experience on our sites, have more original expression. You see some of the same catchphrases used on people arguing on the right side of things. You see it a little on the Left, but the cadence and the words used aren't as resoundingly similar.[401]

From the opposite end of the country, what was most apparent to Peter Bhatia of the Portland *Oregonian* was the

conscious strategy of polarization that's worked so well for the Republicans and for the Bush administration. People shouldn't misunderstand that. It's a conscious strategy to polarize that has worked extremely well for their purposes. Even though it's a 50-50 country, they've got 50 + 1 on pretty much everything, whether you're talking Congress, the Executive or the Judiciary. And that's all you really need in a democracy to control things and they've done it quite well. But because they are executing that strategy and have done it quite brilliantly, it makes it harder for the media to try to unwind all the complexity of things. They're attacking the media, and that's the strategy. Divert people's attention from what really matters, go after a convenient target. They know they've got half the population in their pocket thinking the media is bad.

Although Bhatia said people criticize the Washington press corps as "lap dogs," the criticism ignores the extent to which the administration has controlled journalism or attacked journalists. "You know what? We're human beings. You get whomped so many times at some point, you don't get up off the mat ... I do think that this administration, more than any other in my professional life time, has been good at controlling the news ... More so than any other." [402]

Steve Fox agreed. "This has become a conservative campaign by the Bush administration, to really demonize the media. Perhaps the last defense of an administration way back on its heels, but nonetheless ..." [403]

According to Dan Froomkin, the result was that journalists at the White House wavered in tackling the Bush administration. White House correspondents know when they are being told something that isn't true. And rather than say, "this is not true," they will at best find some Democrat to say, "We don't agree." At worst, they will just report it as stenography. And that's just not acceptable. Because they feel like, saying "it's not true" is fighting words. It takes them out of that place where they're comfortable, and they know if they're too far out of it, their livelihood may be over ... it's not an overt threat, like anybody is going to get fired because of this, but just know: that's where you're safest.[404]

Froomkin's observation recalls Gramsci's hegemony theory: that people pick out a niche, based sometimes on what's comfortable, and then conform to the system. Indeed, until the release of *The Price of Loyalty*, by journalist Ron Suskind, Froomkin said, there had been little critique of the Bush administration because it had used the horror of 9/11 and the threat of terrorism to "completely cow the media ... As a consumer, rather than as a participant, I definitely got the sense that it was, 'Do not criticize the president. The people have no patience for that right now.'"

On the other hand, news people since then have become more aggressive. "When the president said stuff about Social Security that wasn't accurate, the press actually called him on it ... in the same way that [he] implied the Al Qaeda-Saddam link, he implied that privatizing Social Security would actually solve the financial problems of Social Security. And the press coverage didn't let him get away with that. Which is the way it should be!"[405]

One reason the Bush administration's communication succeeded for an extended time is that Republicans generally excel at the control of messages, according to political journalist Amy Walter, while Democrats tend to be more nuanced and less clear. "Democrats try to go and do a little more wooing ... and Republicans just come right out, and it's just like: 'This is it ... Here's the deal' ... Democrats tend to make things more complicated than it needs to be ... get really bogged down in unnecessary details and nuance and the internal debate." Because of Republican clarity, she said, the Republican House Speaker Dennis Hastert kept control of the House even when it was narrowly divided.

The Bush administration was even better at controlling message, and extraordinarily successful in doing so in comparison to the Clinton administration, according to David Broder.

> It seems to me that they are always a step, at least, ahead of us in terms of how do you control the dialog that the public hears ... I wish I had some smart idea about how we could catch up or leap frog them, but we don't. I think these guys are the best we've seen so far. I expect that whoever does it next will probably be even more adept at controlling the message than they have been. But they have been extraordinarily successful in controlling the message. They've done it in the classic ways. They have limited access, and they have decided what the message is that they want to get out, and then they have been very disciplined about conveying on message. I mean there've been a few examples where it's broken down, but very few considering the pressures of the upheavals that have taken place in the world and in the country since they've been in power.

The extent of Bush administration message control, he said, "was particularly vivid because the Clinton Administration was full of people who were shooting off their mouths for their own advantage, and whether it helped Clinton or not. That is not tolerated in this administration." [406]

According to Tom Rosenstiel of the Project for Excellence in Journalism, the Bush administration not only outflanked the press, but overwhelmed the Democratic sources on whom the press has relied, as well. The domination has been so evident that the press was clear that Democratic sources had dried up, even if some Democrats seemed unclear how much they'd been overpowered. Rosenstiel compared the situation to

> a football game in which the Republicans have computer models, they have guys up in the sky boxes videotaping instantly and sending photos down of the alignments. They've got a huge play book and each of the plays is figured out. They know what the first twenty plays they're going to call, in order. And the Democrats are going in the huddle and mapping out the plays with a stick in the dirt! One of these parties is very, very disciplined and the other one

starts over every four years, almost from scratch. But that's a function, I think, not necessarily so much of the infrastructure but of the fact that those [conservative] think tanks have generated ideas. And it really built them up and they're connected and there's kind of a flow. Whereas the Democrats assumed a set of ideas that were inherited and they haven't really thought anew from the ground up. The Republican Party did ... They started from scratch in '64.

Democrats have been utterly blind-sided by this juggernaut, Rosenstiel said. He recalled playing golf with a top Democrat the day after Senator John Kerry lost the 2004 election. The Democrat told Rosenstiel, "'We have to come to grips with the fact that we are not a majority party.' And I thought to myself ... 'You haven't been a majority party for twenty years! It may be that you could win with voter turnout. But that's not the same thing as being a majority party.' I just read Richard Reeves' book about Reagan. In 1980, there were twice as many registered Democrats in the country as there were Republicans. Today, it's 30-30-30, and 30 percent are independents. But that's been a long time in coming. If Democrats are just coming to grips with that now, it means that only now are they kinda hitting rock bottom, so that rebuilding — their 1964 — it hasn't happened yet, or maybe it happened in 2004, some analog to that. But they have not gotten to that point."

Other effects, personal and professional. If the Bush administration polarizing the electorate hampered mainstream journalism, as Bhatia and Judd suggest, other journalists report other effects, personal and professional.

Phil Meyer echoed Helen Thomas:

The right wing has made liberal a dirty word. And lots of people don't understand the meaning of the word. I made a reference in one of my *USA Today* columns to "liberal democracy," which basically means a democracy that has civil rights, as well as the right to vote. And I got a lot of mail from my readers saying liberal democracy is a bad thing. Whenever a *USA Today* reader writes me an angry letter about being a member of the liberal media, I write back and say:

You've got my number. I'm a Volvo-driving, bleeding heart, tax-and-spend, tree-hugging liberal. We can't let them steal the name. When Bill Moyers appears on television he wears a flag in his lapel. He was asked about it and he said, "I'm not going to let them steal it!" I'm not wearing it now, but I've taken to wearing the National Defense Service Medal. It's the minimum medal you can get just for showing up when there's a war going on. I had a very undistinguished military career, but I can wear something that President Bush can't wear![407]

The effects of the polarization hit former Gannett editor Vikki Porter hard. She said that she and her partner, who is also a journalist, were so affected by the right-wing deviantization of gays and lesbians that they considered leaving the country.

The divisive issues of gay marriage ... those issues hit home personally, but politically they are such manipulative and, to me, evil things. Tremendously evil ... since basically the election of George Bush, there has been more of an awareness in our household of the political shifts, to the point where we literally were thinking of moving to Canada...I am just actually discovering this as I'm talking to you about this. Because I truly feel victimized right now, frankly, as a woman, too, because of the abortion issue. I feel women have lost a lot of ground ... Seeing environmental legislation that is trying to clean up California, just being sliced and diced. We literally feel like we need to run away somewhere and hide. But that's just whether you talk about the last five years and Karl Rove; to me George Bush is not the issue ... But I feel that there's somebody behind the curtain. And, as a journalist, I can say, that is probably the most uncovered story.[408]

Like Broder and Froomkin at the *Washington Post*, McManus of the *Los Angeles Times* said that journalists have been outflanked. "I've always felt that mainstream journalists are always one war behind in the arms race. You know, it's sort of like the Syrians against the Israelis. Modernize-modernize-modernize, but they're always a generation ahead of us, because they're spending all their time figuring out how to do it, we're not."[409]

Another revealing set of insights came from Walter Pincus, summarizing an evolution in journalism, not only at the *Washington Post*, but throughout mainstream news. Because Republicans tightly controlled Congress and the executive branch the first six years President Bush was in office, from January 2001 to January 2007, Congress conducted few hearings and exercised almost no oversight of the 9/11 attacks, the Iraq war, or spying on Americans. As a result, those issues received much less news coverage than those debated in the customary congressional forums. In consequence, Pincus said, editors became much more nervous about reporting them. In that situation, the *Post* and other news organizations changed complexion; the quality of coverage changed. In contrast to the crusading that distinguished the *Post* and other news organizations in the 1960s and 1970s, in the summer of 2006, Pincus seemed to be describing a different journalistic setting.

> Congress is the worst. They don't cover Congress in any other way except the central issue under discussion ... and part of it is Congress' fault, part of it ... because we have made it uncomfortable to be in Congress, or to run for political office. We take apart people who do run, and we demean the institution. And we now have people running it who don't care about the institution.

In contrast, in the power struggles of the sixties and seventies over the Vietnam War between the executive branch and the legislative branch, Pincus said members of the House and the Senate would unite to rein in executive power, even when all were of the same party. When it came to holding the executive branch accountable, war opponent Senator J. William Fulbright of Arkansas, chairman of the Senate Foreign Relations Committee, could count on war *pro*ponents Senators Richard Russell of Georgia and John Stennis of Mississippi to support holding hearings to confront the administration of President Johnson, even though all were Democrats. In contrast, by summer 2006, Pincus said,

> Now, it doesn't matter. I mean they essentially, the leaders of the House and Senate — except when it's their own prerogatives ...

they'll do whatever the president wants. They're all part of the Party. So there's no oversight that could embarrass them. I mean, no hearings, nothing. It's *never* been like that!...The worst is this whole business of conferences [in which bills already passed are entirely re-written] and the conference is only Republicans. It's a huge scandal, and we don't write about it, we don't care about it.

The week Pincus and I spoke, for example, David M. Walker, head of the U.S. Government Accountability Office, testified before a House Government Reform subcommittee, heavily criticizing the implementation of President Bush's plan for victory in Iraq. Walker reported that the plan was fundamentally flawed because it assumed that the war could be financed through the revenues of the Iraqi oil industry. As Pincus described it, Walker "looked over the books in Iraq, and he said it took him a second and a half to see how corrupt it was. And then this oil is the whole basis by which they were going to finance a government ... Nobody covered the hearing when it took place. Nobody's gotten it since, except my story. Then my story they held for a couple of days and dumped in the back of the paper."[410]

That story appeared in the *Post* the day before Pincus and I talked. The next day when we spoke, a second story of his was being held, too. "The CIA did a classified study in 2002 that showed that Al Qaida had a plan for organizing prisons, all of which became implemented in Abu Ghraib." The study laid out the scenario for Abu Ghraib, but *Post* editors held that story until two days later.[411] "It's a wonder ... that anything that happened before yesterday ... [gets] in the paper, no matter what the substance is. Unless somebody else picks it up ... And that's because editors are nervous about stepping out on any issue of substance other than sex, and corruption."

While the *Post* continues to do enterprise reporting and still wins Pulitzers for its work, Pincus said, it's falling down on the daily work of holding government accountable. These days, "Enterprise is directed more at winning prizes than changing policy."

Moreover, because the goal of a younger journalist is more likely "to become a manager, not a reporter covering whatever your beat is," the *Post* has become more bureaucratic. While journalists were rotated off the desk when Ben Bradlee was managing editor just as they are today, Pincus said, the point in Bradlee's day was to strengthen not the editorial bureaucracy, but reporting "because reporting is the heart of the paper. You can have the best goddamn editors in the world, but if the news is not reported correctly, the paper's going to be lousy." [412]

Pincus' critique changed by fall 2007, when he noted that reporting from the *Post* and other organizations had changed for the better in the course of a year (the change coinciding, in part, with the election of 2006 that reintroduced divided government, and, in turn, a broadening of articulated official opinion).

> [T]he truth is, since that time [when we spoke in July 2006] we have done more, though perhaps not enough — Dana Priest's Pulitzer on CIA prisons, and more recently, [the] Walter Reed [hospital problem] and others. In general, reporting on the war has certainly taken a tougher turn and not just us, [but] the *New York Times* and others ... But there is still too much reporting of what amounts to administration PR and canned Democratic responses — not real news events, just things done and said to get into the papers and on TV. [413]

A different picture of how much the paper has changed relates to the esprit de corps in the *Post* of yesteryear, Pincus said. On Saturdays, under Bradlee's editorship, a group of people would come in for lunch at a French restaurant to talk about the newspaper.

> It started with about six of us — friends of Ben. And it grew to about twelve to fourteen people. [Publisher] Kay [Graham] used to come, and [editorial page editor] Meg [Greenfield], and everybody else. And it was the one time that everybody talked honestly about each other and what we'd done and the rest of it, because it was a communal effort. You come in on a Saturday now and the only person there is the reporter on duty and the others — the place is empty. And the Sunday paper, which is the biggest paper we have by a third, is essentially filled with stories that were done Thursday and Friday. Everybody wonders why the circulation has dropped ... But, everybody is happy! I mean [at the old *Post*] we were all divorced and crazy, and it didn't pay as well, so you had to do other

things. So now it pays well, a lot of 'em are married to each other, live in the suburbs, and they socialize among themselves.

Pincus attributes the change in organizational climate, especially among younger journalists, to a certain Gannett-izing of the entire newspaper industry. Frank Gannett, he said, was a good reporter who wanted to be an editor, and then a publisher. Other journalists followed his lead, working their way up to the corporate offices. But that is not why people Pincus knew went into the business. "We all went into the business to change the way government works. You say that now — and, you know, they say, 'Oh, you're a crusader.' Of course you're a crusader! That's what it's all about!"[414]

Chapter 30

JOURNALISTS ON KARL ROVE

To what extent have journalists and journalism been affected by the work of Karl Rove?

LA Times bureau chief Doyle McManus answered by recalling how he and most other journalists missed the main story as they covered candidate Bush in the 2000 South Carolina primary campaign. McManus "didn't notice that lurid flyers were being put on windshields in every church parking lot the Sunday before that primary, denouncing John McCain for various sins. Because I wasn't in a church parking lot, I didn't know where to look ... We didn't figure out what happened in South Carolina — McCain didn't figure out what happened — until a week or ten days later. And Karl is one of the most spectacular practitioners of all those skills and arts that any of us have seen ... we're still behind ... we're at a permanent disadvantage."

That disadvantage seemed to get no better by 2004, by which time Rove and Republican National Committee chairman Ken Mehlman, McManus said, had

> reinvented retail politics ... if you look at what they did in Ohio and other swing states. They did an enormous amount of old-fashioned fieldwork, of canvassing, of identifying voters, costly in terms of both money and personnel, labor — that, you know, to some seemed like a throw-back, but turned out to be terrifically effective. We tried to write about it a couple of times in the campaign, but, boy, editors and readers thought that was a crashing bore. "OK, so they're sending people around from door to door. Instead of, you know, having notebooks or clipboards, now they have Palm Pilots and

they'll download the data. OK, fine." We were too thin on the
ground to be able to report adequately on the issue of polling places
in Ohio. To do that properly — Well, I was fighting to get one
reporter in Ohio, for the *LA Times* ... So — I think we are behind
and I think, arguably, and the people who are working for him are
so good and have innovated so successfully and so rapidly that
we're behinder than we used to be.[415]

At *Time* magazine's Washington bureau, journalist Karen Tumulty
jumped as if touched by a hot iron when asked what impact Rove has had
on journalists. Rove's strategy of exciting the base worked well in electing
Bush and re-electing him, Tumulty said. But it wasn't enough, by the
second term, to bulldoze Social Security, the administration's anticipated
next step in assembling a permanent conservative majority.

We had a reporter [Matt Cooper] practically go to jail for his
conversation with Karl Rove, and somebody else [Viveca Novak]
lost her job ... so that's a very touchy subject here. I think a lot of
reporters, and myself included, have found Karl extremely helpful.
But I think his primary influence has been on the policies and the
strategic direction of this administration. [They chose to] fight on
Social Security and he loses it. That influences the kind of coverage
they get. I think the real influences are a sort of much higher altitude
... Rove's model worked as long as it worked. It got Bush re-
elected, because his basic model was this country was so polarized
and the two camps were so entrenched that there just weren't many
swing voters up for grabs. In fact, one time [in 2004] ... we went
into Rove's office and he showed us this little wallet card ... he had
it reduced to a little card that he had laminated and put in his wallet
... it showed how many voters are basically Republicans and how
many voters are basically Democrats, and how many voters are truly
swing voters, and it traced it for like fifteen or twenty years. One
was red, one was blue, and then the swing voters were green. The
swing voter line got smaller and smaller and became basically
almost nothing, while he had all the voters going into these red and
blue camps. So, basically, his whole strategy for the election was,
you know, get our guys out there, which is what Swift Boats did. It

was totally base mobilization and depressed the [vote of the] other side.

That worked until Bush gets re-elected and then, and in part because Karl picked some issues like Social Security, where you didn't have a closely divided country, that model just didn't work ... They tried to convince people there was a crisis, which was just demonstrably not true. The funny thing, too, was that their solution, if anything, made the solvency of the system worse. Iraq, the same. I mean ... you can't play Iraq anymore as a closely divided issue because people aren't closely divided on it any more ... the base might be able to do it for you when Bush's approval rating is 49. When his approval rating is 34, the base isn't enough.[416]

Anne Kornblut, now at *The Washington Post*, said that Rove has been direct with reporters about political tactics, responsive to their e-mail, and seems to respect what journalists do, even as he's sought to circumvent their work. And though Rove and the Right have been highly successful, she said, the Left has been gearing up, partly through the Center for American Progress.

In a strange way, Rove was actually a provider of information as much as he was anything else ... He was very blunt with all of us about strategy. No more than any other political operative, would leak things, no more, no less. It's funny, for all the supposed secrecy of this administration, Karl's actually been one of the most accessible people in that White House. He responds to every e-mail, without delay ...

He was not intimidating toward us. He was occasionally even helpful. And I don't know that he sits around thinking about philosophical matters of journalism. I actually see it more from sort of the grassroots, maybe, you know, he's connected to them. He seems to be one of those people who actually from the outset was pretty straightforward about his mission and how he intended to do it, and we weren't a big piece of it. He was going to go around us and talk to churches and go to the exurbs and talk to talk radio ... But Karl actually has always displayed a sort of strange kind of respect for what we do. I know that's going to sound incongruous, but I know other reporters who feel the same way. He is capable of lying, but that's not his general MO.

Although he continued to shape administration strategy and image, Kornblut said, he seemed to have limited influence over administration policy around Iraq, but focused on getting the administration to speak directly to voters, and supplanting journalists. "They want to manipulate us, sure, but actually what they really want to do is just render us irrelevant." [417]

If Rove's impact on Iraq war policy was less dramatic than in other policy areas, he nevertheless took full advantage of the 9/11 attacks to strengthen the administration politically, according to Tom Edsall. "I think Rove very effectively capitalized on the reaction to 9/11, to make criticism from any source — press, Democrats, into kind of an unpatriotic act. And that did succeed. It wasn't just him; it was a full-scale administration plan. But that worked quite effectively at the *Post* and other institutions … we all saw the whole lead up to the war in Iraq was not given adequate examination by the paper." [418]

According to Tom Rosenstiel, Bush and Rove adopted the language of fundamentalism, and invoked patriotism partly to short-circuit the media, and move the country to war.

> Rove and Bush, as communicators, use the language of religion and fundamentalism. [Bush] talks like someone who's born again, uses that language and that works...he isn't trying to persuade journalists … Everything was changed, of course, by the war … that was one thing that Rove and Bush had going for them. Once you are under attack, the country is on a war footing, you can invoke patriotism and all this rhetoric about treason and criticism helping the enemy, and all of that. That feeds into the feeling that the media is liberal, of course. But it also, always, puts the media on its heels.[419]

Overall, talking about Rove's influence is more like describing the impact of the entire advertising industry, according to Ed Lenert, formerly of the University of Nevada.

"Karl Rove" is like saying Madison Avenue, or saying Hollywood. There is an industrial structure of message production, of which he is like the Michael Eisner [of the Walt Disney Co.] ... He has so many capable lieutenants and so many people committed to the mission of power acquisition that's just like Disney is committed to market share. And these people will have no qualms at doing what's necessary to win because that's what politics in the non-civic sense is about: it's about winning. So, I think we've been tremendously transformed by ... the ability of these people to use the Internet to get their talking points out so that all the commentators and all the conservative shows are all talking about the same points for the same time, using the same kind of loaded language ... where freedom-loving Americans are willing to give up some civil rights for security. And once you phrase the debate that way, it's uphill to argue against it, especially if [Bill] O'Reilly is shouting at you while you say it.[420]

Rove's success, according to Richard Viguerie, begins with his marketing ability. "He was a world class marketer, and for the first time in our life time, you've got somebody that's a communication marketing professional running the administration's political shop, the Republican Party's political shop, and they're just not talking about it."

In contrast, Viguerie recalled visiting with DNC Chairman Terry McAuliffe in August 2004 at the Republican National Convention, telling McAuliffe he understood that the DNC had mailed more prospect letters in the first four months of 2004 than it had the entire decade of the 1990s. McAuliffe acknowledged that that was true, and said it hadn't been done earlier because his predecessors had had a big debt. The DNC effort paid off by November 2004, Viguerie said, when Democrats raised record amounts of money. But according to Viguerie, the following month, at the Orlando winter meeting of the DNC, McAuliffe told delegates

that the Republicans stole a march on them, because while they had done this broadcasting, so to speak — mailing every registered voter over age forty in the country and doing this and that type of thing — Rove, the Republicans had long since done that and now they were drilling straight down, doing narrowcasting, going into a union neighborhood and finding out who was concerned about same-sex marriage, who was concerned about this issue or that and talking directly to that one person. Now, most generals, they say, fight the last war and so Terry was fighting the last war. Now he'll go out and maybe fight this battle in the next election. But hopefully Rove will be ahead of him, because he is a master marketer.[421]

Dan Froomkin commented not about Rove's marketing abilities, but about a tendency toward prevarication.

Another thing that's been so atypical about this administration, is that if you look at your buddy, Karl Rove, and what he's done, they traffic in untruths ... much more ... than in any other administration ... I'm not saying that these guys always lie, but I'm saying they have a reality which they want to get out there and which is absolutely dependent on the media delivering at least most of that message. The fact is that none of us have any really good sense of what the interplay between the reporter and Karl Rove is because it's all done in secret. [The late Robert] Novak was just talking the other day, and he said, "Every single one of my conversations with Karl Rove, this was off the record." That's where he operates.[422]

At National Public Radio, Linda Wertheimer expressed guarded respect for the level of discipline she's seen around Rove, and a concern similar to Froomkin's. "I think we try very hard, in our political reporting, to point out the hand of Karl Rove wherever it can be seen ... But he has brought a kind of professionalism to this new kind of campaigning which is quite remarkable. And until recently or up to a point he has been very successful ... It is part of the Rove philosophy that the campaign continues. They don't stop campaigning. Every decision is based on campaigning ... and one of the things that I have noticed during the reign of Rove: a lotta, lotta lyin' goin' on in politics."

Wertheimer said former Bush opponents Senator John McCain in the 2000 primary campaign and Senator John Kerry in 2004 both thought that campaign lies told about them would not be believed, only to discover that they were "believable to enough people that it made a difference." In Georgia, when disabled Vietnam vet Senator "Max Cleland ran [for re-election] ... the rest of us had just kind of got into the habit of thinking that every day that Max Cleland wakes up in the morning and crawls into that wheelchair is an act of courage," he sets an example to be emulated. But then came the ad campaign run against him, for which Cleland fingered Rove.

Commercials for Cleland's opponent, Saxby Chambliss, Cleland said, "Even put me up there with Osama bin Laden and all that kind of stuff, and said I voted against Homeland Security when I was really one of the authors of the Homeland Security bills."[423]

Nasty politics, Wertheimer said. "It is THAT kind of politics...which is difficult for reporters. You report that the campaign ads are misleading but you write that story once or twice and the ads go on and on. What are you going to do? Are you going to sit up in the press gallery and start chanting, 'Liar, Liar, Pants on Fire?'" [424]

Rove is among the luckiest of politicos, Charles Lewis said, a master of dirty tricks, ruthlessly effective, whose results are not pretty for politics or for journalism.

> In some ways Rove is obviously a brilliant and incredibly interesting fellow, but he also ... happened to be at the right place at the right time, with the right candidate, and the right moment historically. He's got to be the luckiest person on Planet Earth. I think 9/11 helped him, to put it mildly. So did the Florida recount. I mean, it's a little bit like Forrest Gump at every turn. I'm not saying Rove isn't a smart guy, but to lose the popular vote and still win the White House — just take your pick — at every turn it broke a certain way and it always has broken his way, even [not] getting indicted. Everyone was convinced he would be indicted. I mean, he must have, like, ten four-leaf clovers he carries around, because I've never seen anyone this lucky in my life!

Lewis' two favorite Rove moments are the 2000 "South Carolina primary where they smeared John McCain unmercifully," and the scandal for which Rove dodged indictment: the case of outed CIA officer Valerie Plame:

You'll recall there's a seminal moment when McCain erupts in a debate with George W. Bush and accuses him of doing it [an attack of lies]. And then the public sees him angry, McCain, and it worked! Not only did they [Rove and the Bush campaign] manage to defame him all over the state, with hundreds of push polls, and low-grade radio where no one could monitor, but saying things, and all very carefully orchestrated ... Rove has never 'fessed up and acknowledged fully what he did with South Carolina, but if it wasn't for South Carolina, Bush might not have become president.

The Plame affair is the story of South Carolina, again: smearing and trying to destroy dissidents who are criticizing the president and the White House. And here is Karl Rove, caught red-handed, trying to smear, and possibly break federal laws. That's still debatable. There's no question he was smearing Joe Wilson and Valerie Plame. That's actually not a disputed issue, at this point. It's under oath. It's been documented in grand jury testimony ... The issue is that the vice president of the United States, and Karl Rove, together, were scurrilously smearing opponents with journalists. They were giving the orders to smear ... Some guy did an op-ed and he gets smeared by the chief of staff to the vice president? I mean, that's astonishing. And so, Rove was caught red-handed.

Now we live in a culture where we can't remember what happened yesterday, let alone a week or two ago. And Rove has not really suffered. Not only was he not indicted, most Americans don't even recognize what I just said... But both of those are snapshots into the real Karl Rove. He's a dirty trickster. He always was and he always will be. And what's disturbing is, he's always gotten away with it ... Rove has never shown the slightest sign, and from any interviews I've ever read, the slightest introspection or regret or ambivalence or anything. I mean, he's a cold-blooded shark. And he happens to be ruthlessly effective, obviously. No one disputes that ... it's very possible every single thing he's done is not illegal. It's just the way politics are done. So we all say, "Gosh, he's really good, isn't he?" [425]

The level of control over journalism evidenced by Rove's work did not begin with him or with President Bush, according to former NBC Newsman Frank Green. "There's no one who likes Bush less than I do.

But he follows a proud tradition of control of the press, the flow of information. I mean, it was Reagan who did the ear wave. When asked a question he didn't want to answer, he'd say, 'I can't quite hear you,' and leave. It looked like he had contempt for the press. But he was so charming he could kind of get by with it. But [Nixon aide H.R.] Haldeman — that guy is Karl Rove's predecessor. He laid the groundwork for Karl Rove as a ruthless operative."

Green believes that good reporters can still have an impact, but are being kept from doing so "because they're locked out. That's a Rovian control of information ... They really keep a tight control of information ... EPA (for example) can't come out against arsenic. EPA is so tightly politically controlled that even an issue of poison, that should be a science-based slam dunk, gets blocked. Are they convinced their information control is so complete that they can, with a straight face, say arsenic is good for us?"[426]

The genius of Rove, according to columnist EJ Dionne, lies in his capitalizing on the strengths of the Right. "I bow to no one in thinking that Karl Rove is a really smart, effective guy who gets done what he wants to gets done. But I think Karl Rove had a whole movement behind him, parts of which preceded him, and so I think Rove's genius was not to invent all this, but to build on it and help coordinate it. And there is a lot of spontaneous action on the right that doesn't have to be organized" — part of it demonstrated in the sinking of Dan Rather.

> The power of the conservatives is that they've created a very large movement that acts autonomously and intelligently without necessarily having central coordination. These are not automatons; these are millions of very engaged political people who have been involved in this fight. I think the Left, liberals and the Left, have realized the need to organize their folks in a comparable way. The conservatives had a lead on this, because also I think the conservatives felt beleaguered from 1964 on ... I think liberals made the mistake of believing that they really were the establishment and were well behind conservatives in realizing the need for organization, whereas I think conservatives always had the sense that they were an insurgency.[427]

PART VI

SUMMARY AND CONCLUSIONS

Chapter 31

STEALING REALITY

This study began with the question: How could Karl Rove be so effective? To answer, I outlined my experience working with Karl; connected the lessons of Rove to the history of propaganda, the rise of the Right, and communication theory; and interviewed journalists for their insights. I conclude by more closely comparing the journalists' observations to the lessons from history, theory and Rove.

To summarize the journalists' answers, I employ a framework for evaluating research that recommends comparing data with regard to structure, process and outcome.[428]

Structure

From the mid-1960s through the late '70s, substantial investment in network television, newspapers, and news magazines produced a sort of Golden Age[429] in mainstream journalism. The improved technology of television drew the country's attention to civil rights and environmental movements, hampered the 1964 presidential candidacy of Senator Barry Goldwater, highlighted the quagmire of Vietnam and created sensations that produced the departures of President Johnson over Vietnam, and President Nixon in Watergate. Journalists' focus on equal justice and the public interest also aided passage of civil rights legislation. At the same time, feeling shut out of the mainstream media, conservatives began to bypass them, beginning by using direct mail.

By the 1980s, the economic pressures of mergers and acquisitions produced budget cutting in mainstream news, vast layoffs of experienced

Table 4
JOURNALISTS OUTLINE A FRACTURE OF NEWS (SEE TABLES 1-3)
(N=32*)

Respondents unprompted	Respondents prompted (Table 3) for the influence of...		
	Q2 – The Right	Q3 – The Bush administration	Q4 – Karl Rove
Q1 – Biggest changes in Journalism/-ists?	31 – Substantial influence	4 – Secrecy	1-reporters permanently disadvantaged
4 – increased professionalism -better-educated journalists -women, minorities better-represented -greater specialization -fewer "agenda" journalists than in the 1980s	2 – both activist respondents, from Left and Right, affirm (in differing degrees)	8 – Has effectively controlled journalists, journalism	1-"base strategy" became less effective
4 – political Right influences journalism (all four respondents *Washington Post*-related)	1 – a journalistic "silence" linked to budget-cutting		1 – an information provider, who also goes around journalists, direct to voters
	3 – a related, generalized fear in journalism		
	1 – a new postmodernism of the Right		
30 – technology, pressure of capital markets	1 – Right's technology mastery linked to its political and communication dominance		4 – master marketer; used 9/11 to master politics; now an industrial structure greater than Rove himself
5-decline of mainstream media			
4 – news values emptied; less substance in news			
2-rise of political consultants			
2-end of Fairness Doctrine			3 – "traffics in untruths;" yet
2-promise of technology: greater hope; less centralized power	5 – Left pushing back, especially in the blogosphere		2 – lies are not his standard mode of operation

* Explanatory note: Sample size = 32. Because some respondents offered more than one answer for Questions 1 and 2, the answers do not sum to 32. Consequently, this table aggregates the most frequent responses in order to identify common threads among the respondents. At the same time, it also includes some individual answers that seem to provide a helpful perspective. Because a little less than half of respondents had fairly current experience in Washington, D.C., the responses to Questions 3 and 4 number less than half of the responses for Questions 1 and 2.

journalists, and the subordination of mainstream journalism values to the values of capital markets. Because much of the communication of the New Right occurred outside mainstream news, many mainstream journalists not only missed the conservative electoral insurgencies of 1978 and 1980, but the structural advances of the Right — founded on the work of George Creel and Antonio Gramsci — that had propelled them. The market pressures, improved technology, and Ted Turner's entrepreneurialism produced the Cable News Network in 1980. CNN and subsequent imitators emphasized timeliness, sometimes at the expense of accuracy, context, and reflection. While mainstream journalism weakened, conservative political operators grew adept at manipulating broadcast television by mastering the hardware and software of the visual image.

By 2005, mainstream media companies that lost subscribers to newer television and Internet alternatives struggled to develop multimedia platforms themselves to save market share. Improvements in technology, computing, and the splintering of the market strengthened both political consultants and "avowedly partisan media,"[430] especially on the Right. The Right colonized AM radio; Right and Left, using the Internet, increasingly cultivated their own communities of interest, bypassing mainstream news.

Process

The Influence of the Right. In the 1970s, media became increasingly specialized; the Left, increasingly passive at the same moment that the Right began "working the referee," criticizing news media relentlessly. The conservative focus on knitting together its communities of interest and controlling visuals, in particular, by the 1980s, connected, ironically, to the French Left intellectual movement of the 1950s and '60s known as *postmodernism*.

By the 1980s, with mergers and budget-cutting in full bloom, mainstream journalism became quiescent and cautious. The more "the suits," the financial managers[431] cut budgets for news, the more dependent news people became on institutional sources, including the presidency, for access and exclusive interviews. A new, budget-driven urgency to gain access to a more conservative administration undercut journalistic values,

Table 5

JOURNALISTS' OBSERVATIONS LINKED TO CONTEMPORARY HISTORY BY DECADE: EVALUATING CHANGES IN STRUCTURE, PROCESS, AND OUTCOME, 1965-2006

Decade	Structure	Process	Outcome
60s-70s	"Golden Age" of journalism for newspapers, newsmagazines, and network television. 1972: commercial TV networks produce 400 hours of documentaries; *Washington Post* coverage of Watergate sets new standards in investigative journalism; National Public Radio debut	Mainstream commercial media dominate news (as media specialization develops); reporting focuses civil rights; women's, elders, gay rights; the environment; Vietnam and Watergate	Social upheaval and policy change; focus on Vietnam leads to Lyndon Johnson decision not to seek re-election; in Watergate, Richard Nixon resigning residency Conservatives, feeling shut out of mainstream news media, develop direct mail by mastering computing technology; develop new institutions to shape debate, critique the news
70s-80s	Budget-cutting in mainstream news organizations reduces ability to report; debut of CNN, and greater focus on immediate news Rise of conservative think tanks CBS News Division reduced from 2,000-3,000 personnel to a few hundred	Conservative institutions begin reshaping the national agenda, linking together libertarian conservatives, anticommunist neoconservatives, and the Christian Right; postmodern methods deployed, and new institutions continue development in the mode of Antonio Gramsci. Mainstream news becomes more cautious in confronting power	Peak prestige in journalism, journalistic head-swelling; the political Left becomes passive; 1978: four liberal U.S. Senators defeated 1980: Ronald Reagan elected Some in mainstream journalism caught off-guard in the conservative sweep.

Table 5, continued

Decade	Structure	Process	Outcome
80s-90s	Budget-cutting continues in mainstream news, with more pressure for financial return. News organizations with fewer resources become more dependent on institutional sources: a more conservative administration, conservative think tanks, and business.	Journalism begins transforming into entertainment. Reagan administration masters postmodern approach to visual images, especially televisuals	Market logic and technology 'eviscerate news organizations and the profession of journalism.' Conservative ideas increasingly dominate public debate, the product of a Gramscian hegemony Increasing political polarization
	1987: Fairness Doctrine ends		Political Right 'colonizes' AM radic News becomes "talk show culture" 1988: Republican officials turn t.v. news' own cameras on reporters to beat the press
		1992: Republicans splinter over tax hikes; splintering foretells a return to activating conservative base in years to come	Bill Clinton, elected by a plurality, unable to enact health care reform, tacks right on taxes, welfare

Table 5, continued

Decade	Structure	Process	Outcome
90s-2006	The Right dominates Congress; increasingly, the Judiciary, and lobbying. Mainstream media begin moving to Internet platforms.	1998: Bill Clinton-Monica Lewinsky becomes first great Internet story; "Drudged" becomes a verb.	Kenneth Starr appointed special prosecutor; Clinton impeached. Lewinsky story stains journalism.
	Advances in technology and computing enable better attention to market splinter, strengthening a trend to partisan media.	Ascent of Fox News, MoveOn.org, and an array of others	Mainstream media increasingly weakened; financial model no longer clear; newspaper columns, books, more influenced by Right. Political consultants strengthened.
		2000: Left awakens to being outflanked by the Right	Right and Left criticize and bypass mainstream news. News values of fairness, justice wane.
		Sept. 11 reinforces broadcast media focus on flag, terrorism to boost ratings	Karl Rove, Bush administration, the Right use 9-11 to increase political control, cow the media, propel war in Iraq; ultimately, "Swift Boat" Democrat John Kerry in 2004.
	Technology that strengthened the Right is deployed by Left to articulate, organize in the blogosphere	2006: commercial network TV news produces no documentaries	24-hour cable networks set news agenda Mainstream news is no longer the central text; 'the core of meaning changes'

on the one hand, while the conservative assault on mainstream media grew stronger and better organized, on the other. Once the Fairness Doctrine ended in 1987, talk radio went right-wing. Right-wing media criticism (e.g., Accuracy in Media, Media Research Center, American Family Association, American Center for Law & Justice) and right-wing media (e.g., Fox News, *Washington Times*, *Weekly Standard*, *American Spectator*) grew with the burgeoning of think tanks on the Right. The more the right-wing think tanks grew and the greater budget pressures became, the more journalistic foci shifted from the reporting of substance to reporting the less expensive, easier-to-cover stories: money, sex and celebrity.[432]

The trends of the 1980s accelerated over the next two decades as technology, more than substance, drove the news to greater speed, less reflection. Ultimately, the twenty-four-hour cable networks, rather than the larger and more prestigious news organizations, began to set the news agenda. Routine reporting of the government's work went often under reported or ignored. Trivia dominated the news; pop culture prevailed; but so did Republicans, who were more advanced in the uses of technology. Mainstream news editors became more sensitive to criticism from the Right and its active blogosphere. By 2000, the Left seemed to awaken and became more active. But after 9/11, broadcast stations, national and local, focused less on news and more on consultants' advice to fly the flag to boost ratings and ad revenue. Moreover, the reporting of political campaigns became less about content; campaigns themselves, less about substance than about controlling image and the tactics of winning, directed by political consultants. Images prevailed over substance: Dukakis in the tank in 1988; or the Swift Boating of John Kerry in 2004. Politicians increasingly bypassed media by their own means, unobstructed by campaign finance law.

The Bush administration, which several journalists called the most secretive in their experience, especially post 9/11 threatened government leakers with jail and journalists with treason, while it used the rhetoric of terrorism to blunt dissent. In response to the administration's measures, journalists sought to better protect themselves, especially in discussions of national security, by exercising new care in citing sources.[433]

Republican "talking points" began showing up with more frequency on talk radio and in new media,[434] as well as in mainstream news. As journalists described a relentless right-wing campaign against them and their profession, journalists covering the White House began backing off their toughness to maintain a comfort zone, even about critical issues of war and peace. The Bush White House remained a step ahead of journalists in controlling and limiting information; one respondent considered leaving the country; and even at the *Washington Post,* editors held up, altered, or buried important stories about government conduct.

With Karl Rove, journalists said they've been at a disadvantage — even a permanent disadvantage. They reported being unaware, at first, of how John McCain had been victimized in the 2000 primary in South Carolina; or how John Kerry was Swift-Boated and destroyed in Ohio four years later. Or how, in parallel form, the administration outed and smeared its own covert CIA officer, Valerie Plame,[435] who lost her job as the result of an administration campaign to undercut her husband, Ambassador Joseph Wilson, for unveiling administration untruths in the run-up to war about Iraq seeking uranium for a nuclear weapon.

During his 2000 presidential campaign Bush promised to be a "uniter, not a divider;" Rove's polarizing approach won his boss the presidency by a single vote in the Supreme Court, although he lost the election by a half-million votes. In the White House, Rove was prompt and helpful in assisting some journalists, although he seemed to require the same off-the-record protections journalists were now affording other sources, who feared being outed as leakers. At the same time, he pursued a strategy of connecting directly to grassroots constituencies, to render journalism irrelevant. He did so by a consummate use of technology: the hardware of computing, and the analytical power of databases; and the software of language, using both fundamentalism and patriotism. He used 9/11 and the Iraq war to change the conventional wisdom in order to secure constituencies and votes, disable journalists and put the media on its heels. Two journalists interviewed, both women, said Rove was engaging and generally truthful; three others, two men and a woman, suggested that Rove lies.

Outcome

From a Golden Age in the 1960s and '70s, mainstream journalism in the 1980s found itself cornered by a combination of technology and market logic that eviscerated news organizations and the profession itself.[436] The political polarization of the 1990s stained journalism; "Drudged" — the impact of right wing blogger Matt Drudge targeting political actors on his web site — became a verb. News as central text from which Americans make meaning became supplanted by alternative media.[437] By 2006, a film of frogs mating could not be shown on at least one television network. Most respondents affirmed the rightward tilt Ben Bagdikian described (Table 3).

Mainstream media seemed more under the influence of conservatism. Book publishing, as well as newspaper columns, became more influenced by the Right. Mainstream media were no longer the lifeguards of politics; their financial status and prestige declined. Their practitioners seemed intimidated; afraid to publish news detrimental to the administration for fear of flak, or to expose untruths about the Iraq war for fear of being called biased; or, by confronting power, losing market share in a tightening market. As mainstream media weakened, political consultants displaced journalists as the fourth branch of government, and became for the first time term-long office-holders at the highest levels of the executive branch.

The *Washington Post*, as an exemplar of these phenomena, seemed to move to the right along with the nation's capital. The *Post* no longer had a labor beat, or a beat covering the poor. One journalist observed in one of the newer stars at the paper a sense of devotion to the *Post* as a corporate organization, as opposed to a devotion to reporting the truth. What should have been essential stories — including the lead-up to the Iraq war— went under reported while *Post* editorials supported it, and two of its op-ed columnists did so, sometimes with factual error.[438] The more the administration succeeded in framing the conventional wisdom, the more editors of the *Post's* news pages seemed afraid to go beyond it.

Overall, mainstream journalism itself seemed to shift to the right, the apparent result of three factors: a well-organized, long-term, conservative campaign; the imperatives of technology itself, and conservatives'

Table 6
STEALING REALITY: LESSONS IN THEORY AND PRACTICE

Theory

The American political Right arose by using the government's World War I propaganda model, perfected by the methods of the European intellectual Left:

- Italian communist Antonio Gramsci's theory of intellectual hegemony: constructing a system of institutions to master the conventional wisdom.
- The postmodernism of the French Left: "The discourse of truth is quite simply impossible." To dominate the conventional wisdom, dominate the images.

Practice

The revolution in the Right's mastery in only thirty years is suggested by comparing discourse from the Richard Nixon and George W. Bush administrations.

Nixon's former Attorney General John Mitchell said: "Watch what we do, not what we say." In contrast, the Bush administration turned Mitchell's dictum 180 degrees, in effect to: Watch what we say, not what we do.

For example, the Bush administration justified a pre-emptive U.S. military strike on Iraq by conflating Sept. 11 with Saddam Hussein. By copying the fear-inducing visuals of the American Cold War and nuclear bombs and pasting them on Iraq, it advanced and perpetuated its war policy. And by training the armor of coercion on opponents, often anonymously, it eliminated or stifled dissent.

Lessons:
- Reality is pliable, shapeable, even reversible
- Images count, more than reality.
- The political Right, later partly coordinated by Karl Rove, mastered these issues beginning in the 1960s; organizationally, the political Left appears to be a generation behind.
- Mainstream journalism — fractured in organization, budgetary resources and comprehension of these issues, and surrounded by Right's system of institutions — has been outflanked, perhaps permanently.

command of it; and the subjugation of mainstream reporting to capital markets.

Theory and Practice

That mainstream news now acts less as lifeguard[439] or referee[440] speaks partly to the fracture of news as outlined above, and partly to the loss of an effective political opposition: the news sources of the Left in the first six years of the Bush administration were shut out by the Right. The Left appears to be a generation behind the Right in its organization. The Right so dominated the Bush administration that the Environmental Protection Agency, for example, couldn't set an allowable limit for arsenic in drinking water,[441] much less grapple with global warming. The Bush administration did not regulate Big Tobacco, then sought to lower tobacco company liability in the marketing of cigarettes that caused cancer and heart disease to millions. The administration launched a congressionally accepted, pre-emptive war against Iraq based on evidence it constructed. Conservative judges upended the principle of one man, one vote in campaign finance by declaring unlimited campaign contributions legal in the name of free speech. Karl Rove's genius lay in building on the conservative message machinery that rendered fiction into fact, and better coordinating it. But the mastery of conservatives lay in adopting the lessons of Antonio Gramsci.

Antonio Gramsci and hegemony theory. Gramsci asked: why do people fail to act in their collective best interests? Rove's associate, Grover Norquist, answered the question in speaking to Young Republican Club women at Smith College in 2005.

"The biggest shift in demography," Norquist said, "is the number of people who own shares of stock directly. In 1980, 20 percent owned stocks directly. Today, it's 60 percent of adults, and 70 percent of voters." Pausing, then scanning the room for effect, Norquist said: "This changes behavior ... not all of a sudden ... but this changes who you are." For every five thousand dollars in stock a person purchases, he continued, that individual is 18 percent more likely to be Republican. "If one then buys a gun, one is significantly more Republican ... Every year, more Americans own stock, and every year, more Americans own stock, and more ... this," he repeated, "changes behavior." [442]

The more that individuals focus on individual wealth and security, Norquist seemed to suggest, the less concerned they become about vast wealth at the top, the impoverishment of the poor at the bottom, or the economic stagnation of the middle class — and the more conservative they become. The secret to rendering Americans politically inert is to focus them on shopping, winning the lottery, or growing their 401Ks or pensions through mutual funds: people who focus on individual gain lose track of the greater good. How can there be class warfare if no one focuses on class ?[443] How can there be a focus on the greater good when the meticulously-built institutions of the Right — the American Enterprise Institute, the Heritage Foundation, the Federalist Society, the Cato Institute, and some 500 others — construct the conventional wisdom around individual gain, down to the level of a primary and secondary education focus on test scores, and college education aimed at technical issues, not the liberal arts and critical thinking? How can those concerned with the greater good find a platform when the media of the Right — Fox News, the American Spectator, the range of journals and web sites of the Right, and virtually all of AM talk radio, focus on marginalizing them? [444]

Postmodernism. Rove and the Right dominated the news by exercising discipline over the creation of the conventional wisdom and by using their own media, beginning with direct mail, to communicate it, while market consolidations and the requirements of profitability sapped mainstream journalism of its strength. But in addition, the Right adopted the thinking of the sort of people Rove sought to vilify for their opposition to the Bush war in Iraq: the French intellectual left. One insight into this came in an article by journalist Ron Suskind, quoting an unidentified administration official.

> In the summer of 2002, after I had written an article in *Esquire* that the White House didn't like about Bush's former communications director, Karen Hughes, I had a meeting with a senior adviser to Bush. He expressed the White House's displeasure, and then he told me something that at the time I didn't fully comprehend — but which I now believe gets to the very heart of the Bush presidency.
>
> The aide said that guys like me were "in what we call the reality-based community," which he defined as people who "believe that solutions emerge from your judicious study of discernible reality." I nodded and murmured something about enlightenment principles and empiricism. He cut me off. "That's not the way the world really works anymore," he continued. "We're an empire now, and when we act, we create our own reality. And while you're studying that reality — judiciously, as you will — we'll act again, creating other

new realities, which you can study, too, and that's how things will sort out. We're history's actors . . . and you, all of you, will be left to just study what we do."[445]

Implicit in that statement is a departure from the usual poll-oriented, advertising-and-public relations, scientific research-grounded approaches to political communication. What's described, instead, is an approach to communication and philosophy called postmodernism. Although the meaning of the term is complex, it originated with such French thinkers as Jean Baudrillard and Michel Foucault. Suskind's passage resonates, in particular, with Baudrillard. To interpret, Baudrillard asserts that the more we depend on mediated images for our view of reality, the farther from reality we stray. The more the world is mediated, the farther removed it becomes from the authentic. The more that mediated images are substituted for the real, the more such images undercut the authentic, the more their construction displaces reality, and the more likely that those who construct it may dominate. Through such a process, Baudrillard concludes, "The discourse of truth is quite simply impossible." [446]

In the abstract, that idea may simply appear — abstract. Its importance, however is this: if one can challenge and control reality, then one can do literally anything, including making one's opponents appear to be that which they are not.

We can begin to grasp the revolutionary nature of this idea if we consider the words of Richard Nixon's attorney general, John Mitchell, a generation ago. In the midst of the brewing Watergate scandal, Mitchell famously told reporters: "Watch what we do, not what we say." To begin to understand how far the Bush administration succeeded in advancing postmodern theory to insulate itself from attack, Mitchell's slogan might now be turned inside out, to: "Watch what we say, not what we do."

By continuously conflating images of 9/11 with fears of nuclear attack in the United States, Bush administration officials succeeded, less than thirty years after Mitchell spoke, in getting most Americans to think, at least for a time, that what was important is not what officials of the Bush administration did, but what they said. For example, to justify attacking Iraq, Saddam Hussein is linked to al-Qaeda; or Saddam Hussein has weapons of mass destruction; or Saddam Hussein poses a direct threat to the United States; or Saddam Hussein *had* a program to build weapons of mass destruction; or, the world is better off without Saddam Hussein. The continuous images of the 9/11 attacks, conflated with the fear of a domestic mushroom cloud, undercut the real and substituted a postmodern, and highly authoritarian, "reality."

To explain it another way, E. J. Dionne cites the story of psychologist Kenneth Gergen (brother of political leadership specialist David Gergen), who frames the question in baseball terms: how do you tell the difference between a pre-modern, modern, and post-modern umpire?

When it comes to balls and strikes, the premodern umpire says: "I call them as they are."

The modern umpire says, "I call them as I see them."

The postmodern umpire says, "They don't exist until I call 'em."

Postmodern reality, in sum, exists partly because authority declares it to be so.

Postmodern reality, however, also depends on just how mediated "reality" becomes. Media theorist Barry Vacker, a former Texan, provides another example by reviewing the career of George W. Bush.

According to Vacker, Bush became the mediated face of the Texas Rangers, its general manager, the son of the forty-first president, dressed in cowboy boots and seated in the stands behind the dugout with other Texans; a personable promoter. The images of the apparently successful Bush, engaged in the crowd and the all-American game, became part of a campaign staged for television successfully enough that Arlington, Texas taxpayers in 1991 approved a half-cent sales tax to pay for more than two-thirds the cost to erect "The Ballpark at Arlington," for Bush's Rangers. The stadium itself was constructed to resemble a 1920s-era brick urban stadium, something that never existed in Texas, Vacker noted, another imitation, this one of an idealized past. The stadium, in turn, is filled with television screens in the outfield, in corporate suites, bars, restaurants, and vending areas — mediating the game, producing more image imitations, reflecting the spectacle, validating stadium and game, the postmodern equivalent of a Roman arena. And, magically, Vacker noted, the team began to win its first division titles and go to the playoffs, after a generation of losing. The new, successful, mediated image ultimately enabled Bush, the general manager, to sell the image itself to become, first, a multimillionaire; then governor, and president. According to Vacker, the more that images stray from the original, the more self-referential they become. Each ultimately becomes a self-referring copy, a tautology of circulating images that legitimate each other.[447]

2006, 2008, 2010 and Beyond

To read American journalism at this writing in 2010 is to forget that Democrats seemed more confident about their chances of recapturing the White House and reversing the Republican losses of 2006 and 2008.[448] Democrats maintained such confidence at their peril.[449] Rove and Bush won the election of 2000 even though they came up a half-million votes short—after the Supreme Court decided in Bush's favor. A few blinks later, facing a divided country from the White House, Rove reduced the administration's legitimacy problem by linking Bush to congressional Democrats. By lowering taxes and passing the "No Child Left Behind" Act, Congress legitimated the unelected Bush as "a uniter, not a divider."

Yet, while reckoning with the legitimacy problem, Bush ignored the Middle East. Bush had claimed he would "avoid nation-building." But in the next blink, the terror of 9/11 gripped the country, and Rove transformed Bush into an internationalist, "a wartime president," attacking terrorists and promising to rebuild Afghanistan (and later, Iraq). Propelled by patriotism, Bush's image approval swelled to 70 to 80 percent. Rove seized that opportunity, too, pushing Bush to unprecedented midterm campaigning in 2002. Rove used Bush's new popularity to lock up new majorities in Congress, new governorships, and redistricting to favor Republicans around the country for the next decade. His numbers finally secure, Bush moved against Saddam Hussein.

Two years later, the war in Iraq a disaster, Rove seized even that opportunity, for a time, and the administration reversed course again. Instead of going it alone, the administration declared a deadline for a political turnover, and ceded nation-building to a UN it once declared "irrelevant." Suddenly, the diplomatic machinery, too, began working for Bush, while the administration banned images of American coffins coming home. At the 2004 G-8 summit in Georgia, the administration won accolades from allies it had shut out. In February and March 2007, even as it began a surge of troops while fending off congressional attempts to withdraw them, the administration reversed its policy course again. By removing defense secretary Donald Rumsfeld and undersecretary Paul Wolfowitz from the Defense Department, Bush reduced the influence of neoconservatives who'd encouraged him to strike in Iraq. At the same time, the administration resumed diplomatic initiatives propelled by Secretary of State Condoleeza Rice, including talks with Iran, Syria, and North Korea, the "axis of evil" with which Bush had declared he would not negotiate. The administration did so even as a jury convicted the vice president's former chief of staff, I. Lewis "Scooter" Libby, for lying and obstruction of justice in covering up administration political attacks on Ambassador Wilson and his wife, former CIA operative Valerie Plame. In sum, anyone who believes she has Karl Rove in her sights decidedly underestimates Rove and overstates her aim. The fact that he is no longer in the White House is even less material today than in Austin, when Rove, "the Prime Minister," ran the politics of the Bush administration from the office of Karl Rove + Co. Rove is at his most powerful when he is out of the public eye.

Rove almost invariably ignores the conventional. In message production, he rolls with his own poll-tested symbols, semiotics, story line, and frame, forcing news people to run with *them*. The approach is ironically similar to that of Nikolai Lenin, who argued that the place of journalism is not to critique the government, but to structurally support it.[450] And so, in the 2004 presidential campaign, Rove's forces eliminated dissent: opponents who sought to get tickets to Bush rallies simply couldn't get them. Bush had it both ways. While screening out dissent on the one hand, his advance people framed a blue-shirt-sleeved president as a common man, on the other. At the same time, Bush television ads framed Sen. John Kerry as the elitist (and Kerry made it possible by being taped wind-surfing off the Massachusetts coast: sail flipping insouciantly in the breeze). As Rove put it in our class: "How you look is as important as what you say."

The ability to reverse reality is Rove's signature. In 2004 he stripped Kerry of the advantage of his Silver-Star-winning service in Vietnam, thereby deflecting focus from Bush's checkered service in the Texas Air National Guard. By unleashing the Swift Boat Veterans, Rove so discredited Kerry that Kerry's own supporters stayed home, while the attacks reinvigorated the Right.

The Elections of 2006 and 2008

In retrospect, Bush's self-described "thumping" in the 2006 midterm elections that shifted the majority in both houses of Congress to the Democrats seems less a win for Democrats than a failure by Republicans. The results appeared to be a referendum, in part, on administration policy in Iraq and Hurricane Katrina. But even those policy setbacks might have been overcome had it not been for Republican scandals that steadily built to election day: money laundering and conspiracy charges against former House Republican majority leader Rep. Tom DeLay; the conviction of former lobbyist Jack Abramoff, which helped to bring down former Rep. Bob Ney; the bribery and corruption scandal of former Rep. Randy (Duke) Cunningham; the sex scandal of Rep. Mark Foley. Even then, Rove noted that an overall shift of only 77,611 votes around the country would have kept the House of Representatives in Republican hands.[451]

A larger danger for conservatives beyond their losses in 2008 is that their base may be splintering.[452] However, Republican primary voters still appeared to be clear on their direction: in March 2007, about 39 percent said they wanted the next presidential contender to *continue* the policies of George W. Bush; another 39 percent wanted policies that were even more conservative.[453] Despite the early successes of Barack Obama in outflanking the Right, its base seems alive, well, and sticking right. Rove, by dint of his strength as networker of the Right and architect of the Bush victories, remains uniquely capable of knitting together Bush supporters and the Right. In the meantime, the superstructure that the Right built over generations — the foundations, nonprofits, news media, political consultants — remains intact. Moreover, as Grover Norquist told a group of College Republican women at an event at Smith College, the fortunes of the Republican party depend, in part, on the voters of Latinos. The numbers show that "if thirty percent of Hispanics vote Republican, we'll (Republicans) run the country for the next thirty to fifty years."[454] Even in 2006, Latinos wooed by George Bush went Republican by 30 percent.[455] In 2008, Latinos gave Republican John McCain 31 percent.[456]

And just as Rove and the Bush administration showed policy flexibility when they began their term, they showed it again after losing a congressional majority. Bush in 2007 called for scale-backs in private-sector executive pay; the administration throttled back its insistence on firing some U.S. attorneys (while Rove asserted their right to do so); the State Department opened a diplomatic initiative to Syria and Iran over the Middle East; and domestically, betraying new flexibility on the issue of sexual abstinence for young people, former Rove client/Texas Governor Rick Perry moved to require HPV vaccinations for girls and women age eleven and older. Reversing course, the administration began diplomatic moves with North Korea and Iran, and began discussing a phased pull-out from Iraq.

Democrats, through the Center for American Progress, were organizing, raising money, and focusing public attention on the Iraq war and national security policy, health care, and income security. But Democrats remain years behind. Splintered or not, the Right has hundreds of think tanks, research groups, and media organizations in place. They continue controlling message, research, and ideas to dominate the conventional wisdom. With Democrats' gains in 2006 and 2008, the challenges from the Left — at least to mainstream news — seemed to be taking hold, especially in the blogosphere. Yet even with splintering on the Right, conservative institutions remain in place, with no sign their dominance is waning. That structure for the creation and dominance of ideology seems likely to sustain the Right and undercut the Left for many years to come.

"Thor." Political attacks are a Rove trademark; direct mail, the device by which the Right developed, and Rove launched many attacks. Yet, I wanted to believe Rove when he denied being or knowing "Thor," who'd set off the attack on me, over the Internet (Chapter 24). But when I tuned in to C-SPAN one day, who should I see speaking but Rove, recognizing: Mark "Thor" Hearne, the National General Counsel for Bush/Cheney '04 Inc. "I ran into Thor Hearne as I was coming in," Rove told a lawyers association, as he began his speech. "He was leaving; he was smart, and he was leaving to go out and enjoy the day."[457]

Hearne was executive director of the American Center for Voting Rights (ACVR), according to blogger Brad Friedman, "a Republican front group created by high-level GOP operatives expressly for the purpose of spreading disinformation to sidetrack the election reform movement in this country"[458] — another of the hundreds of institutions set up to advance the interests of the Right. When I called Hearne's office, his assistant denied the Lucianne.com post was Hearne's. Later, when friends e-mailed me a story that said that the parents of Grover Norquist had considered naming him Thor,[459] I called Norquist's office, spoke to his press spokesman, sent him the Lucianne.com fax, but received no callback. In short, the identity of "Thor" remains a mystery.

Beneficiary and coordinator. Karl Rove has succeeded wildly in his work — partly through unsurpassed talent, drive, confidence and experience as political operative; partly because he may be the most voracious reader of political communication theory in practical politics today; partly because he's a one-man network for the Right. A chief beneficiary of the decades-long effort by the Right to undercut the New Deal, he is now its chief strategist. Rove built on that longer effort by absorbing the methods of the Left. He learned that by commanding the full power of political communication, one no longer needs large majorities, or, even "reality."

Rove's work, in combination with the rise of the Right and the effect of market forces, has emasculated mainstream American journalism. "The press are like sheep," he told our class; they can be led, like four-legged ruminants. Indeed, how could any political consultant resist the opportunity to turn history 180 degrees, to frame views opposite those most would consider "real," turning opponents' greatest strengths — even heroic armed service — into their worst nightmares? If Rove's success began with his talent at debate, his mastery came in acting on scholarship that recognizes, as John Lennon sang, that "Nothing is real" — that truth and meaning are as reversible as a raincoat.

Journalism reported the administration's conventional wisdom on Iraq with murderous results. By summer 2004, the *Washington Post* and the *New York Times* acknowledged they'd been misled. Small wonder, then, that news people and citizenry alike remained confused, for years after.

When the intelligence community was blamed for the failures in detecting weapons of mass destruction in Iraq, the administration convened a blue-ribbon commission, but *specifically barred it* from looking at the politically radioactive question: did the administration gin up the intelligence it wanted in order to go to war?[460] In short: if one controls images and story line, one cannot but succeed?

If the assault on truth is evident in the response of the national media, it's subtler at the state level, where it's less apparent, more readily hidden, and less subject to scrutiny. In Iowa, which went narrowly for Bush in 2004, for example, consider the state's most important newspaper, the formerly Pulitzer Prize-winning *Des Moines Register,* now owned by the Gannett chain. The *Register*, for one, appeared even more misled by the Swift Boat Veterans[461] than the *Times* and *Post* were misled in Iraq. In a Sunday lead story, it declared that the Swift Boat Veterans had placed no radio ads in Iowa. Yet when I heard the ads repeatedly on Iowa radio stations as I drove across the state that same weekend and pointed out the error in writing in a letter to the editor, the paper offered neither acknowledgment, nor *mea culpa*, nor correction.[462] As Rove said in class, "Nothing works like repetition" (see chapter 7).

Rove and I connected at the University of Texas partly because we were focused on similar phenomena. I'd reached saturation as a journalist in mainstream news organizations that reflected middle-of-the-road, social consensus points of view, but screened out the views of all sorts minorities. I'd sought in my work as a journalist to include more of them, and in my graduate work, to understand why the news often didn't reflect them. Rove, too, comprehended the range of views, but carefully chose those to insert into the conventional wisdom to accomplish his political aims, even when that meant promoting an unjustified war to achieve them.

In 1922, Walter Lippmann wrote "news and truth are not the same."[463] A generation after Lippmann's death, Rove and the Right proved that, in fact, truth is infinitely pliable and shapeable. They demonstrated, moreover, that the postmodernism of the French Left, and the hegemony theory of an Italian communist, could be adopted through an intellectual jiu-jitsu to defeat the Left. That is perhaps among Rove's greatest victories: he used the tools of his intellectual opponents, some of their greatest strengths, to defeat them.

Rove's work affirms the insight of Shakespeare's Macbeth, that "nothing is, but what is not."[464] Indeed, when it comes to postmodern reality and news, a new fundamental seems to apply: a lie is not a lie, when one controls the means to make it true: the framing, imaging, and cultivation of the conventional wisdom. At that point, with that level of mastery, journalism, journalists, and even most opponents can be rendered inert.

Scholars of literary history have made it clear that when it came to plot and language even Shakespeare stole. Rove and the Right, at least for a time, appear to have used the tools of the Left to advance the Right, and they succeeded in stealing reality, itself.

Chapter 32

Reality Adjustments:
Rove's Memoir

In spring semester 2010, I decided, as a learning exercise, to ask my eleven graduate students in research methods at St. Mary's University to read a draft of this book and Karl Rove's new memoir, *Courage and Consequence*. In his book, Rove repeatedly denounces others as "hypocrites" and "liars." The students and I discussed Rove's book on March 24 and April 8, 2010. Each student independently drafted a response and discussed the issues in class. After they presented, so did I.

Needless to say, most of the students comments were critical. Here's a sampling.

- Rove's book is "accessible to adolescents and clearly indicates his displeasure for Democrats and his esteem for Republicans with well-placed adjectives throughout ... . There is no discussion on the more scientific basis for his instruments of guiding public opinion ... Most of the controversies are handled ... with spin ... it would have been nice to read his disgust at those tactics in the stratum of competition; it would have been wonderful to read his thoughts on the science, with his declaration that the science is more effective than the mud."
- "Rove's book sounds candy-coated. He paints Bush as a highly intellectual, sensitive, thoughtful man and I think even past supporters do not believe that. Rove is very quick to name drop ... I see it as a very sophomoric story with little reality, specifics or statistical proof ... He paints the Democratic Party with a very broad black brush. The few accusations that are leveled against

the Republicans are briefly touched upon, blamed on misinformation or outright lies by the other side ... "

- "It was hard to believe that EVERYTHING Rove did was for the good of humanity and good will, although he made it seem that way. All in all I enjoyed ... its 'candor' and historical approach."
- "He is only telling one side of the story. He is so persuasive and knows how to stir emotions so well, he succeeds in getting his 'message' across, even though we know it is not true."
- "Rove frequently portrayed himself as the victim when he was blamed for ... dirty politics ... Rove provided his share of evidence which showed that he was not the perpetrator, but who knows what information that was omitted to keep himself looking innocent."
- Rove "tried to create the illusion of honesty in a few self-revealing, emotional passages and harmless confessions, attempting to set the stage for believability later on ... Rove never addresses the fact that Bush ended with a huge deficit."

But these comments did not tell the whole story. It was more complicated than that. Another student said that Rove's book "still doesn't explain why we went to war in Iraq." Al-Qaeda may have been a threat to the United States beginning in 1993, she said, "but he still didn't connect Iraq with 9/11 — I'm still not satisfied. He blames 9/11 for redefining the Bush presidency."

Yet, immediately after those comments, she paused, reflecting further: "Maybe Bush wasn't such a bad president. The book demonstrates how he's (Rove's) so powerful and persuasive, with good explanations ... whoever criticizes, he takes on, and makes his argument seem justified." Although she had produced a strong critique herself, she then, ironically, doubted her own thinking, because Rove's memoir had seemed persuasive, even though it didn't answer her question.

Indeed, most of the students in our seminar said they found Rove's argument persuasive, even when it diverged from their own experience.

After the students finished their presentations, I said Rove's memoir defends him and the Bush administration by omitting or altering facts, and attacking others who would force him to face them. In doing so, the memoir underscores Rove's dictum when he taught at the University of

Texas: *It doesn't matter what the story is if you can promote the right picture.* Some of the contradictions between Rove's picture and the public record include:

- *Bush legitimacy.* Rove blames Democrats for the idea that Bush won the presidency illegitimately, saying he expected bipartisanship from Democrats, especially after 9/11 (305). Rove omits that (1) Bush lost the election of 2000 by 543,895 votes, yet won the electoral vote when the Supreme Court by a vote of five to four halted the recounting of votes in Florida; (2) The U.S. Civil Rights Commission found that Florida election officials (who declared Bush won by 537 votes) permitted pre-election voter registration-scrubbing that disenfranchised thousands of black voters (who opposed Bush by a margin of 9-1), yet who accounted for more than half of Florida's 180,000 spoiled votes; (3) Black voters were ten times more likely than non-blacks to have their ballots rejected, even though "error rates stemming from uneducated, uninformed, or disinterested voters account for less than 1 percent of the problems;"[465] and (4) The voter disenfranchising was authorized by the official charged with overseeing Florida's election: Florida Secretary of State Katherine Harris, who served as Bush-Cheney Florida campaign co-chair.

- *Taxes, Deficits, the Economy, and Education.* According to Rove, the Bush tax cuts in 2001 and 2003 produced "the longest period of economic growth since President Reagan," and substantial growth in gross domestic product and labor productivity; and pushed the U.S. economy from $9.7 trillion in 2001 to $14.2 trillion in 2008. "That $4.5 trillion in growth alone is bigger than the entire Japanese economy" (236). Deficits that occurred, Rove maintains, were due to the recession when Bush took office, and Bush's response to the attacks of 9/11. Rove attributes the financial decline late in the Bush administration to Democrats who failed to back the regulating of Fannie Mae and Freddie Mac (410). "Democratic critics were wrong about Bush economics," Rove declares, "and many were hypocrites." (236-237). Meantime, in education, he says student test scores improved, thanks to the No Child Left Behind Act, "one of the great modern domestic policy successes." (237).

It is true that gross domestic product has grown steadily across all administrations since the 1970s. What Rove omits is that in 2008, the last year of the Bush presidency, American household net worth fell 18 percent, $11 trillion — a decline in a single year that more than doubled the Japanese economy, and equaled the annual output of Germany, Japan and the U.K. combined.[466] (In 2009, U.S. household net worth rose 5.4 percent.[467]) According to the Federal Reserve Bank of St. Louis, from a high the last quarter of 2007 to a low point in the first quarter of 2009, American industrial production fell 15 percent; bank loan failures were up four-fold; unemployment more than doubled; and the U.S. dollar tied its forty-year low against the Japanese yen.[468] As unemployment went up, home foreclosures went up dramatically.[469]

During the administration's first term, then Federal Reserve Chairman Alan Greenspan said that the Bush tax cuts were appropriate only if federal deficits went down.[470] Instead, they went up; by the end of the Bush administration deficits were 50 percent higher than at any time in recent history.[471] The deficits were largely accounted for by the Bush tax cuts, the wars in Afghanistan and Iraq, and the economic downturn.[472] At the same time, the administration avoided or sought to curb economic and other regulation, even as financial markets were in the early stages of a meltdown that threatened another Great Depression.[473]

As the economy expanded on paper, through the unregulated trading of collateralized debt obligations and credit default swaps, the Bush administration failed to regulate both banking and securities markets. Concentrations of financial wealth reached near all-time highs[474] and income inequality grew as high as it had been in the 1920s.[475]

In education, the Bush focus on individual responsibility — notably high-stakes testing for students — obscured what educators have known for 100 years: the strong correlation between poverty and educational achievement. In the meantime, students' general knowledge *declined* as public schools grew worse.[476]

- *The Environment.* Rove declares that Bush withdrew from the Kyoto accords on global emissions because the treaty would have harmed the U.S. economy, and because it did not include some developing countries (241). Yet, Rove writes that under "President Bush, the nation's air, water, and land got cleaner ... environmental improvement ... moved at a faster pace than under President Clinton ... historians will conclude [Bush] was forceful and innovative about protecting the environment" (242-243).

  Indeed, Bush did establish the world's largest marine conservation in Hawaii in 2006. Otherwise, however, his environmental record manifested a different reality. In 2002-3, Bush weakened regulations governing air pollution; he redefined carbon dioxide, the primary cause of global warming, so that it was not considered a pollutant subject to regulation under the Clean Air Act; he opened millions of acres of public land in the West to oil and gas drilling; repealed the Roadless Area Conservation Rule, through which the U.S. Forest Service had sought to protect the last "wild lands" in national forests; advocated for more nuclear power plants; interfered with climate change science; and kept more than a dozen states from implementing tougher vehicle emission standards than those in federal law.[477] Rove's portrait of Bush as environmental protector contrasts with the view of the Sierra Club, which declared that Bush had "compiled one of the worst environmental records of any President in the history of the United States."[478]

- *Rove's Hit Parade.* Rove denies involvement in a number of political hits, from Texas to Washington and elsewhere. He also recalls his youthful anger at Richard Nixon for Watergate (40). But Rove omits mention of part of his basic training: He once worked with Watergate dirty trickster Donald Segretti, who went to prison for his crimes in the 1972 campaign. At the time, Rove escaped prosecution, if not brief investigation. Just a few years ago, however, he came close to indictment in the case of Valerie Plame. Rove minimizes his connection to influence peddler Jack Abramoff (63) — yet he met Abramoff in his limousine away from the White House, and failed to avoid detection.[479] Rove now indicates he's a church-going believer; yet, asked by a reporter why he'd told me that he was an agnostic, he misled the reporter about our friendship[480] — though he'd previously acknowledged our friendship in writing.

- *9/11, the War in Iraq.* Rove portrays 9/11 as an administration-defining surprise. But he acknowledges that because of presidential intelligence briefings, chief of staff Andy Card immediately suspected al-Qaeda (250). Then Rove omits certain facts: (1) the president had had a briefing that warned of attack the previous month, while he vacationed in Texas; (2) the title of the briefing memo, presented to the president Aug. 6, 2001, was "Bin Laden Determined to Attack Inside the United States;" (3) the briefing included mention that "Bin Laden ... wanted to retaliate in Washington;" that FBI information "indicates patterns of suspicious activity in this country consistent with preparations for hijackings or other types of attacks, including recent surveillance of federal buildings in New York," and that a group of bin Laden supporters were "in the U.S. planning attacks;" and (4) that twelve times in the seven years before 9/11, the CIA reported that hijackers might use airplanes as weapons.[481]

    Omitting mention of those warnings, Rove next argues that because of 9/11, Bush considered Saddam Hussein "a threat to America's national security" — and intimates that UN inspection officials Hans Blix and Mohammed el-Baradei supported the Bush view of Iraq as a mortal threat (303).

    Except that they did not. Blix told the U.N. Security Council that his agency found no evidence of weapons of mass destruction, despite 700 inspection trips to Iraq.[482] El-Baradei was convinced Iraq had not resumed its nuclear weapons program, which the International Atomic Energy Administration dismantled in 1997. Nevertheless, Bush administration officials, Blix said, "chose to ignore us."[483]

    Indeed, Vice President Cheney, Defense Secretary Rumsfeld, their staffs, and the CIA fostered the creation of intelligence to sell the Secretary of State on selling the United Nations Security Council on the war. Rove quotes Secretary of State Colin Powell's chief of staff, retired Col. Larry Wilkerson, that Powell "was convinced by what the agency and members of the IC [intelligence community] were able to present to him." (341)

But Rove neglects to mention that Wilkerson said Powell ultimately fell for a story line concocted by "a cabal between the vice president of the United States, Richard Cheney, and the secretary of defense, Donald Rumsfeld."[484] Rove, it seems, bought the story, too, as he wrote me in early March 2003.

Rove calls Democrats hypocrites for arguing that the administration lied about the war, (341), partly because they affirmed the case for war at the time. Rove omits that they were persuaded, just like Secretary Powell, on the basis of faulty intelligence the administration produced for the occasion.

Nor, Rove says, was there any torture during the war — only "EITs" (enhanced interrogation techniques) — blessed by administration attorneys (295-299). How could such an acronym violate the Geneva conventions?

Finally, Rove omits mention of the White House Iraq Group — the group through which he marketed and sold the war, illegitimately, world-wide. When it became clear that there were no WMDs, the group looked for other justifications, to shift the argument: "The world is better off without Saddam Hussein," Rove declared.

* *Rove's Book.* Just as Rove's version of the Iraq war varies from reality, so too there's variation in the framing of his memoir. Rove says his book's title refers to Bush as a man of "courage and conviction" (xvi) and "courage and consequence" (520). Yet, Rove's face dominates the book's cover and the title "Courage and Consequence: My Life as a Conservative in the Fight" obviously refers to him, not Bush.

Perhaps, in a postmodern world, one *can* have it both ways; for if we can invent our reality regardless of the facts, then journalism and history are passé. But unless one is committed to finding and expressing the truth as best one can determine it, how can one act reasonably in the world, let alone have *any* enduring and meaningful relationship?

Philosophical questions aside, having sold the war, Rove is among those responsible for 4,400 American dead in Iraq and many thousands more wounded and disabled; and hundreds and thousands of Iraqi dead, about whom Rove's book is utterly silent.

Immediately after my presentation, most of my students nodded, as if agreeing with what I'd said — even though many had seemed to agree with Rove, just before I spoke. Although they nodded in agreement with me, I suspected it was less the facts that had swayed them than the *sound* of the accumulated evidence as I delivered it. They made their judgments not on the specifics or logic of what I presented, but on how the argument *seemed* to be.

Nor are they alone. As I learned in writing this book, the reality in which we live and upon which we base our decisions every day is not just manipulable — it's utterly reversible. Our political reality has been, and continues to be, stolen.

ENDNOTES

[1] Lecture notes, Feb. 10, 1998

[2] Notes on KR and BI telephone conversation, January 20, 1998.

[3] Lecture notes, January 20 to April 28, 1998

[4] For example, Harold E. Hughes, "Hughes — Peril to Democracy in Secret Military Policies," Los Angeles Times News Service, in the *Des Moines Register*, Aug. 14, 1973, op-ed page.

[5] Chapter 22.

[6] Richard L. Berke and Fran Bruni, "Architect of Bush Presidency Still Builds Bridges of Power, *The New York Times*, February 18, 2001, 1.

[7] Philip Schlesinger, "The Sociology of Knowledge." Paper presented at a meeting of the British Sociological Association, March 24, 1972.

[8] Bill Israel, fax to Karl Rove, Jan. 8, 1998.

[9] Karl Rove, e-mail to Bill Israel, "First class meeting," Jan. 19, 1998 12:48:04 -0600

[10] Timothy Crouse, *Boys on the Bus.*(New York: Ballantine Books, 1973.

[11] Robert A. Caro, *Master of the Senate: the Years of Lyndon Johnson*, New York: Vintage Books, 2003, 115-116.

[12] "GOP Probes Official as Teacher of Tricks," *The Washington Post*, August, 13, 1973, cited in James Moore and Wayne Slater, *Bush's Brain: How Karl Rove Made George W. Bush Presidential*, Hoboken, N.J.: John Wiley and Sons, 2003, 135.

[13] David Talbot, "Creepier than Nixon," Salon Magazine, http://dir.salon.com/story/news/ feature/2004/03/31/dean/index1.html?pn=2, 2

[14] Presidential Campaign Activities of 1972, Senate Resolution 60, Hearings before the Select Committee on Presidential Campaign Activities of the United States Senate, Ninety-Third Congress, First Session, Watergate and Related Activities, Phase II: Campaign Practices, Book 11, Washington, D.C.: U.S. Government Printing Office, 1973, p. 4641.

[15] Notes on KR and BI telephone conversation, January 20, 1998.

[16] Lecture notes, January 27, 1998.

[17] Ibid.

[18] "We dog-eared Richards' book!" exclaimed Republican operative Dale Laine, to smiles from Rove. By that Laine meant that the book's careful reading was an important part of opposition research for the Bush campaign. Ibid.

[19] For campaign context, see James Moore and Wayne Slater, *Bush's Brain: How Karl Rove Made George W. Bush Presidential.* Hoboken, N.J.: John Wiley & Sons, Inc, 2003, 168; and Lou Dubose, Jan Reid, and Carl M. Cannon, *Boy Genius: Karl Rove, the Brains Behind the Remarkable Political Triumph of George W. Bush*, New York: Public Affairs, 2003, 69.

[20] Lecture notes, Feb. 10, 1998

[21] Media scholar Kathleen Hall Jamieson explains: "Visual, dramatic moments are more likely than talking heads to get news play...Indeed, as CBS's Lesley Stahl reported in 1984, the Reagan presidency pioneered the use of visuals to counter the "facts." If support for nursing homes had just been cut, one could contain the fallout by appearing with seniors in a nursing home according to Reagan logic." See Jamieson's *Dirty Politics: Deception, Distraction, and Democracy* New York: Oxford University Press, 1992, 4.

[22] Lecture notes Feb. 3, 1998.

[23] Lecture notes, Feb. 17, 1998

[24] David W. Moore, *The Superpollsters: How They Measure and Manipulate Public Opinion in America.* New York: Four Walls Eight Windows, 1995.

[25] Thomas Patterson, *Out of Order.* New York: Knopf, 1993.

[26] American Association of Public Opinion Research, " AAPOR Statement on "Push Polls," May 19, 2004; see www.aapor.org/pdfs/2004/pushpolls.pdf

[27] "A Press Warning from the National Council on Public Polls," press release, May 22, 1995; see: http://www.ncpp.org/push.htm

[28] Lecture notes, Feb. 24, 1998

[29] Television has represented a presidential campaign's single largest investment. Robert V. Friedenberg, *Communication Consultants in Political Campaigns: Ballot Box Warriors.* Westport, Conn.: Praeger, 1997, 154-155.

[30] See Jamieson. The commercial was not only highly effective, but highly misleading, as Jamieson records in Chapter 1, "Attack Campaigning."

[31] To view, see: http://www.cnn.com/ALLPOLITICS/1996/candidates/ad.archive/

[32] To view, see: http://www.cnn.com/ALLPOLITICS/1996/candidates/ad.archive/

[33] "Meet the Press," NBC Television Network, February 8, 1998.

[34] Lecture notes April 14, 1998.

[35] Garth S. Jowett and Victoria O'Donnell, *Propaganda and Persuasion.* Newbury Park, Calif.: SAGE Publications, Inc., 1986, and Garth S. Jowett and Victoria O'Donnell, *Propaganda and Persuasion.* third edition, Thousand Oaks, Calif.: SAGE Publications, Inc., 1999, 76.

[36] Tom Stites, "Is Media Performance Democracy's Critical Issue?" Speech to the Media Giraffe Conference, University of Massachusetts Amherst, June 30, 2006. Available at http://www.mediagiraffe.com/

[37] Lecture notes Feb. 3, 1998.

[38] David Halberstam, *The Best and the Brightest.* New York: Random House, 1972, 515. Cited in Peter J. Kuznick, "Scientists on the Stump," *Bulletin of the Atomic Scientists,* Vol. 60, No. 6, November/December 2004, 28-35; see: http://www.thebulletin.org/article.php?art_ofn=nd04kuznick

[39] http://en.wikipedia.org/wiki/Daisy_(television_commercial)

[40] See Kathleen Hall Jamieson, *Dirty Politics: Deception, Distraction, and Democracy.* New York: Oxford University Press, 1992, 19.

[41] According to one author, "most assume [that the ad] was actually made by the Bush campaign rather than the PAC." Kerwin C. Swint, *Mudslingers: The Top 25 Negative Political Campaigns of All Time.* Westport, Conn.: Praeger, 2006, 157.

[42] Jamieson., p.22.

[43] Researchers Robert McClure and Thomas Patterson call this "meltdown;" ibid.

[44] Ibid., 33.

[45] Swint, vii, 157.

[46] Dubose, Reid and Cannon, 142.

[47] Barbara Bradley Hagerty, "Conservative Black Clergy Make Waves from Pulpit," *All Things Considered*, April 6, 2006; available at: http://www.npr.org/templates/story/story.php?storyId=5328555

[48] Stephen Ansolabehere and Shanto Iyengar, *Going Negative: How Attack Ads Shrink and Polarize the Electorate*. New York: The Free Press, 1995. Chapter 5.

[49] Besides Jamieson and Ansolabehere and Iyengar, see, for example, James A. Thurber, Candice J. Nelson, and David A. Dulio, *Crowded Airwaves*, Washington, D.C.: Brookings Institution Press, 2000; and Richard R. Lau and Gerald M. Pomper, *Negative Campaigning: An Analysis of U.S. Senate Elections*, Lanham-Boulder-New York-Toronto-Oxford: Rowman and Littlefield Publishers, Inc.: 2004.

[50] Lecture notes March 3, 1998.

[51] Mike Allen, Ship Carrying Bush Delayed Return; Carrier That Spent Night off San Diego Could Have Gone Straight to Home Port, *Washington Post*, May 8, 2003; Page A29 http://www.washingtonpost.com/ac2/wp-dyn?pagename=article&node=&contentId=A27574-2003May7&notFound=true

[52] Tom Teepen, COMMENTARY: Carrier landing blurs military, civilian line, Cox News Service, May 8, 2003

[53] Ed Stephan, "U.S. Military Deaths in Bush's Iraq Quagmire," available at http://www.edstephan.org/USfatalities.html

[54] Casualties–Iraq Operation Iraqi Freedom, available at: http://icasualties. org/Iraq/Index.aspx

[55] Iraq Coalition Casualty Count, http://icasualties.org/oif/default.aspx; Casualties in Iraq; The Human Cost of Occupation, http://www.antiwar.com/casualties/#wounded

[56] http://www.antiwar.com/casualties/index.php#count; and Elisabeth Rosenthal, "Study Puts Iraqi Deaths of Civilians at 100,000," *International Herald Tribune*, October 29, 2004. http://www.nytimes.com/2004/10/29/international/europe/29casualties.html?ex=1175400000&en=5384eaa72019a06c&ei=5070; and Updated Iraq Survey Affirms Earlier Mortality Estimates, *Mortality Trends Comparable to Estimates by Those Using Other Counting Methods*, October 11, 2006. http://www.jhsph.edu/publichealthnews/press_releases/2006/burnham_iraq_2006.html See also: Iraq Deaths, Just Foreign Policy, http://www.justforeignpolicy.org/iraq

[57] "Democrats Continue Criticism Of Bush's Aircraft Landing," The Bulletin's Frontrunner, Bulletin Broadfaxing Network, Inc., May 9, 2003

[58] Kim Landers, "Bush Holds Back on Bold Statements on Iraq," The World Today, May 2, 2006; see: http://www.abc.net.au/worldtoday/content/2006/s1628701.htm

[59] Lecture notes, March 10, 1998.

[60] "Spin doctors" had become so ubiquitous in such events, Dave McNeely added, that "It's reached a point in which one of the reporters went up to a spin doctor and said, "Spin me!" Reporters like debates, Dave told students, because of the possibility of mistakes, because they may expose candidates on some issues, and because "You get to see the candidate actually do something" — as opposed to the steady day-to-day of contrived campaign appearances that reveal little beyond what's already known.

[61] Lecture notes, March 24, 1998.

[62] Lecture notes, April 21, 1998.

[63] Texas Monthly, July 1, 1999. http://www.texasmonthly.com/preview/1999-07-01/feature24. See also "3 from GOP vying to take on Edwards, *Bryan-College Station Eagle*, Feb. 22, 2004; http://www.theeagle.com/campaign2000/localregional/

022204congressional.htm

[64] See John W. Gonzalez, "Procedure flaw dooms abortion notification bill," *Houston Chronicle*, May 27, 1997. Available at: http://www.chron.com/cgi-bin/auth/story/content/chronicle/page1/97/05/28/fallout.html

[65] See Moore and Slater, *Bush's Brain*, Chapter 1, 19-21.

[66] Anita Miller, editor, *The Complete Transcripts of the Clarence Thomas-Anita Hill Hearings*. Chicago: Academy Chicago Publishers, 1994.

[67] Ibid.

[68] Anita Hill, *Speaking Truth to Power*, New York: Doubleday, 1997, p. 194.

[69] Miller, 76.

[70] Jane Mayer and Jill Abramson, *Strange Justice: The Selling of Clarence Thomas*. Boston/New York: Houghton Mifflin, 1994, 297.

[71] Miller, 6.

[72] David Keene interview, in Andrea Seabrook, "Republicans Turn to Blogs to Deliver a Message," All Things Considered, National Public Radio, February 18, 2005, available at: http://www.npr.org/templates/story/story.php?storyId=4504846

[73] Lecture of Feb. 3, 1998.

[74] See Herbert J. Gans, *Deciding What's News: A Study of CBS Evening News, NBC Nightly News, Newsweek, and Time*. New York: Pantheon, 1979, chapter 2.

[75] Lecture notes April 7, 1998.

[76] Anne E. Kornblut, "Post-9/11, Rove Went to Market Forms Show Card Worth at least $1M," Boston Globe, June 15, 2002, A5.

[77] "T.R.? He's No T.R.," *New York Times*, February 11, 2007; http://www.nytimes.com/2007/02/11/opinion/11sun1.html?ex=1328850000&en=8b311014eee420a6&ei=5088&partner=rssnyt&emc=rss; Robert Vandermark, "What About Teddy Roosevelt's Legacy?" *Daytona News-Journal*, February 26, 2006; http://www.net.org/editorials/teddy_roosevelt.vtml

[78] Karl Rove, "Re: your sausage," e-mail to Bill Israel, March 27, 1998 17:14:09 -0600

[79] Bill Israel, "Your sausage," e-mail to Karl Rove, Mar 30, 1998 8:45 AM

[80] Karl Rove, "RE: your sausage," e-mail to Bill Israel, March 30, 1998 13:34:56-0600

[81] Dubose, Reid and Cannon, 113-116.

[82] Karl Rove, "RE: are you there?" e-mail to Bill Israel, Mar 27, 1999 20:22:10 -0600

[83] Jowett and O'Donnell, 1986, 16.

[84] Jowett and O'Donnell, 1986, 17-18.

[85] Ibid, 24.

[86] Jowett and O'Donnell, 1999, 49.

[87] Jowett and O'Donnell, 1999, 49-50.

[88] Jowett and O'Donnell, 1999, 50-51.

[89] Jowett and O'Donnell, 1999, 53.

[90] Jowett and O'Donnell, 1999, 53.

[91] Jowett and O'Donnell, 1999, 53.

[92] Jowett and O'Donnell, 1999, 54.

[93] Jowett and O'Donnell, 1999, 59.

[94] Jowett and O'Donnell, 1999, 59.

[95] Jowett and O'Donnell, 1999, 60.

[96] Jowett and O'Donnell, 1999, 54-55.

[97] Jowett and O'Donnell, 1999, 63.

[98] Jowett and O'Donnell, 1999, 63-64.

[99] Jowett and O'Donnell, 1999, 65.

[100] Elizabeth L. Eisenstein, "Some Conjectures about the Impact of Printing on Western Society and Thought: A Preliminary Report," *Journal of Modern History 40* (1968),1-56.

[101] http://www.luther.de/en/ws.html

[102] Max Weber, "Politics as a Vocation," available at: http://www.ne.jp/asahi/moriyuki/ abukuma/weber/lecture/politics_vocation.html

[103] Jowett and O'Donnell, 1999, 72-73.

[104] Carl von Clausewitz, *On War*, ed. and trans. Michael Howard and Peter Paret. Princeton, N.J.: Princeton University Press, 1976, 184-185. Cited in William M. Darley, "War Policy, Public Support, and the Media," *Parameters 35* (Summer 2005), 126.

[105] Jowett and O'Donnell, 1999, 78.

[106] Jowett and O'Donnell, 1999, 78-79.

[107] Jowett and O'Donnell, 1999, 79.

[108] George Creel, "Propaganda and Morale," *The American Journal of Sociology*, Vol. 47, No. 3 (Nov. 1941), 344.

[109] Creel, 343, 351. "Strong and clear as the seven trumpets of rams' horns that blew before Jericho" and as essential as "a high call to the idealism that is the soul of the race."

[110] Michael Schudson, *Discovering the News*. New York: Basic Books, 1978, 132-135.

[111] James E. Pollard, *The Presidents and the Press*. New York: Octagon Books, 1973, 569-600, and John Anthony Maltese, *Spin Control: The White House Office of Communications and the Management of Presidential News*. Chapel Hill and London: The University of North Carolina Press, 1992, 4.

[112] Creel, 340.

[113] Jowett and O'Donnell, 1986, 97. Creel insisted the CIP was "at pains to avoid even the appearance of manufacturing hate. We issued no atrocity stories, such as the mutilation of women and babies, alleged crucifixions, etc. ... The temptation was there, of course, for the baser emotions are far more easily stirred than mental processes." Creel, 347.

[114] Creel, 1941, 346.

[115] George Creel, *How We Advertised America*. New York: Arno Press, 1972, 21-22.

[116] Stuart Ewen in *PR! A Social History of Spin*. New York: Basic Books, 1996, 112.

[117] The developer of this idea was Antonio Gramsci, whose work is more thoroughly explained later in chapter 12.

[118] Carl Boggs, *The Two Revolutions: Antonio Gramsci and the Dilemmas of Western Marxism*. Boston, MA.: South End Press, 1984, 161.

[119] Todd Gitlin, *The Whole World Is Watching. Mass Media in the Making and Unmaking of the New Left*. Berkeley: University of California, 1980, 10.

[120] Ewen, 111-123.

[121] Ewen, 119-121.

[122] Gibson Bell Smith,"Guarding the Railroad, Taming the Cossacks; The U.S. Army in Russia, 1918 — 1920." *Prologue*, Winter 2002, Vol. 34, No. 4. Available at: http://www.archives.gov/publications/prologue/2002/winter/us-army-in-russia-1.html, and George Creel, *War, the World and Wilson*. New York: Harper and Brothers, 1920, 205.

[123] Creel, *How We Advertised America*, ix.

[124] Jowett and O'Donnell, 1999, 163, 219-221.

[125] From Lasswell, *Propaganda Technique in the World War*, 1927, 220-221.] In Jowett and O'Donnell, 1986, 98.

[126] Creel, 1972, 16.

[127] Creel, 1972, 16-18.

[128] Creel, 1972, 24.

[129] Walter Lippmann, *Liberty and the News*, New York: Harcourt, Brace, and Howe, 1920, 56-58, 69-104.

[130] Lippmann, *Liberty and the News*, 72-94.

[131] Walter Lippmann, Public Opinion. New York: Macmillan, 1922, 158.

[132] Dante Germino, *Antonio Gramsci, Architect of a New Politics*. Baton Rouge: Louisiana State University Press, 1990, 198.

[133] Germino, xvii-xviii.

[134] Declaration of Independence, available at: http://www.archives.gov/national-archives-experience/charters/declaration_transcript.html

[135] Benedetto Fontana, *Hegemony and Power: On the Relation between Gramsci and Machiavelli*. Minneapolis: University of Minnesota Press, 1993, 140-141.

[136] Stuart Hall, "Culture, the Media and the 'Ideological Effect,'" in *Mass Communication and Society*, ed. James Curran, Michael Gurevitch, and Janet Woollacott, Beverly Hills: Sage, 1979, 314-348; cited in Gitlin, *The Whole World Is Watching*, 253.

[137] Fontana, 141.

[138] Fontana, 141.

[139] Fontana, 141.

[140] W. Lance Bennett, *News: The Politics of Illusion* (3rd edition). White Plains, N.Y.: Longman, 1996, 163. See also Section III of this book.

[141] Fontana, 141; Gitlin, 282.

[142] Walter L. Adamson, *Hegemony and Revolution. A Study of Antonio Gramsci's Political and Cultural Theory*. Berkeley: University of California Press, 1980, 236.

[143] Adamson, 231.

[144] Adamson, 226.

[145] Adamson, 207.

[146] Adamson, 207.

[147] Adamson, Chapter 7.

[148] Harold Lasswell, *Propaganda Technique in the World War*. New York: Knopf, 1927.

[149] Jowett and O'Donnell, 1986, 98-101.

[150] Jowett and O'Donnell, 1986, 101.

[151] Jowett and O'Donnell, 1999, 231-233.

[152] Jowett and O'Donnell, 1986, 102-108.

[153] Boggs, *The Two Revolutions*, 153-154.

[154] Oliver Thomson, *Mass Persuasion in History*. Edinburg: Paul Harris, 1977; cited in, Jowett and O'Donnell, 1999, 235.

[155] Jowett and O'Donnell, 1999, 237.

[156] Jowett and O'Donnell, 1986, 102-112.

[157] Ibid.

[158] Jacques Ellul, *Propaganda*. New York: Alfred A. Knopf, 1972, 3-4. Ellul specified psychology and sociology, but said that effective propaganda takes over mass communication, literature, and history, as well.

[159] Ellul, 4-6.

[160] Ibid.

[161] Ibid., 62.

[162] Ellul, 62.

[163] Ellul, 63-66.

[164] Pollard, v.

[165] Ewen, 116; Creel, *How We Advertised America*, Chapter 1.

[166] "Radio Corporation of America, U.S. Radio Company," The Museum of Broadcast Communications, http://www.museum.tv/archives/etv/R/htmlR/radiocorpora/radiocorpora.htm

[167] Franklin D. Roosevelt, Inaugural Address, March 4, 1933, as published in Samuel Rosenman, ed., *The Public Papers of Franklin D. Roosevelt, Volume Two: The Year of Crisis, 1933.* New York: Random House, 1938, 11—16; text available at http://historymatters.gmu.edu/d/5057/

[168] For example, the day after the election of Ronald Reagan in 1980, staff member David Gergen prepared a study comparing the first hundred days of every administration since FDR, that "showed that the successful presidents were those who immediately established a clear and simple agenda." Maltese, 180.

[169] "Franklin D. Roosevelt (1882-1945)," Eleanor Roosevelt National Historic Site, Hyde Park, New York http://www.nps.gov/archive/elro/glossary/roosevelt-franklin.htm

[170] The author wishes to acknowledge the importance to this part of this narrative of the work of Stuart Ewen in *PR! A Social History of Spin.* The portion of the narrative relies on p. 235.

[171] Ewen, Chapter 14.

[172] Daniel Hallin, *The Uncensored War: The Media and Vietnam.* New York: Oxford University Press, 1986, 59.

[173] Ewen, 289.

[174] Jacques Ellul, *Propaganda; the Formation of Men's Attitudes.* New York, Knopf, 1965, 66-67.

[175] Ewen, Chapter 14. A major portion of the narrative that follows is from Ewen's chapter.

[176] Ewen, 264-276.

[177] Ewen, 316.

[178] Ibid., 316-317.

[179] Ewen, 307-336, 382.

[180] Ellul, 67.

[181] Ellul, 66-67.

[182] Gilbert C. Fite, Richard B. Russell, Jr., Senator from Georgia. Chapel Hill: University of North Carolina Press, 2002, 229.

[183] Ellul, 67.

[184] Robert A. Caro, *Master of the Senate: The Years of Lyndon Johnson,* New York: Vintage Books, 2003, 248.

[185] Caro, Chapters 10-11.

[186] "Cointelpro," http://www.icdc.com/~paulwolf/cointelpro/cointel.htm

[187] Taylor Branch, *Parting the Waters, America in the King Years, 1954-63.* New York: Simon and Schuster, 1988.

[188] Mahmoud Mamdani, *Good Muslim, Bad Muslim: America, the Cold War, and the Roots of Terror.* New York: Pantheon Books, 2004.

[189] Melvin A. Goodman, "Revamping the CIA," *Issues in Science and Technology.* Dallas: National Academy of Sciences, University of Texas at Dallas, Jan. 9, 2002. Available at: http://www.issues.org/18.2/goodman.html

[190] Ibid.

[191] George Washington, "Farewell Address," 1796, http://usinfo.state.gov/usa/infousa/facts/democrac/49.htm

[192] Dwight D. Eisenhower, "Farewell Address," January 17, 1961. Available at: http://www.eisenhower.archives.gov/farewell.htm

[193] The Soviet Union lost twenty-four million people during World War II, more than the combined total wartime losses of the United States (316,000) and the United Kingdom (383,000). Josef Stalin sought to insulate the USSR from nuclear attack and settle the German question by expanding the Soviet frontier through Eastern Europe into Germany. Recognizing Western spheres of influence, Stalin told French and Italian communist parties they'd have to win at the ballot box, not under arms. David Reynolds, professor of international history, Cambridge University, United Kingdom, in "From Hot War to Cold War: A Panel Discussion," The University of Tennessee, Howard H. Baker Jr. Center for Public Policy, March 30, 2006.

[194] Hedrick Smith, *The Power Game: How Washington Works*. New York: Ballantine Books, 1989.

[195] Daniel Yergin, *Shattered Peace: The Origins of the Cold War and the National Security State*. Boston: Houghton Mifflin, 1977, 5-6.

[196] Sproule, 223.

[197] Richard A. Viguerie and David Franke, *America's Right Turn, How Conservatives Used New and Alternative Media to Take Power*, Chicago and Los Angeles: Bonus Books, 2004, 128-131.

[198] Viguerie and Franke, Chapter 8; William A. Rusher, *The Rise of the Right*. New York: William Morrow and Co., 1984; see also Rusher, *The Coming Battle for the Media: Curbing the Power of the Media Elite*. New York: William Morrow and Co., 1988.

[199] Interview with Edward Fouhy, June 30, 2006.

[200] Susan and Bill Buzenberg, eds., *Salant, CBS, and the Battle for the Soul of Broadcast Journalism: the Memoirs of Richard S. Salant*. Boulder: Westview Press, 1999, 6-7.

[201] Gladys Engel Lang and Kurt Lang, *The Battle for Public Opinion: the President, then Press, and the Polls During Watergate*. New York: Columbia University Press, 1983, 31-32.

[202] Sidney Blumenthal, *The Rise of the Counter-Establishment: from Conservative Ideology to Political Power*. New York: Times Books, 1986, 32.

[203] William E. Simon, *A Time for Truth*. New York: Reader's Digest Press ; McGraw-Hill, 1978, 229.

[204] David Brock, *The Republican Noise Machine*. New York: Crown Publishers, 2004, 43.

[205] Rusher, *The Rise of the Right*, 89-91.

[206] Richard A. Viguerie, interview June 29, 2006.

[207] Ibid.

[208] Ibid.

[209] Richard A. Viguerie, *The New Right: We're Ready to Lead.*. Falls Church, Virginia: The Viguerie Company, 1981, 34-35.

[210] Viguerie, *The New Right*, 37.

[211] Viguerie, interview June 29, 2006.

[212] Viguerie and Franke, 71.

[213] Viguerie, *The New Right*, 39.

[214] Viguerie, *The New Right*, 54.

[215] Jeff Horwitz, "My Right-Wing Degree," Salon Magazine, May 25, 2005. http://dir.salon.com/story/news/feature/2005/05/25/blackwell/print.html?pn=1

[216] Blumenthal, 42-43.

[217] Peter Steinfels, *The Neoconservatives: The Men Who Are Changing America's Politics*. New York, Simon and Schuster, 1979, 11.

[218] Ibid.

[219] Rusher, *The Coming Battle for the Media*, 48-61.

[220] The study ignored other scholarship which shows that even the biases of liberal journalists are unlikely to emerge in mainstream news because content is bounded by the training of journalists, by the routines of journalism itself, by the organizations for which journalists work (often led, in the case of newspapers, by publishers who editorialize in conservative directions), by the interests of sources and advertisers, and by the prevailing ideology — which by the late 1970s was becoming more conservative. Gans, *Deciding What's News*. See also Pamela Shoemaker and Steven Reese, *Mediating the Message: Theories of Influences on Mass Media Content*. White Plains, NY: Longman, 1991.

[221] "Our Background," The Federalist Society for Law and Public Policy, downloaded January 2, 2007, from http://www.fed-soc.org/AboutUs/ourbackground.htm

[222] David D. Kirkpatrick, "In Alito, G.O.P. Reaps Harvest Planted in '82," *The New York Times*, January 30, 2006.

[223] "Right Wing Organizations," Right Wing Watch, People for the American Way; http://www.pfaw.org/pfaw/general/default.aspx?oid=3149

[224] Eric Alterman, *What Liberal Media: The Truth about Bias and the News*. New York: Basic Books, 2003, 249-250.

[225] Tom Hamburger and Peter Wallsten, One *Party Country: the Republican Plan for Dominance in the 21st Century*. Hoboken, N.J.: John Wiley and Sons, Inc., 2006, 214-215.

[226] Karl Rove, American Enterprise Institute, May 15, 2006, transcript, *Washington Post online*. http//www.washingtonpost.com/wp-dyn/content/article/2006/05/15/AR2006051500635.html

[227] Karl Rove, Federalist Society speech, November 12, 2005. Note that date should be November 10, 2005. http://www.realclearpolitics.com/Commentary/com-11_12_05_KR.html

[228] Karl Rove, speech to The Federalist Society, November 10, 2005. Transcript Copyright 2005 Congressional Quarterly, Inc.

[229] Rusher, 36.

[230] Rusher, 36; Viguerie, *The New Right: We're Ready to Lead*. Falls Church, Va.: Viguerie Co., 1980, 42-43.

[231] Brock, 46.

[232] "Buying a Movement," Executive Summary, A Report by the People For the American Way Foundation, 1996, http://www.pfaw.org/pfaw/general/default.aspx?oid=2053

[233] Rusher,127.

[234] Viguerie, *The New Right*, 70-72.

[235] Ibid., 8.

[236] Viguerie and Franke, 135-136.

[237] John H. McManus, *Market-Driven Journalism: Let the Citizen Beware*. Thousand Oaks, Calif.: Sage, 1994; Ben H. Bagdikian, *The Media Monopoly*. Boston: Beacon, 2004.

[238] Interview with former CBS News correspondent Jackie Judd, August 29, 2006. Judd moved to the Washington Bureau of ABC News in 1987, after five years at CBS News.

[239] Interview with Charles Lewis, June 29, 2006.

[240] Viguerie and Franke, 195.

[241] Ibid., Chapter 10.

[242] Ibid.

[243] "Network TV Audience, Evening News Viewership, All Networks, November 1980 to November 2005," The State of the News Media 2006, An Annual Report on American Journalism. Project for Excellence in Journalism. http://www.stateofthenewsmedia.org/

2006/chartland.asp?id=211&ct=line&dir=&sort=&col1_box=1

[244] "Cable TV Public Attitudes, Where People Go for National/International News, Network vs. Cable," The State of the News Media 2006, An Annual Report on American Journalism. Project for Excellence in Journalism. http://www.stateofthenewsmedia.org/2006/chartland.asp?id=232&ct=line&dir=&sort=&col1_box=1&col2_box=1col3_box=1

[245] "Cable TV Audience, Cable News Daytime Average Audience, 1998-2005 by Channel," The State of the News Media 2006, An Annual Report on American Journalism. Project for Excellence in Journalism. http://www.stateofthenewsmedia.org/2006/chartland.asp?id=518&ct=line&dir=&sort=&col1_box=1&col2_box=1&col3_box=1

[246] Brock, 2.

[247] George Lakoff, *Don't Think of an Elephant! Know your Values and Frame the Debate.* White River Junction, VT.: Chelsea Green Publishing, 2004, 16.

[248] EJ Dionne, "A New Bias in the Media." *Boston Globe*, Dec. 9, 2002, A17.

[249] Andrea Seabrook, "Republicans Turn to Blogs to Deliver a Message," *All Things Considered, National Public Radio,* February 18, 2005, available at: http://www.npr.org/templates/story/story.php?storyId=4504846

[250] Theodore H. White, *Breach of Faith: the fall of Richard Nixon.* New York: Atheneum, 1975, 25-26/

[251] "A Good Leak," *Washington Post,* editorial page, April 9, 2006, B6.

[252] Bagdikian, ix-x.

[253] Brock, 10-11.

[254] "Bill Brock, the then-chairman of the Republican Party, he told me ... after the debacle of Watergate, that there was such humiliation and embarrassment nation-wide among Republicans, and they had taken such a shellacking in '74 in those midterm elections that they really, seriously, were debating changing the name of the party, cause they felt that it would be stained forever." Interview with Charles Lewis, June 29, 2006.

[255] David Plotke, *Building a Democratic Political Order: Reshaping American Liberalism in the 1930s and 1940s.* New York: Cambridge University Press, 1996.

[256] Brock, 50.

[257] Brock, 49-51.

[258] Telephone interview with E. J. Dionne, August 7, 2006.

[259] Jeff Horwitz, "My Right Wing Degree," Salon.com, May 25, 2005. http://dir.salon.com/story/news/feature/2005/05/25/blackwell/print.html; James Moore and Wayne Slater, Bush's Brain: How Karl Rove Made George W. Bush Presidential," Hoboken, N.J.: John Wiley and Sons, 2003, 129-130; Lou Dubose, Jan Reid and Carl M. Cannon, *Boy Genius.* New York: Public Affairs, 2003, 9-10.

[260] James Ridgeway, "Grime Pays: Boy Makes Bad; a Karl Rove Chronological Tour, Making All Local Stops," *Village Voice,* July 19, 2005. http://www.villagevoice.com/news/0529,ridgeway,66005,6.html

[261] Presidential Campaign Activities of 1972, Senate Resolution 60, Hearings before the Select Committee on Presidential Campaign Activities of the United States Senate, Ninety-Third Congress, First Session, Watergate and Related Activities, Phase II: Campaign Practices, Book 11, Washington, D.C.: U.S. Government Printing Office, 1973, 4635-4638.

[262] "GOP Probes Official as Teacher of Tricks," *The Washington Post,* August, 13, 1973, cited in James Moore and Wayne Slater, *Bush's Brain:* 135.

[263] Moore and Slater, *Bush's Brain,* 26.

[264] Dubose, *Boy Genius,* 12.

[265] David Talbot, "Creepier than Nixon," Salon Magazine, http://dir.salon.com/story/news/feature/2004/03/31/dean/index1.html?pn=2, 2

[266] Dubose, *Boy Genius*, 12.

[267] Presidential Campaign Activities of 1972, 4635-4638.

[268] Moore and Slater, *Bush's Brain*, 139.

[269] Dubose, *Boy Genius*, 21.

[270] Moore and Slater, 148.,

[271] Dubose, *Boy Genius*, 42.

[272] Ibid. 38-41.

[273] Moore and Slater, *Bush's Brain*, 27.

[274] Moore and Slater, *Bush's Brain*, 53; interview with Wayne Slater, Feb. 23, 2007.

[275] Ibid., 31-59.

[276] Moore and Slater, *Bush's Brain*, 87-89.

[277] Dubose, *Boy Genius*, 44.

[278] Ibid., 44-45.

[279] Moore and Slater, *Bush's Brain*, Chapter 5.

[280] Ibid., 173-182.

[281] Wayne Slater, "Rivals Again Fault Bush Over Rumors; Governor and Aides Deny Starting, Spreading Rumors," *Dallas Morning News*, December 2, 1999, reprinted in Moore and Slater, *Bush's Brain*, 25-27.

[282] Moore and Slater, *Bush's Brain*, 196.

[283] Dubose, *Boy Genius*, 72.

[284] Moore and Slater, Bush's Brain, 225-226.

[285] Dubose, Reid, and Cannon, 101-102.

[286] Steve Barnes, "National Briefing | Southwest: Texas: Prison For Ex-Official," Nov. 1, 2003, http://query.nytimes.com/gst/fullpage.html?res=9C05EEDB1330F932A35752C1A9659C8B63&n=Top%2fReference%2fTimes%20Topics%2fPeople%2fM%2fMorales%2c%20Dan

[287] Moore and Slater, *Bush's Brain*, 228.

[288] John W. Dean, *Worse than Watergate: the Secret Presidency of George W. Bush*. New York: Little, Brown and Co., 2004.

[289] Edward Epstein, "Colleagues cool to Feingold's bid to censure Bush, But Watergate figure John Dean says action could prevent abuses of power," *San Francisco Chronicle*, April 1, 2006, http://www.sfgate.com/cgi-bin/article.cgi?file=/c/a/2006/04/01/MNGTRI1V221.DTL

[290] Moore and Slater, *Bush's Brain*, 25.

[291] Dubose, Reid, and Cannon, 140.

[292] Dubose, Reid, and Cannon, 142-143.

[293] Moore and Slater, *Bush's Brain*, 14-15; see also John Antigua, "Miami's rent-a-riot. Remember last week's ugly protest of the hand recount? Aalen all over? Guess again — Washington GOP operatives were running this circus." *Salon*. http://archive.salon.com/politics/feature/2000/11/28/miami/index.html; and Al Kamen, "Miami 'Riot' Squad: Where Are They Now?" *Washington Post*, Jan. 24, 2005; A13. www.washingtonpost.com/wp-dyn/articles/A31074-2005Jan23.html. Participant Joel Kaplan dubbed the event the "Brooks Brothers Riot," and he became a White House policy adviser; Matt Schlapp became White House political director; Garry Malphrus became deputy director of the White House Domestic Policy Council; and Rory Cooper worked at the White House Homeland Security Council and the Presidential Inaugural Committee.

[294] On Jan. 18, 2002, Rove appeared to tell GOP handlers to exploit Bush's war in Afghanistan for the fall election. "We can go to the country on this issue because they trust the Republican Party to do a better job of protecting and strengthening America's military might and thereby protecting America." Dubose, Reid, and Cannon, 216.

[295] Bob Woodward, *State of Denial: Bush at War, Part III*. New York: Simon and Schuster, 2006, 49-52.

[296] Ron Suskind, *The One Percent Doctrine: Deep Inside America's Pursuit of its Enemies since 9/11*. New York: Simon and Schuster, 2006, 2.

[297] James Moore and Wayne Slater, *The Architect: Karl Rove and the Master Plan for Absolute Power*. New York: Crown, 2006, 89-91, 217.

[298] Moore and Slater, *The Architect*, 39.

[299] E-mail, Bill Israel to Karl Rove, Friday, May 25, 2001, 00:54:00, "Subject: retirement, anyone?"

[300] E-mail, Karl Rove to Bill Israel, Saturday, May 26, 2001 10:32:42, "Subject: Re: retirement, anyone?"

[301] B'tselem, the Israeli Information Center for Human Rights in the occupied territories; http://www.btselem.org/English/Statistics/Casualties.asp.

[302] Bob Woodward, *Plan of Attack*. New York: Simon and Schuster, 2004, 9.

[303] Ron Suskind, *The One Percent Doctrine*. New York: Simon and Schuster, 2006, 1-2.

[304] Thomas E. Ricks, *Fiasco: the American Military Adventure in Iraq*. New York: Penguin, 2006, 30.

[305] Ricks, 38.

[306] Craig Unger, "The War They Wanted, the Lies They Needed," *Vanity Fair*, July 2006: 92.

[307] Ricks, 55.

[308] James Moore and Wayne Slater, *The Architect: Karl Rove and the Master Plan for Absolute Power*. New York: Crown, 2006, 204.

[309] Ricks, 52-54.

[310] Sam Gardiner, *Truth from These Podia: Summary of a Study of Strategic Influence, Perception Management, Strategic Information Warfare and Strategic Psychological Operations in Gulf II* (October 8, 2003), 51. Downloaded from *U.S. News and World Report* web-site: http:// www.usnews.com/usnews/politics/whispers/documents/ truth_1.pdf+Gardiner+and+%22Truth+from+these+Podia%22&hl=en&gl=us&ct=cln k&cd=1&client=safari. See also: Michael Isikoff and David Corn, *Hubris: the Inside Story of Spin, Scandal, and the Selling of the Iraq War*. New York: Crown, 2006, 29.

[311] Isikoff and Corn, 29.

[312] Ricks, 54.

[313] Ricks, 51.

[314] "Top Bush officials push case against Saddam," Late Night Edition with Wolf Blitzer, CNN, September 8, 2002. http://archives.cnn.com/2002/ALLPOLITICS/09/08/ iraq.debate/index.html

[315] Michael Gordon and Judith Miller, "U.S. Says Hussein Intensified Quest for A-Bomb Parts," *The New York Times*, September 8, 2002, 1.

[316] The Editors, "The Times and Iraq," *The New York Times*, May 26, 2004, A10.

[317] Ibid.

[318] Ibid.

[319] Howard Kurtz, "The Post on WMDs: An Inside Story; Prewar Articles Questioning Threat Often Didn't Make Front Page," *Washington Post*, August 12, 2004, A1.

[320] Ibid.

321 Ibid.

322 Christoffer Carstanjen.

323 Bill Israel, "A policy of neglect and cowardice, a pay-off of death," *Massachusetts Daily Collegian*, September 12, 2001.; available at: http://works.bepress.com/bill_israel/

324 Bill Israel, "Attacks were the predictable result of American policy," *Boston Globe*, Sept. 13, 2001, A29.

325 Israel, "A policy of neglect."

326 E-mail, Bill Israel to Karl Rove, "Subject: learning from the opposition?" Friday, September 14, 2001, 21:31:14.

327 Lucianne.com post as downloaded from the site September 16, 2001: http://works.bepress.com/bill_israel/ The full document, including 20 pages of ensuing posts, are no longer publicly available at Lucianne.com.

328 Chapter 9.

329 http://www.freerepublic.com/focus/f-news/524487/posts

330 James Taranto, "Journalism profs against America," in *WSJ.com Opinion Journal from the Wall Street Journal*, http:///works.bepress.com/bill_israel/

331 See partial, abbreviated directory of comments downloaded Sept. 19, 2001 at the end of the *Collegian* op-ed, at: http://works.bepress.com/bill_israel. Full list not migrated to http://www.dailycollegian.com/

332 University administrations have a long history of failing to support the First Amendment rights of professors. See David Demers, *The Last Professor of the Enlightenment: An American Odyssey* (unpublished book manuscript, 2011).

333 People for the American Way, "Right Wing Watch," "Right Wing Organizations," "Collegiate Network," http://www.pfaw.org/pfaw/general/default.aspx?oid=16241

334 http://www.isi.org/cn/members/papers.aspx

335 The Collegiate Network has received at this writing, from the years 1995-2005, $5.8 million in grants from conservative foundations such as the Sarah Scaife Foundation, the Lynde and Harry Bradley Foundation, the Kirby Foundation, Carthage Foundation, and the John M. Olin Foundation, among others. "Right Wing Watch, Right Wing Organizations, Collegiate Network," http://www.pfaw.org/pfaw/general/default.aspx?oid=16241#5

336 T. Kenneth Cribb, Jr., http://www.isi.org/about/our_leadership/leadership.html

337 Paul Hollander, "The Resilience of the Adversary Culture." The *National Interest*, Summer, 2002; available at: http://www.findarticles.com/p/articles/mi_m2751/is_2002_Summer/ai_87720938/pg_1

338 Christopher Chow, "Student Panel Discusses Campus Reaction to 9/11," Accuracy in Academia.org; http://www.academia.org/campus_reports/2002/summer_2002_5.html

339 "Watch: Covering the War on Terror,"http://watch.windsofchange.net/themes_14.htm

340 Thomas D. Segel, "Those Seeking a "Liberal" Education Often Receive A "Radical" One Instead," Washington Dispatch, http://www.freerepublic.com/focus/f-news/892829/posts

341 Moore and Slater, *Bush's Brain*, 270-271.

342 Gardiner, 11.

343 Gardiner, 27.

344 John Kampfner, "Saving Private Lynch story 'flawed,'" BBC Online, May 15, 2003. http://news.bbc.co.uk/2/hi/programmes/correspondent/3028585.stm

345 Ibid.

346 "Psssst . . . Can I Get a Bomb Trigger?" (chart) Week in Review, *The New York Times*, Sept. 15, 2002.

347 Gardiner, 29.

[348] Gardiner, 29.

[349] Gardiner, 30.

[350] Ibid.

[351] Ibid.

[352] Ibid., 28-32.

[353] Ibid., 34-36.

[354] James Gordon Meek, Kenneth R. Bazinet, and Thomas M. DeFrank, "Hit Squad: White House Group Targeted Iraq Policy Critics," *New York Daily News*, reprinted in *Pittsburgh Post-Gazette*, October 20, 2005, A-10.

[355] Barton Gellman, "A Leak, Then a Cascade; Did a Bush loyalist overstep the bounds in protecting the administration's case for war in Iraq and obstruct an investigation?" *Washington Post*, October 30, 2005, A1.

[356] Ibid.

[357] Thomas M. DeFrank, "Bush Whacked Rove on CIA Leak," *New York Daily News*, Oct. 19, 2005, 10.

[358] Indictment, Count 1 (Obstruction of Justice), *United States of America v. I. Lewis Libby*, 7. http://www.usdoj.gov/usao/iln/osc/documents/libby_indictment_28102005.pdf

[359] Walter Pincus, "Anonymous Sources: Their Use in a Time of Prosecutorial Interest," *Nieman Reports*, July 6, 2005. http://www.niemanwatchdog.org/index.cfm?fuseaction= Showcase.view&showcaseid=0019

[360] Matthew Cooper, Massimo Calabresi, and John F. Dickerson, "A War on Wilson?" *Time*, July 17, 2003.http://www.time.com/time/nation/article/0,8599,465270,00.html

[361] Daniel Hallin, *The Uncensored War: The Media and Vietnam*. New York: Oxford University, 1986, 158, 265.

[362] http://www.usatoday.com/news/world/iraq/2006-10-10-iraq-dead_x.htm

[363] Lippmann, *Liberty and the News*, 39-40.

[364] W. Lance Bennett, Regina G. Lawrence, and Steven Livingston, "None Dare Call it Torture," *Journal of Communication* 56. no.3 (September 2006): 482.

[365] "Politics" lecture notes, February 3, 1998, chapter 1.

[366] Deepa Kumar, review of *War, Media, and Propaganda*, Yahya R. Kamalipour and Nancy Snow, eds., in *Journalism Educator* 61, no.2 (Summer 2006): 216-218.

[367] Donald L. Shaw, "The Rise and Fall of American Mass Media: Roles of Technology and Leadership." Second annual Roy W. Howard Lecture. Bloomington, IN: the Roy W. Howard Project, School of Journalism, Indiana University, 1991, 1-40.

[368] Barry Vacker, "Global Village or World Bazaar?" In Alan B. Albarran, David H. Goff, Understanding the Web: Social, Political, and Economic Dimensions of the Internet. Ames, Iowa: Blackwell, 2003, Chapter 10.

[369] Philip Meyer interview, June 30, 2006.

[370] In a related offshoot, Philip Meyer noted in his book, *Vanishing Newspapers*, that Richard Maisel in 1972 observed a proliferation of specialized media, with specialized points of view. Moreover, the American Society of Newspaper Editors in 1996 began to distance itself from the idea of objectivity. See also William Lawrence Israel, *Ritual Killings? American Journalism and the Treatment of Dissent*, doctoral dissertation, University of Texas at Austin, 1999, Chapter 1, p. 8.

[371] Thomas forthrightly outlined her views in her remarks for this book, and in her own book, *Watchdogs of Democracy? The Waning Washington Press Corps and How It Has Failed the Public*. New York: Lisa Drew/Scribner, 2006.

[372] Viguerie interview, June 29, 2006.

[373] Press interview, July 18, 2006.

[374] Lewis interview, June 29, 2006.
[375] Ibid.
[376] Fouhy interview, June 30, 2006.
[377] Meyer interview, June 30, 2006. See also Philip Meyer, "Journalism Must Evolve — and Quickly; Science Provides a Model, with Objectivity at its Heart,"*USA Today*, September 23, 2004, 21A. http://www.usatoday.com/educate/college/careers/journalism/articles/J9-23-04.ht
[378] Porter interview, June 30, 2006.
[379] Chris Daly interview, June 28, 2006.
[380] Doyle McManus interview, July 11, 2006.
[381] Thomas Edsall interview, July 14, 2006.
[382] "*Wash. Post* Published Four Op-eds Attacking Prosecution and Trial of Libby, None Supporting Them," Media Matters for America, February 21, 2007 6:02pm EST, http://mediamatters.org/items/200702210007
[383] Jack Nelson interview, July 15, 2006.
[384] Barbara Matusow interview, July 15, 2006.
[385] Broder interview, July 17, 2006.
[386] Linda Wertheimer interview, July 17, 2006.
[387] Brodeur interview, June 29, 2006.
[388] Kornblut interview, July 22, 2006.
[389] Rosenstiel interview, June 28, 2006.
[390] Green interview, September 15, 2006.
[391] Pincus interview, July 18, 2006.
[392] Thomas interview, June 29, 2006.
[393] Judd interview, August 29, 2006.
[394] Lenert interview, June 29, 2006.
[395] Dionne interview, August 7, 2006.
[396] Daly interview, June 28, 2006.
[397] Fouhy, ibid.
[398] McManus first pointed up the practice. Mathews then elaborated his intentions and his public advocacy of the practice. E-mail, Jay Mathews to Bill Israel, "Re: Doyle McManus," December 26, 2006.
[399] E-mail, Doyle McManus to Bill Israel, January 15, 2007.
[400] Nelson interview, July 15, 2006.
[401] Brodeur, ibid.
[402] Bhatia interview, June 29, 2006.
[403] Steve Fox interview, June 30, 2006.
[404] Dan Froomkin interview, July 15, 2006.
[405] Ibid.
[406] Broder interview, ibid.
[407] Meyer interview, ibid.
[408] Porter interview, June 30, 2006.
[409] Doyle McManus interview, July 11, 2006.
[410] Walter Pincus, "Corruption Cited in Iraq's Oil Industry," *Washington Post*, July 17, 2006, A12.
[411] Walter Pincus, "Detainees Used Al-Qaeda Prison Manual, Report Says, Washington Post, July 20, 2006," A12.
[412] Pincus interview, July 18, 2006.
[413] E-mail, Walter Pincus to Bill Israel, August 12, 2007.
[414] Pincus interview, ibid.
[415] McManus interview, ibid.

[416] Tumulty interview, July 17, 2006.

[417] Kornblut interview, ibid.

[418] Thomas Edsall interview, July 14, 2006.

[419] Rosenstiel interview, ibid.

[420] Lenert interview, ibid.

[421] Viguerie interview, ibid.

[422] Froomkin interview, ibid.

[423] Eric Boehlert, "The President Ought to Be Ashamed," Salon.com, November 21, 2003, 3. http://dir.salon.com/story/news/feature/2003/11/21/cleland/index_np.html

[424] Wertheimer interview, ibid.

[425] Lewis interview, ibid.

[426] Green interview, ibid.

[427] Dionne interview, ibid.

[428] See as an evaluation model: Avedis Donabedian, *An Introduction to Quality Assurance in Health Care.* New York: Oxford University Press, 2003, chapter 4.

[429] Meyer, interview, June 30, 2006.

[430] McManus interview, July 11, 2006.

[431] Lewis interview, June 29, 2006.

[432] Green interview, September 15, 2006.

[433] McManus interview, July 11, 2006.

[434] Daly interview, June 28, 2006; Brodeur interview, June 29, 2006.

[435] Lewis interview, June 29, 2006. "The Plame affair is the story of South Carolina, again: smearing and trying to destroy dissidents who are criticizing the president and the White House. And here is Karl Rove, caught red-handed, trying to smear, and possibly break federal laws." See chapter 11.

[436] Ibid.

[437] Brodeur interview, June 29, 2006; chapter 10.

[438] Sussman interview, January 19, 2007; chapter 10.

[439] Tumulty interview, July 17, 2006.

[440] Meyer interview, Ibid.

[441] Katharine Q. Seelye, "Often Isolated, Whitman Quits as E.P.A. Chief," *New York Times,* May 21, 2003, 1.

[442] Author's notes from a speech by Grover Norquist at Nielson Library, Smith College, Northampton, Massachusetts, November 4, 2005. See also Bill Israel, "Democracy Under Siege," *Daily Hampshire Gazette,* Northampton, Mass., January 30, 2006, 4.

[443] See Rove's discussion of "demagnetizing issues," chapter 2.

[444] See Rove's discussion of "demagnetizing issues," chapter 2.

[445] Ron Suskind, "Without a Doubt," *New York Times Magazine,* October 17, 2004, 44.

[446] Jean Baudrillard, "The Ecstasy of Communication," in C. Jencks, ed., *The Post Modern Reader.* London: Academy Editions; New York: St. Martin's, 1992.

[447] Conversations with Barry Vacker, Temple University, 2006-2007.

[448] See, for example, Sidney Blumenthal, "Generation Dem: Beyond the failure of Karl Rove, the momentous 2006 elections signaled the emergence of a younger, bluer America that could reshape politics for years to come," *Salon.com,* Nov. 30, 2006; http://www.salon.com/opinion/blumenthal/2006/11/30/2006_election_trends/, and Adam Nagourney and Megan Thee, "G.O.P. Voters Voice Anxieties On Party's Fate," *New York Times,* March 13, 2007, 1.

[449] Democrats would do well to remember Rove's debate dictum: "Lower your expectations of how you'll perform, no matter how good you are," chapter 3.

[450] J. Herbert Altschull, *Agents of Power: the Media and Public Policy.* White Plains, NY: Longman, 1995.

[451] Peter Baker, "Rove Remains Steadfast in the Face of Criticism," *Washington Post*, November 12, 2006, 1.

[452] See, for example, Richard A. Viguerie, *Conservatives Betrayed: How George W. Bush and Other Big Government Republicans Hijacked the Conservative Cause.* Los Angeles: Bonus Books, 2006.

[453] Nagourney and Thee, March 13, 2007, 1.

[454] Author's notes from a speech by Grover Norquist at Nielson Library, Smith College, Northampton, Massachusetts, November 4, 2005. See also Bill Israel, "Democracy Under Siege," *Daily Hampshire Gazette*, Northampton, Mass., Jan. 30, 20006, 4.

[455] Ibid.

[456] Mark Hugo Lopez, "The Hispanic Vote in the 2008 Election," The Pew Hispanic Center, November 5, 2008, updated November 7, 2008. Downloaded May 31, 2009.

[457] "Rove Thanks Republican Lawyers for Their Work on 'Clean Elections,'" Raw Story.com, April 10, 2006, http://www.rawstory.com/news/2006/ Rove_thanks_Republican_lawyers_for_their_0410.html ; C-SPAN appears not to have archived the speech.

[458] Brad Friedman, "Phony GOP 'Voting Rights' Group Delivers Onslaught of Disinfo Today!," August 2, 2005, http://www.bradblog.com/?p=1651.

[459] Ronald Kessler, "One More Deep Throat Rendezvous," *Newsmax.com*, Jan. 10, 2007, http://www.newsmax.com/archives/articles/2007/1/9/180126.shtml

[460] Joshua Micah Marshall, Talking Points Memo, Nov. 5, 2005; http://www.talkingpointsmemo.com/archives/006933.php

[461] Thomas Beaumont, "Ads hurt Kerry bid, split vets in Iowa," *The Des Moines Register*, Sunday, Aug. 29, 2004, 1.

[462] Bill Israel, unpublished letter to the editor, *Des Moines Register*, August 29, 2004.

[463] Walter Lippmann, "News, Truth, and a Conclusion," Chapter 24, *Public Opinion.* New York: Macmillan, 1922/1965), 226-229.

[464] William Shakespeare, *Macbeth*, Act I, Scene III.

[465] Executive Summary, "Voting Irregularities in Florida During the 2000 Presidential Election," http://www.usccr.gov/pubs/vote2000/report/exesum.htm

[466] S. Mitra Kalita, "Americans See 18% of Wealth Vanish." *Wall Street Journal*, March 13, 2009; http://online.wsj.com/article/SB123687371369308675.html; downloaded March 23, 2010.

[467] Jeff Bater, Dow Jones Newswires, "US Household Net Worth Rises Third Straight Quarter," Fox Business News, March 11, 2010, http://www.foxbusiness.com/story/ markets/industries/real-estate/update-household-net-worth-rises-straight-quarter/; downloaded March 23, 2010.

[468] See "Economic Research, Federal Reserve Bank of St. Louis," available at: http://research.stlouisfed.org/fred2/; downloaded March 23, 2010.

[469] "Industry News: U.S. Foreclosure Rates Surge as Unemployment Continues to Rise," American Banking News, October 28, 2009. http://www.americanbankingnews.com/ 2009/10/28/u-s-foreclosure-rates-surge-as-unemployment-continues-to-rise/; downloaded March 23, 2010.

[470] St. Petersburg Times, http://www.politifact.com/truth-o-meter/statements/2010/mar/02/ hillary-clinton/greenspan-gave-approval-tax-cuts-only-if-deficits-/; downloaded March 23, 2010.

[471] "Uncharted Waters," chart of Federal Budget Deficit as a Percent of GDP. http://www.powerlineblog.com/archives/assets_c/2009/01/Deficit%20Chart.php; downloaded March 23, 2010.

[472] Kathy Ruffing and James R. Horney, "Where Today's Large Deficits Come From: Economic Downturn, Financial Rescues, and Bush-Era Policies Drive the Numbers." Center on Budget and Policy Priorities, Revised February 17, 2010. http://www.cbpp.org/cms/index.cfm?fa=view&id=3036 downloaded March 23, 2010.

[473] Bill Fleckenstein, "Voodoo debt and the coming recession." Contrarian Chronicles, MSN Money, Sept. 25, 2006. http://articles.moneycentral.msn.com/Investing/ ContrarianChronicles/VoodooDebtAndTheComingRecession.aspx; downloaded March 23, 2010; and Robert Pear, "Bush Directive Increases Sway on Regulation," *New York Times*, January 30, 2007. http://www.nytimes.com/2007/01/30/washington/30rules.html downloaded March 23, 2010.

[474] G. William Domhoff, "Wealth, Income, and Power," September 2005 (updated February 2010). http://sociology.ucsc.edu/whorulesamerica/power/wealth.html downloaded March 23, 2010.

[475] Kenneth F. Scheve and Matthew J. Slaughter, "A New Deal for Globalization." Foreign Affairs, July–August, 2007, 1-2; cited in Tom Juravich, *At the Altar of the Bottom Line: the Degradation of Work in the 21st Century*. Amherst and Boston: The University of Massachusetts Press, 2009.

[476] Diane Ravitch, former assistant secretary of education to President George H.W. Bush, *The Death and Life of the Great American School System: How Testing and Choice Are Undermining Education*. New York: Basic Books, 2010.

[477] "The Bush Environmental Legacy: 9 Landmark Decisions." PBS' "NOW." Week of Feb. 22, 2008. http://www.pbs.org/now/shows/408/legacy.html downloaded March 23, 2010.

[478] Pressroom, "Profile: George W. Bush." The Sierra Club. http://www.sierraclub.org/ pressroom/presidential_endorsement/profile_bush.asp downloaded March 23, 2010.

[479] James Moore and Wayne Slater. *The Architect: Karl Rove and the Master Plan for Absolute Power*. New York: Crown, 2006; and Kate Klonick, "House Committee Report: Abramoff Through Rove Influenced White House Policy," TPM Muckraker, June 9, 2008. http://tpmmuckraker.talkingpointsmemo.com/2008/06/ house_committee_report_rove_ti.php downloaded March 23, 2010.

[480] Michael Getler, "The Gift That Keeps on Giving," The Ombudsman Column, August 24, 2007 http://www.pbs.org/ombudsman/2007/08/the_gift_that_keeps_on_giving.html downloaded March 23, 2010.

[481] Bill Moyers Journal, PBS, September 14, 2007. http://www.pbs.org/ moyers/journal/09142007/transcript1.html downloaded March 24, 2010.

[482] Newsmaker: Hans Blix, PBS Newshour, March 17, 2004. http://www.pbs.org/newshour/ bb/international/jan-june04/blix_3-17.html downloaded March 24, 2010.

[483] "U.S. Iraq war wasn't justified, U.N. weapons experts say." CNN.com, March 22, 2004. http://www.cnn.com/2004/US/03/21/iraq.weapons/ downloaded March 24, 2010.

[484] Brian Knowlton, "Former Powell Aide Says Bush Policy Is Run by 'Cabal,'" *New York Times* online, October 21, 2005. http://www.nytimes.com/2005/10/21/politics/ 21wilkerson.html downloaded March 24, 2010.

BIBLIOGRAPHY

Adamson, Walter L. *Hegemony and Revolution: A Study of Antonio Gramsci's Political and Cultural Theory.* Berkeley Calif.: University of California Press, 1980.

Allen, Mike."Anti-Taliban Drive Centers on Role of Women; White House Campaign Highlights Regime's Mistreatment; First Lady to Address Nation," *Washington Post*, November 16, 2001, A34.

_____. "Ship Carrying Bush Delayed Return; Carrier That Spent Night off San Diego Could Have Gone Straight to Home Port," *Washington Post*, May 8, 2003, A29. Available at: http://www.washingtonpost.com/ac2/wp-dyn?pagename=article&node=&contentId=A27574-2003May7&notFound=true

Alterman, Eric. *What Liberal Media?: The Truth about Bias and the News.* New York: Basic Books, 2003.

Altschull, J. Herbert. *Agents of Power: the Media and Public Policy.* White Plains, NY: Longman, 1995.

American Association of Public Opinion Research, "AAPOR Statement on "Push Polls," May 19, 2004. Available at: www.aapor.org/pdfs/2004/pushpolls.pdf.

Ansolabehere, Stephen and Shanto Iyengar. *Going Negative: How Attack Ads Shrink and Polarize the Electorate.* New York: The Free Press, 1995.

Associated Press. "Bush Sidesteps Away From Far Right Causes, Touts His Independence," *St. Louis Post-Dispatch*, May 26, 200, A15.

"Homo Narrans: Story-telling in Mass Culture and Everyday Life," *Journal of Communication* 35, no. 4 (1985), 73.

Bagdikian, Ben H. *The Media Monopoly.* Boston: Beacon Press, 2004.

_____. *The New Media Monopoly.* Boston: Beacon Press, 2004.

Baker, Peter. "Rove Remains Steadfast in the Face of Criticism," *Washington Post*, November 12, 2006, 1.

Beaumont, Thomas. "Ads Hurt Kerry Bid, Split Vets in Iowa," *The Des Moines Register*, Sunday, Aug. 29, 2004, 1.

Bennett, W. Lance. *News: The Politics of Illusion*. Third edition. White Plains, N.Y.: Longman, 1996.

_____, Regina G. Lawrence, and Steven Livingston, "None Dare Call it Torture," *Journal of Communication* 56. no.3 (September 2006), 482.

Berke, Richard L. and Fran Bruni, "Architect of Bush Presidency Still Builds Bridges of Power," *New York Times*, February 18, 2001 Sunday, 1.

Bernays, Edward L. *Propaganda*. New York: Horace Liveright, 1928.

_____. *Public Relations*. Norman, Okla.: University of Oklahoma Press, 1952.

Blumenthal, Sidney. *The Rise of the Counter-Establishment: From Conservative Ideology to Political Power*. New York: Times Books, 1986.

Boehlert, Eric "The President Ought to Be Ashamed," Salon.com, November 21, 2003, 3. http://dir.salon.com/story/news/feature/2003/11/21/cleland/index_np.html

Boggs, Carl. *The Two Revolutions: Antonio Gramsci and the Dilemmas of Western Marxism*. Boston, MA.: South End Press, 1984.

Branch,Taylor. *Parting the Waters, America in the King Years, 1954-63*. New York: Simon and Schuster, 1988.

Breed, Warren "The Mass Media and Socio-Cultural Integration," *Social Forces* 37, no.1 (1958/59), 109/116.

_____. "Social Control in the Newsroom: A Functional Analysis." *Social Forces* 33, no. 4 (May 1955) 326-335.

Brock, David. *The Republican Noise Machine*. New York: Crown Publishers, 2004.

"Buying a Movement," Executive Summary, A Report by the People For the American Way Foundation, 1996, http://www.pfaw.org/pfaw/general/default.aspx?oid=2053

Buzenberg, Susan and Bill, eds., *Salant, CBS, and the Battle for the Soul of Broadcast Journalism: The Memoirs of Richard S. Salant*. Boulder, Colo.: Westview Press, 1999.

"Cable TV Audience, Cable News Daytime Average Audience, 1998-2005 by Channel," The State of the News Media 2006, An Annual Report on American Journalism. Project for Excellence in Journalism. http://www.stateofthenewsmedia.org/2006/chartland.asp?id=518&ct=line&dir=&sort=&col1_box=1&col2_box=1&col3_box=1

"Cable TV Public Attitudes, Where People Go for National/International News, Network vs. Cable," *The State of the News Media 2006*, Annual Report on American Journalism. Project for Excellence in Journalism. http://www.stateofthenewsmedia.org/2006/chartland.asp?id=232&ct=line&dir=&sort=&col1_box=1&col2_box=1col3_box=1

Casualties of War: The Human Cost of Occupation, http://www.antiwar.com/ casualties/#wounded

Carlyle, Thomas. *On Heroes and Hero Worship.* London: Oxford University Press, 1846, 1963.

Caro, Robert A. *Master of the Senate: the Years of Lyndon Johnson,* New York: Vintage Books, 2003.

Cater, Douglass. *The Fourth Branch of Government.* Boston: Houghton Mifflin, 1959.

Chow, Christopher. "Student Panel Discusses Campus Reaction to 9/11," Accuracy in Academe.org; http://www.academia.org/campus_reports/2002/ summer_2002_5.html

Clausewitz, Carl von. *On War,* 1832. Reprint ed. and trans. Michael Howard and Peter Paret. Princeton, N.J.: Princeton University Press, 1976.

CNN.com "War in Iraq: Forces: U.S. & Coalition/Casualties, available at: http://www.cnn.com/SPECIALS/2003/iraq/forces/casualties/

Cohen, Stuart and Jock Young, eds. *The Manufacture of News: Social Problems, Deviance and the Mass Media,* revised edition. Beverly Hills: Sage, 1974.

"Cointelpro," http://www.icdc.com/~paulwolf/cointelpro/cointel.htm

Cook, Timothy E. *Governing with the News. The News Media as a Political institution,* Chicago: University of Chicago Press, 1998.

Cranberg, Gilbert, Randall Bezanson, and John Soloski. *Taking Stock: Journalism and the Publicly Traded Newspapers Company.* Ames: Iowa State University Press, 2001.

Creel, George. "Propaganda and Morale," *The American Journal of Sociology* 47, no. 3 (Nov. 1941), 340.

_____. *How We Advertised America.* 1920. Reprint, New York: Arno Press, 1972.

_____. *War, the World and Wilson.* New York: Harper and Brothers, 1920.

Curran, James, Michael Gurevitch and Janet Woollacott, eds. *Mass Communication and Society.* Beverly Hills: Sage, 1979.

Darley, William M. "War Policy, Public Support, and the Media," *Parameters 35,* Summer 2005, 126.

Declaration of Independence, available at: http://www.archives.gov/national-archives-experience/charters/declaration_transcript.html

"Democrats Continue Criticism Of Bush's Aircraft Landing," *Bulletin's Frontrunner,* Bulletin Broadfaxing Network, Inc., May 9, 2003.

Dionne, E. J. "A New Bias in the Media," *Boston Globe,* Dec. 9, 2002, A17.

Dubose, Lou, Jan Reid, and Carl M. Cannon. *Boy Genius: Karl Rove, the Brains Behind the Remarkable Political Triumph of George W. Bush.* New York: Public Affairs, 2003.

Eisenhower, Dwight D. "Farewell Address," January 17, 1961. Available at: http://www.eisenhower.archives.gov/farewell.htm

Edelman, Murray. *The Symbolic Uses of Politics.* Urbana and Chicago: University of Illinois, 1985.

The Editors, "The Times and Iraq," *New York Times*, May 26, 2004, A10.

Eisenstein, Elizabeth L. "Some Conjectures about the Impact of Printing on Western Society and Thought: A Preliminary Report," *Journal of Modern History 40* (1968).

Ellul, Jacques. *Propaganda: The Formation of Men's Attitudes.* New York, Knopf, 1965, 1972.

Ericson, Richard V., Patricia Baranek, and Janet Chan. *Negotiating Control: A Study of News Sources.* Toronto: University of Toronto Press, 1989.

Entman, R. "Framing: Toward clarification of a fractured paradigm," *Journal of Communication* 43, no.4 (1993).

Ewen, Stuart. *PR! A Social History of Spin.* New York: Basic Books, 1996.

Farrell, T. B. "Narrative in Natural Discourse: On Conversation and Rhetoric," *Journal of Communication* 35, no. 4 (1985), 126.

Fishman, Mark. *Manufacturing the News.* Austin: University of Texas Press, 1980.

Fontana, Benedetto. *Hegemony and Power: On the Relation between Gramsci and Machiavelli.* Minneapolis: University of Minnesota Press, 1993.

"Franklin D. Roosevelt (1882-1945)," Eleanor Roosevelt National Historic Site, Hyde Park, New York. Available at: http://www.nps.gov/archive/elro/glossary/roosevelt-franklin.htm

Friedenberg, Robert V. *Communication Consultants in Political Campaigns: Ballot Box Warriors.* Westport, Conn: Praeger, 1997.

Fuller, Jack. *News values: Ideas for an Information Age.* Chicago: University of Chicago, 1996.

Gandy, Oscar. *Beyond Agenda Setting.* Norwood, N.J.: Ablex, 1982.

Gans, Herbert J. *Deciding What's News: A Study of CBS Evening News, NBC Nightly News, Newsweek, and Time.* New York: Pantheon, 1979.

_____. *Deciding What's News,* New York: Pantheon, 1979

Gardiner, Sam. *Truth from These Podia: Summary of a Study of Strategic Influence, Perception Management, Strategic Information Warfare and Strategic Psychological Operations in Gulf II* (October 8, 2003). Downloaded from *U.S. News and World Report* web-site: http://www.usnews.com/usnews/politics/whispers/documents/truth_1.pdf+Gardiner+and+%22Truth+from+these+Podia%22&hl=en&gl=us&ct=clnk&cd=1&client=safari

Gellman, Barton. "A Leak, Then a Cascade," *Washington Post*, October 30, 2005, A1.

Germino, Dante. *Antonio Gramsci, Architect of a New Politics*. Baton Rouge: Louisiana State University Press, 1990.

Gitlin, Todd. *The Whole World Is Watching: Mass Media in the Making and Unmaking of the New Left*. Berkeley: University of California Press, 1980.

"A Good Leak," *Washington Post*, editorial page, April 9, 2006, B6.

Goodman, Melvin A. "Revamping the CIA," *Issues in Science and Technology*. Dallas: National Academy of Sciences, University of Texas at Dallas, Jan. 9, 2002. Available at: http://www.issues.org/18.2/goodman.html

Graham, Bradley. "Air Force Analysts Feel Vindicated on Iraqi Drones," *Washington Post*, September 26, 2003, A23.

Hagerty, Barbara Bradley. "Conservative Black Clergy Make Waves from Pulpit," *All Things Considered*, April 6, 2006. Available at: http://www.npr.org/templates/story/story.php?storyId=5328555

Halberstam, David. *The Best and the Brightest*. New York: Random House, 1972.

Hall, Stuart. "Culture, the Media and the 'Ideological Effect,'" in *Mass Communication and Society*, James Curran, Michael Gurevitch, and Janet Woollacott, eds. Beverly Hills: Sage, 1979.

Hallin, Daniel. *The Uncensored War: The Media and Vietnam*. New York: Oxford University Press, 1986.

Hamburger, Tom and Peter Wallsten. One *Party Country: The Republican Plan for Dominance in the 21st Century*. Hoboken, N.J.: John Wiley and Sons, Inc., 2006.

Herman, Edward S. "The Propaganda Model: a Retrospective," *Journalism Studies* 1, no. 1, 102-103.

_____ and Noam Chomsky, *Manufacturing Consent: The Political Economy of the Mass Media*. New York: Praeger, 1988.

Hess, Stephen. *The Washington Reporters: Newswork*. Washington, D.C.: Brookings Institution, 1981.

Hill, Anita. *Speaking Truth to Power*. New York: Doubleday, 1997.

Hofstetter, C.R. *Bias in the News*, New York: Ohio State University Press, 1976.

Hollander, Paul. "The Resilience of the Adversary Culture," *The National Interest*, Summer, 2002. Available at: http://www.findarticles.com/p/articles/mi_m2751/is_2002_Summer/ai_87720938/pg_1

Horwitz, Jeff. "My Right-Wing Degree," *Salon*, May 25, 2005. http://dir.salon.com/story/news/feature/2005/05/25/blackwell/print.html?pn=1

Iraq Coalition Casualty Count, http://icasualties.org/oif/default.aspx

Isikoff, Michael and David Corn, *Hubris: the Inside Story of Spin, Scandal, and the Selling of the Iraq War*. New York: Crown, 2006.

Israel, Bill. "A Policy of Neglect and Cowardice, a Pay-off of Death," *Massachusetts Daily Collegian*, September 12, 2001; http://dailycollegian.com/2001/09/12/a-policy-of-neglect-and-cowardice-a-pay-off-of-death/

Israel, William Lawrence. Ritual Killings? *American Journalism and the Treatment of Dissent*. Dissertation, University of Texas at Austin, 1999.

Ivins, Molly. Column for January 22, 1998, Creator's Syndicate, distributed by the Associated Press, New York.

Jamieson, Kathleen Hall. *Dirty Politics: Deception, Distraction, and Democracy*. New York: Oxford University Press, 1992.

Jensen, Klaus Bruhn. "News as Ideology: Economic Statistics and Political Ritual in Television Network News," *Journal of Communication* 37, no.1 (1987), 8-27.

Johnstone, John W. C., Edward J. Slawski, William W. Bowman. *The News People: A Sociological Portrait of American Journalists and their Work*. Urbana: University of Illinois Press, 1976.

Jowett, Garth S. and Victoria O'Donnell. *Propaganda and Persuasion*. Newbury Park, Calif.: Sage Publications, Inc., 1986. Third edition, 1999.

Kampfner, John. "Saving Private Lynch story 'flawed,'" BBC Online, May 15, 2003. http://news.bbc.co.uk/2/hi/programmes/correspondent/3028585.stm

Kessler, Ronald. "One More Deep Throat Rendezvous," *Newsmax.com*, Jan. 10, 2007; http://www.newsmax.com/archives/articles/2007/1/9/180126.shtml

Kiefer, Francine. "How the White House Uses (Gasp!) Polls," *Christian Science Monitor*, June 15, 2001.

Kirkpatrick, David D. "In Alito, G.O.P. Reaps Harvest Planted in '82," *New York Times*, January 30, 2006.

Kumar, Deepa. Review of *War, Media, and Propaganda*, Yahya R. Kamalipour and Nancy Snow, eds., in *Journalism Educator* 61, no. 2 (Summer 2006): 216-218.

Kurtz, Howard. "The Post on WMDs: An Inside Story; Prewar Articles Questioning Threat Often Didn't Make Front Page," *Washington Post*, August 12, 2004, A1.

Kuznick, Peter J."Scientists on the Stump," *Bulletin of the Atomic Scientists* 60, no. 6 (November/December 2004), 28-35. Available at: www.thebulletin.org/article.php?art_ofn=nd04kuznick

"Lady Macbeth — Arlene Wohlgemuth," *Texas Monthly*, July 1, 1999. Available at: http://www.texasmonthly.com/preview/1999-07-01/feature24

Lakoff, George. *Don't Think of an Elephant! Know your Values and Frame the Debate.* White River Junction, VT.: Chelsea Green Publishing, 2004.

Landers, Kim. "Bush Holds Back on Bold Statements on Iraq," *World Today*, May 2, 2006. Available at: http://www.abc.net.au/worldtoday/content/2006/s1628701.htm

Lang, Gladys Engel and Kurt Lang. *The Battle for Public Opinion: the President, then Press, and the Polls During Watergate.* New York: Columbia University Press, 1983.

Lasswell, Harold. *Propaganda Technique in the World War.* New York: Knopf, 1927.

Lippmann, Walter. *Liberty and the News.* New York: Harcourt, Brace and Howe, 1920.

_____. *Public Opinion.* Macmillan,1922. Reprint, New York: Free Press/Simon and Schuster, 1997.

Lucaites, J.L. and C. M. Condit. "Re-constructing Narrative Theory: A Functional Perspective," *Journal of Communication* 35, no. 4 (1985), 90-108.

Mamdani, Mahmoud. *Good Muslim, Bad Muslim: America, the Cold War, and the Roots of Terror.* New York: Pantheon Books, 2004.

Mander, M.S. "Narrative Dimensions of the News: Omniscience, Prophecy, and Morality," *Communication* 10 (1987), 63.

Manoff, Robert and Michael Schudson, eds. *Reading the News.* New York: Pantheon, 1986.

Matusow, Barbara. *The Evening Stars: The Making of the Network News Anchor.* Boston: Houghton Mifflin, 1983.

McCombs, Maxwell, Edna Einsiedel, and David Weaver. *Contemporary Public Opinion: Issues and the News.* Hillsdale, N.H.: Erlbaum, 1991.

Mayer, Jane and Jill Abramson. *Strange Justice: The Selling of Clarence Thomas.* Boston/New York: Houghton Mifflin, 1994, 297.

McGee, M. C. and J. S. Nelson. "Narrative Reason in Public Argument," *Journal of Communication* 35, no. 4 (1985), 139-155.

McManus, John H. *Market-Driven Journalism: Let the Citizen Beware.* Thousand Oaks, Calif.: Sage, 1994.

Meek, James Gordon, Kenneth R. Bazinet, and Thomas M. DeFrank. "Hit Squad: White House Group Targeted Iraq Policy Critics," *New York Daily News*, reprinted in *Pittsburgh Post-Gazette*, October 20, 2005, A10.

Miller, Martha T., ed. *The Complete Transcripts of the Clarence Thomas-Anita Hill Hearings.* Chicago: Academy Chicago Publishers, 1994.

Milton, John. *Areopagitica,* 1644. Available at Renascence Editions, http://www.uoregon.edu/~rbear/areopagitica.html

Moore, David W. *The Superpollsters: How They Measure and Manipulate Public Opinion in America.* New York: Four Walls Eight Windows, 1995.

Moore, James and Wayne Slater. *Bush's Brain: How Karl Rove Made George W. Bush Presidential,* Hoboken, N.J.: John Wiley and Sons, 2003.

_____. *The Architect: Karl Rove and the Master Plan for Absolute Power.* New York: Crown, 2006.

Moore, Martha T. and Laura Parker. "Observers See Big Threat in Small Klan Groups," *USA Today,* June 26, 1998, 2A.

Moore, Michael. *Downsize This!* New York: Crown Publishers, 1996.

"Network TV Audience, Evening News Viewership, All Networks, November 1980 to November 2005," *The State of the News Media 2006,* Annual Report on American Journalism. Project for Excellence in Journalism. http://www.stateofthenewsmedia.org/2006/chartland.asp?id=211&ct=line &dir=&sort=&col1_box=1

"Number of U.S. Daily Newspapers," State of the News Media 2004, Journalism.org. http://www.stateofthenewsmedia.org/chartland.asp?id= 167&ct=line&dir=&sort=&col1_box=1&col2_box=1&col3_box=1&col4 _box=1

"Our Background," The Federalist Society for Law and Public Policy. Downloaded January 2, 2007, from http://www.fed-soc.org/AboutUs/ourbackground.htm

Patterson, Thomas. *Out of Order.* New York: Knopf, 1993.

Pincus, Walter."Corruption Cited in Iraq's Oil Industry," *Washington Post,* July 17, 2006, A12.

_____. "Detainees Used Al-Qaeda Prison Manual, Report Says, *Washington Post,* July 20, 2006," A12.

Plotke, David. *Building a Democratic Political Order: Reshaping American Liberalism in the 1930s and 1940s.* New York: Cambridge University Press, 1996.

Pollard, James E. *The Presidents and the Press.* New York: Octagon Books, 1973.

Presidential Campaign Activities of 1972, Senate Resolution 60, Hearings before the Select Committee on Presidential Campaign Activities of the United States Senate, Ninety-Third Congress, First Session, Watergate and Related Activities, Phase II: Campaign Practices, Book 11, Washington, D.C.: U.S. Government Printing Office, 1973.

"A Press Warning from the National Council on Public Polls," Press release, May 22, 1995. Available at: http://www.ncpp.org/push.htm

"Quiz Show Scandals," The Museum of Broadcast Communication, http://www.museum.tv/archives/etv/Q/htmlQ/quizshowsca/quizshowsca.htm

"Radio Corporation of America, U.S. Radio Company," The Museum of Broadcast Communications, http://www.museum.tv/archives/etv/R/htmlR/radiocorpora/radiocorpora.htm

Ransford, Leslie. *Narrative Framing of Science News*. Thesis, University of Texas at Austin, 1993.

Ratcliffe, R. G. "The Execution of Karla Faye Tucker; Bush Prayed for Guidance before Denying Tucker's Appeal," *Houston Chronicle*, Feb. 4, 1998, A10.

Reynolds, David. "From Hot War to Cold War: A Panel Discussion," University of Tennessee, Howard H. Baker Jr. Center for Public Policy, March 30, 2006.

Ricks, Thomas E. *Fiasco: the American Military Adventure in Iraq*. New York: Penguin, 2006.

"Right Wing Organizations," Right Wing Watch, People for the American Way;
Tracing the Story of Journalism in the United States," The Write Site. http://www.writesite.org/html/tracing.html

Roosevelt, Franklin D. "Four Freedoms Speech," State of the Union address, January 6, 1941. Available at: http://www.fdrlibrary.marist.edu/od4frees.html

Rosenman, Samuel, ed. *The Public Papers of Franklin D. Roosevelt, Volume Two: The Year of Crisis, 1933*. New York: Random House, 1938.

Rosten, Leo C. *The Washington Correspondents*. New York: Harcourt, Brace and Company, 1937.

"Rove Thanks Republican Lawyers for Their Work on 'Clean Elections,'" Raw Story.com, April 10, 2006, http://www.rawstory.com/news/2006/Rove_thanks_Republican_lawyers_for_their_0410.html

Rove, Karl. Speech at American Enterprise Institute, May 15, 2006. Transcript, *Washington Post online*. http//www.washingtonpost.com/wp-dyn/content/article/2006/05/15/AR2006051500635.html

_____. Speech to The Federalist Society, November 12, 2005 [should read November 10]. http://www.realclearpolitics.com/Commentary/com-11_12_05_KR.html

_____. *Speech to The Federalist Society*, November 10, 2005. Transcript copyright 2005 Congressional Quarterly, Inc.

Rusher, William A. *The Coming Battle for the Media: Curbing the Power of the Media Elite*. New York: William Morrow, 1988.

_____. *The Rise of the Right*. New York: William Morrow, 1984.

Schlesinger, Philip. "The Sociology of Knowledge." Paper presented at a meeting of the British Sociological Association, March 24, 1972.

Schudson, Michael. *Discovering the News*. New York: Basic Books, 1978.

_____. *The Power of News*. Cambridge, Mass.: Harvard University Press, 1995.

Schur, E. M. *The Politics of Deviance: Stigma Contests and the Uses of Power.* Englewood Cliffs, N.J.: Prentice-Hall, 1980.

Scowcroft, Brent. "Don't Attack Saddam," *Wall Street Journal*, Aug. 15, 2002, op-ed page.

Seabrook, Andrea. "Republicans Turn to Blogs to Deliver a Message," *All Things Considered*, National Public Radio, February 18, 2005. Available at: http://www.npr.org/templates/story/story.php?storyId=4504846

Segel, Thomas D. "Those Seeking a 'Liberal' Education Often Receive A 'Radical' One Instead," *Washington Dispatch*, http://www.freerepublic.com/focus/f-news/892829/posts

Shaw, Donald L. "The Rise and Fall of American Mass Media: Roles of Technology and Leadership." Second annual Roy W. Howard Lecture. Bloomington, IN: Roy W. Howard Project, School of Journalism, Indiana University, 1991.

Shoemaker, Pamela J. and Stephen D. Reese, S.D. *Mediating the Message: Theories of Influences on Mass Media Content.* White Plains, N.Y.: Longman, 1991.

Simon, William E. *A Time for Truth.* New York: Reader's Digest Press, McGraw-Hill, 1978.

Smith, Gibson Bell. "Guarding the Railroad, Taming the Cossacks: The U.S. Army in Russia, 1918—1920." *Prologue* 34, no.4 (Winter 2002). Available at: http://www.archives.gov/publications/prologue/2002/winter/us-army-in-russia-1.html

Smith, Hedrick. *The Power Game: How Washington Works.* New York: Ballantine Books, 1989.

Steinfels, Peter. *The Neoconservatives: The Men Who Are Changing America's Politics.* New York: Simon and Schuster, 1979.

Stephan, Ed. "U.S. Military Deaths in Bush's Iraq Quagmire." Available at http://www.ac.wwu.edu/~stephan/USfatalities.html

Stites, Tom. "Is Media Performance Democracy's Critical Issue?" Speech to the Media Giraffe Conference, University of Massachusetts Amherst, June 30, 2006. Available at http://www.mediagiraffe.com/

Stout, David. "A Nation Challenged: the First Lady; Mrs. Bush Cites Women's Plight under Taliban," *New York Times*, November 18, 2001, 1B Sunday.

Suskind, Ron. *The One Percent Doctrine: Deep Inside America's Pursuit of its Enemies since 9/11.* New York: Simon and Schuster, 2006.

Swint, Kerwin C. *Mudslingers: The Top 25 Negative Political Campaigns of All Time.* Westport, Conn.: Praeger, 2006.

Talbot, David. "Creepier than Nixon," *Salon*, http://dir.salon.com/story/news/feature/2004/03/31/dean/index1.html?pn=2

Taranto, James. "Journalism Profs against America," in *WSJ.com Opinion Journal from the Wall Street Journal*, http://www.opinionjournal.com/best/?id=95001149

Teepen, Tom. "Commentary: Carrier Landing Blurs Military, Civilian Line," Cox News Service, May 8, 2003.

The Federalist Papers, "Federalist 10," Library of Congress, available on "Thomas," http://thomas.loc.gov/home/histdox/fed_10.html

Thomason, O. *Mass Persuasion in History*. Edinburg: Paul Harris, 1977.

Tuchman, Gaye. *Making News: A Study in the Construction of Reality*. New York: Free Press, 1978.

Tumber, Howard, ed. *Media Power, Professionals and Policies*. London and New York: Routledge, 2000.

Vacker, Barry. "Global Village or World Bazaar?" Chapter 10, pp. 211-237, in Alan B. Albarran and David H. Goff, *Understanding the Web: Social, Political, and Economic Dimensions of the Internet*. Ames, Iowa: Blackwell, 2000.

Viguerie, Richard A. *The New Right: We're Ready to Lead*. Falls Church, Virginia: The Viguerie Company, 1981.

_____ and David Franke. *America's Right Turn: How Conservatives Used News and Alternative Media to Take Power*. Chicago and Los Angeles: Bonus Books, 2004.

Unger, Craig. "The War They Wanted, the Lies They Needed," *Vanity Fair*, July 2006, 92.

"Wash. Post Published Four Op-eds Attacking Prosecution and Trial of Libby, None Supporting Them," Media Matters for America, February 21, 2007 6:02pm EST, http://mediamatters.org/items/200702210007

Washington, George. "Farewell Address," 1796. Available at: http://usinfo.state.gov/usa/infousa/facts/democrac/49.htm

"Watch: Covering the War on Terror," http://watch.windsofchange.net/themes_14.htm

Weaver, David H. and G. Cleveland Wilhoit. *The American Journalist in the 1990s: U.S. News People at the End of an Era*. Mahwah, N.J.: Lawrence Erlbaum, 1996.

Weber, Max. "Politics as a Vocation," available at: http://www.ne.jp/asahi/moriyuki/abukuma/weber/lecture/politics_vocation.html

_____. *The Protestant Ethic and the Spirit of Capitalism*, 1930. Reprint, London and New York: Routledge, 2001.

Weil, Gordon L. *America Answers A Sneak Attack: Alcan and Al Qaeda*. Los Angeles: The Americas Group, 2005.

White, Theodore H. *Breach of Faith: The Fall of Richard Nixon.* New York: Atheneum, 1975.

Woodward, Bob. *Plan of Attack.* New York: Simon and Schuster, 2004.

_____. *State of Denial: Bush at War, Part III.* New York: Simon and Schuster, 2006.

Yergin, Daniel. *Shattered Peace: The Origins of the Cold War and the National Security State.* Boston: Houghton Mifflin, 1977.

Zoroya, Gregg. "Study Estimates 600,000 Iraqis Dead by Violence," *USA Today*, October 11, 2006. Available at: http://www.usatoday.com/news/world/iraq/2006-10-10-iraq-dead_x.htm

Acknowledgments

For insights that made this work possible, I wish to acknowledge, first, Karl Rove, whose genius became evident during our work together, who became my friend, and whose abilities I respect, even as we disagree as to principles, goals, and methods, and have parted company.

I owe a substantial debt to Stuart Ewen of New York University, whose book *PR! A Social History of Spin* (New York: Basic Books, 1996) inspired my thinking and frames part of my argument; and to David Brock, whose *Republican Noise Machine* (New York: Crown Publishers, 2004) filled in important pieces.

Thirty-two journalist-respondents — some of whom have won Pulitzer and MacArthur awards — gave generously of their time and insights and helped to document journalism's drift to the right. I thank, in alphabetical order: Peter Bhatia, David Broder, Scott Brodeur, Chris Daly, E. J. Dionne, Jon Donley, Tom Edsall, Ed Fouhy, Steve Fox, Dan Froomkin, Frank Green, Brant Houston, Ellen Hume, Jeff Jarvis, Jackie Judd, Anne Kornblut, Ed Lenert, Charles Lewis, Barbara Matusow, Doyle McManus, Phil Meyer, Jack Nelson, Walter Pincus, Vikki Porter, Bill Press, Tom Rosenstiel, Barry Sussman, Helen Thomas, Karen Tumulty, Richard Viguerie, Amy Walter, and Linda Wertheimer.

Jim Moore and Wayne Slater, the great Rove biographers, now friends, provided ongoing insight, encouragement, and help.

I particularly thank political columnist Dave McNeely, through whom I met and came to work with Karl. Dave's review caught errors and improved the manuscript.

From my days at the University of Texas at Austin, I thank Professor Rusty Todd, who asked me to work with Dave and Karl; and, especially, Professors Chuck Whitney (now of Northwestern University), Maxwell

McCombs, Gene Burd, the late James Tankard, and Lester Kurtz (now of George Mason University); and the Honorable William P. Hobby Jr.

At the University of Massachusetts Amherst, Professors John Nelson and John Lombardi (now president of the Louisiana State University system) gave steady, supportive advice. Dr. Mary Deane Sorcinelli and the staff of the Center for Teaching; and the librarians at UMass Amherst, especially Dr. James Kelly and Director of Libraries Jay Schafer, encouraged this work and made me welcome — as did librarians at Amherst, Smith, Hampshire, and Mt. Holyoke Colleges. UMass Journalism faculty read drafts and proposals, offered suggestions, noted I was due a sabbatical (I thank former Provost Charlena Seymour for supporting it), supported bringing Rove biographer Jim Moore to campus, and connected me with a fine editor. Former Vice Provost for Research Paul Kostecki encouraged and connected me to Paul C. Johnson and Cindy Ryan at Arizona State University, who facilitated research privileges there. I thank an anonymous outside reviewer for aptly noting the need to contextualize Rove's work and that of the political Right in the history of propaganda.

At St. Mary's University, San Antonio, I thank many colleagues and friends for their helpful support and encouragement: Professors Rose Cutting, Peggy Curet, Richard Pressman, Ann Semel, Bernard Lee, Bob O'Connor, Terri Boggess, Dennis Bautista, Kevin Welch, and Elijah Akhahenda; Deans Janet Dizinno and Henry Flores; Vice President André Hampton; President Charles Cotrell; and Professors Dan Bjork, Larry Hufford, Jerry Poyo, Aaron Tyler, and Robert Skipper. I thank the members of my spring 2010 graduate seminar for tackling some issues and providing feedback.

Editor Nancy Doherty over the course of months breathed insight and precision into this project. Her abilities, care, and interest greatly improved the manuscript. Thank you, Nancy!

I thank colleagues and Professors Jarice Hanson (Temple University and UMass Amherst), Michael Bugeja (Iowa State University), and Col. Charles Breslin Jr. (retired, U.S. Army War College) for inviting me to present as this work developed. I thank Frank Green, Sue Ellen Bisgaard and the late Professor Soren Bisgaard (UMass Amherst); Professor Emeritus Anne Woodtli (University of Arizona) and Professor James

Mueller (University of North Texas); Professors Nicholas McBride, Nancy Folbré, and Tom O'Brien (UMass Amherst); and Ronald Chrisman of the University of North Texas Press — for helpful readings, suggestions, and moral support.

I thank Ilo Howard for transcription support; Steve Baker, Brett Ingram, Richard Beck, and Claudia Israel for bibliographic and editorial support; Robert Campagna, Candace Windel, Gay Simpson, Margaret Thomas, Katherine and Bernie Cleveland, Peter Bittel and Erin Edwards, Gloria Feldt and Alex Barbanell, Lisa Stark and Bruce Dan; and many other friends and colleagues who patiently made suggestions or put up with my absence while I wrote. At the UMass Information Technology program, I thank, in particular, Professors Charlie Schweik, Rick Adrion, Glenn Caffery, Craig Nicolson, and Copper Giloth. I thank former editors Brenda Hadenfeldt and Bess Van Renen for their encouragement for this project and their support.

For help in grappling with legal issues, I thank attorneys Michael Albert, David Anderson, Steve Bickerstaff, Joseph W. Cotchett, Shirley Z. Johnson, Irving Picard, Candace Windel, and others not named; and the Honorable William P. Hobby Jr. I reserve particular thanks for my publisher, professor and scholar David Demers, who saw the promise of the book and encouraged me forward. As since the days of John Peter Zenger, there remains promise for this society as long as journalists, publishers, and social scientists seek out and tell the truth.

It's to my family — the extended families of Wini Israel and Theresa Breslin — that I owe special thanks for supporting me during this project, despite my missing family events, outings, and time together — thank you, everyone!

I want to recognize those who kindled my interest in politics and journalism: great teachers Helen Schwarz, Edith Pollock, and Royce Barnum; and, journalists and important others at the *Sioux City* (Iowa) *Journal*: Clyde Van Dyke, Alex Stoddard, Louise Zerschling, Robert Dodsley, Kenneth Sanders, Erwin Sias, Elizabeth Sammons, and Louise Sammons Freese. I also thank the four friends who persuaded me to go with them to a Young Republicans National Convention in Omaha: Doug Dashner, Doug Haney, Rick Rhebb, and Grover Sardeson.

This book is dedicated, in part, to the memory of U.S. Senator Harold E. Hughes of Iowa and Park Rinard, Hughes' remarkable administrative assistant, who brought me to Washington, D.C., to work as press secretary during the Watergate years.

Finally, for suggesting an evaluation research model; for serving as second reader of the journalists' data; for steadfast encouragement throughout the long road to publication; and for supporting me with time, talent, treasure, and love, I thank my wife, Eileen Breslin.

INDEX

F

G

H

O

P

Q-R

U

V

W

X-Z

ABOUT THE AUTHOR

Bill Israel (Ph.D., University of Texas at Austin) is an associate professor of Journalism and Political Communication and director of Graduate Communication Studies at St. Mary's University in San Antonio, Texas.

Professor Israel studies the interplay of media and power. He began pursuing this line of research by reporting for newspapers, magazines, radio, television, and online. He worked as reporter, editor, photojournalist or anchor for the *Sacramento Bee, San Francisco Chronicle and Examiner, Dallas Morning News, USA Today, The New York Times,* CBS Radio, ABC-TV, and other regional news outlets. He also worked as press secretary for politicians in Iowa, California, and Washington, D.C.

At the University of Texas at Austin, where he earned his advanced degrees, Israel taught "Politics and the Press" with Republican political strategist Karl Rove. Israel's book, *A Nation Seized*, connects what Rove taught to the bigger issues, including the rise of propaganda and the political Right, the fracture of mainstream news, and the phenomenon Israel calls "stealing reality."

As a faculty member at the University of Massachusetts Amherst, Israel was honored by the president of the UMass system for his work in developing an innovative Information Technology minor, without a major department, open to students in every discipline. He lives with his wife, Eileen Breslin, in San Antonio, Texas. He can be reached at bisrael@stmarytx.edu.